WORDSWORTH AND THE ENLIGHTENMENT IDEA OF PLEASURE

Ancient questions about the causes and nature of pleasure were revived in the eighteenth century with a new consideration of its ethical and political significance. Rowan Boyson reminds us that philosophers of the Enlightenment, unlike modern thinkers, often represented pleasure as shared rather than selfish, and she focuses particularly on this approach to the philosophy and theory of pleasure. Through close reading of Enlightenment and Romantic texts, in particular the poetry and prose of William Wordsworth, Boyson elaborates on this central theme. Covering a wide range of texts by philosophers, theorists and creative writers from over the centuries, she presents a strong defence of the Enlightenment ideal of pleasure, drawing out its rich political, as well as intellectual and aesthetic, implications.

ROWAN BOYSON is a Lecturer in the Department of English at King's College London.

T0382598

CAMBRIDGE STUDIES IN ROMANTICISM

This series aims to foster the best new work in one of the most challenging fields within English literary studies. From the early 1780s to the early 1830s a formidable array of talented men and women took to literary composition, not just in poetry, which some of them famously transformed, but in many modes of writing. The expansion of publishing created new opportunities for writers, and the political stakes of what they wrote were raised again by what Wordsworth called those 'great national events' that were 'almost daily taking place': the French Revolution, the Napoleonic and American wars, urbanization, industrialization, religious revival, an expanded empire abroad and the reform movement at home. This was an enormous ambition, even when it pretended otherwise. The relations between science, philosophy, religion and literature were reworked in texts such as *Frankenstein* and *Biographia Literaria*; gender relations in *A Vindication of the Rights of Woman* and *Don Juan*; journalism by Cobbett and Hazlitt; poetic form, content and style by the Lake School and the Cockney School. Outside Shakespeare studies, probably no body of writing has produced such a wealth of comment or done so much to shape the responses of modern criticism. This indeed is the period that saw the emergence of those notions of 'literature' and of literary history, especially national literary history, on which modern scholarship in English has been founded.

The categories produced by Romanticism have also been challenged by recent historicist arguments. The task of the series is to engage both with a challenging corpus of Romantic writings and with the changing field of criticism they have helped to shape. As with other literary series published by Cambridge, this one will represent the work of both younger and more established scholars, on either side of the Atlantic and elsewhere.

For a complete list of titles published see end of book.

WORDSWORTH AND THE ENLIGHTENMENT IDEA OF PLEASURE

ROWAN BOYSON

CAMBRIDGE
UNIVERSITY PRESS

CAMBRIDGE
UNIVERSITY PRESS

University Printing House, Cambridge CB2 8BS, United Kingdom

Cambridge University Press is part of the University of Cambridge.

It furthers the University's mission by disseminating knowledge in the pursuit of
education, learning and research at the highest international levels of excellence.

www.cambridge.org
Information on this title: www.cambridge.org/9781107566415

© Rowan Boyson 2012

First published 2012
First paperback edition 2015

A catalogue record for this publication is available from the British Library

Library of Congress Cataloguing in Publication data
Boyson, Rowan.
Wordsworth and the enlightenment idea of pleasure / Rowan Boyson.
p.   cm. – (Cambridge studies in romanticism ; 95)
ISBN 978-1-107-02330-7 (Hardback)
1. Wordsworth, William, 1770–1850–Philosophy.   2. Wordsworth,
William, 1770–1850–Criticism and interpretation.   3. Pleasure in literature.
4. Pleasure–Philosophy.   5. Enlightenment.   I. Title.
PR5892.P5B69 2012
821'.7–dc23
2012017170

ISBN 978-1-107-02330-7 Hardback
ISBN 978-1-107-56641-5 Paperback

Contents

Acknowledgements

Many people have helped me in writing this book. Paul Hamilton supervised my doctoral research: I am enormously grateful to him for leading me into deeper philosophical waters, for persuading me to make Wordsworth my key study and for his wicked wit. Several years earlier I caught Nigel Leask's enthusiasm for Romanticism and was inspired by his historical curiosity and theoretical acuity. The graduate classes and supervisions of Lorraine Daston, Simon Schaffer and Fred Parker helped my ideas on pleasure to germinate. At Queen Mary, University of London, I was encouraged by Markman Ellis, Cora Kaplan and Annie Janowitz, who also read chapters. I made many great friends there, especially Molly Macdonald and Suzanne Hobson. Ross Wilson and Simon Swift have been inspiring and generous correspondents. Financial support from the Arts and Humanities Research Council, and the staff and the uplifting space of the British Library, enabled me to undertake the research on which this book is based.

Subsequently, King's College, Cambridge elected me to a Junior Research Fellowship and filled my daily life of working on this book and new projects with reminders of the link between community and pleasure. Conversations with many King's fellows, especially Stefan Uhlig, Pete de Bolla, Victoria Harris and Chris Brooke, have given me new intellectual directions and practical advice. The opportunity to teach wonderful students at King's and through the Pembroke–King's Programme and the University Summer School helped rekindle and clarify my ideas.

I would like to express my gratitude to Neil Vickers and Simon Jarvis, who examined my dissertation with the utmost intelligence and care: though I may not finally have written the book that they might have preferred, their responses continue to reverberate in my mind and will inform much of my future work. The two anonymous readers of my book manuscript for Cambridge University Press gave me a sense that peer review can be almost magical: their pages of engaged criticism and pragmatic suggestions gave orientation and consolation as I rewrote and rethought. Thanks also to Jim Chandler, Linda Bree, Linda Randall and Josephine Lane at Cambridge University Press.

The friendship of Jo Hemmings and Martin Ellory has nourished me through highs and lows. From the bottom of my heart I thank Daniel Wilson for his brilliant editorial suggestions on numerous drafts, his relish of life, his humour and his love. My parents Liz Boyson and Hugo Rose brought me, Frances and Bella up in sociable happiness, and I dedicate this book to them.

Introduction

So I say it again and again, pleasure is shared.[1]

The modern idea of pleasure is primarily individualistic: indeed, modernity is often characterized (and criticized) as the moment which legitimized individual pleasures, rather than transcendent ends, such as God, family or society. The argument of this book, however, is that there is a counter-strain of thought in Enlightenment philosophy and in Wordsworth's poetry, in which pleasure is considered as inherently communal rather than private or solipsistic. The book seeks to retrieve this almost-forgotten idea about how pleasure might register a feeling of collective dependence and interaction, and might be generated from a feeling of community.

Pleasure is a remarkably mobile term, moving between different intellectual and theoretical domains with great ease. It is one of the most basic and yet little-studied facets of eighteenth-century feeling, both ubiquitous and complex in the period: pleasure appeared in almost all areas of British, French and German thought, from theology to the luxury debates, epistemology, science and aesthetics, to education and the new political economy.[2] In particular, pleasure is the common ground of both eighteenth-century aesthetics and political philosophy. We have long been accustomed to viewing the early eighteenth century as a period when the problem of how and why we take pleasure in nature and art was first formulated in a recognizably modern way. We also see the eighteenth century as a period heavily invested in the problem of sociability: how people compete, sympathize and depend on one another. And utilitarianism, which attempted to re-vision social structures in order to produce the greatest 'felicity' of the greatest number, emerged in the late eighteenth century. Pleasure reaches across all these fields. The question of how exactly pleasure and sociability might be related to one another was a burning question for a host of eighteenth- and early nineteenth-century writers, and a question whose political and poetical contours, as well as its legacies, are traced in this book.

I

My procedure is to explore the idea of pleasure and some cognate terms, including happiness, bliss, joy and interest, in a selection of eighteenth-century philosophical texts and novels, before making an extended case-study of Wordsworth's poetry and prose. The book thus offers a speculative, conceptual exploration of pleasure. It is concerned with pleasure not as the umbrella term for quite different activities – the pleasures *of* wine, sex, dancing, card-playing, botanizing – but with 'pleasure' itself as a single, contested and *philosophical* idea.[3] Part of my argument is that we must – indeed, can only – understand pleasure's charged intellectual and political history by reading its usage closely in selected texts. Today's neuroscientists claim to be approaching a full biological picture of mental affect, a definite understanding of what pleasure *is*. Yet, from an alternative point of view, pleasure is not a 'concept' that one can finalize, as the analytic philosopher Leonard Katz suggests in his modest and open-ended definition: 'pleasure is something biological, psychological, and experiential which remains in large part unknown, the nature or category of which it is inappropriate to stipulate a priori'.[4] The only thing we can be sure of as regards pleasure, Katz claims, is that humans have a 'natural basic capacity to refer to it': we seem to have an innate capacity to have a 'good feeling' and to note this, and to communicate about it.[5] Even such a minimal definition does, however, alert us to the critical and theoretical possibilities that pleasure opens up: themes of anthropology, communicability and universality that are explored historically and theoretically throughout this book. Although the meanings of pleasure are explored progressively and dialectically in each chapter, I would like first to set out some provisional ideas about the cluster of terms centrally in play in this book. In the rich tradition of histories of words and concepts (Raymond Williams, C.S. Lewis and William Empson), I offer some brief notes on the etymology of the terms and some of their philosophical incarnations. The chapters to follow will complicate these definitions through a series of close literary and theoretical readings.

KEYWORDS

Pleasure

The history of the word 'pleasure' does not show dramatic or very clearly defined shifts in usage, unlike, for instance, other aesthetic and emotional terms such as envy, altruism and the sublime. A brief tour of four definitions – the *Oxford English Dictionary* (*OED*), Locke's *Essay*, Johnson's *Dictionary* and Diderot and D'Alembert's *Encyclopédie* – introduces the positive and negative valences of the word, and its long association with the ideas of will, power and force, which, as subsequent chapters demonstrate, all inform the way it mediates between individual and community.

The *OED* describes how our Middle English word is derived from Old French, *plesir*, *plaisir*, from the Latin *placere*, to please. 'Pleasure' appears to carry both a neutral sense from the fourteenth century ('The condition of consciousness or sensation induced by the enjoyment or anticipation of what is felt or viewed as good or desirable; enjoyment, delight, gratification') and an unfavourable one from at least the early sixteenth century ('Sensuous enjoyment as a chief object of life or end in itself. Opp. *business*. Sometimes personified as a female divinity'). Its second main signification is in terms of will ('How one is pleased or wills in reference to any action contemplated; that which is agreeable to one or in conformity with one's wish or will; one's will, desire, choice'). This (now less common) usage reveals something of a Janus quality to the word, because the *OED*'s definition 1c ('In strictly physical sense: The indulgence of the appetites; sensual gratification') has implications of the loss of rational will and the dominance of appetite.

John Locke's *Essay concerning Human Understanding* (1689) makes pleasure a building block of knowledge, one of the 'simple ideas of both sensation and reflection', alongside pain, power, existence and unity.[6] Pleasure is a general term for what we now might call 'positive affect': 'satisfaction, delight, pleasure, happiness', Locke says, are 'still but different degrees of the same thing'.[7] Locke argues that 'they join themselves to almost all our ideas … there is scarce any affection of our senses from without, any retired thought of our mind within, which is not able to produce in us *pleasure* or *pain*'.[8] Pleasure has been 'annexed' to objects, ideas and thoughts by God, the better to awaken our faculties and ambitions from an otherwise idle state, a 'lazy lethargic dream'.[9] When he returns to the topic later in the *Essay*, he emphasizes that pleasure and pain are 'two very considerable' simple ideas, but notes that 'they cannot be described, nor their Names defined; the way of knowing them is, as of the simple *Ideas* of the Senses, only by Experience'.[10] Despite this ineffability, they are central: all the passions and even 'good and evil' may only be understood as rooted in pleasure and pain.[11]

Samuel Johnson's 1755 *Dictionary* definition is somewhat less positive, in line with the pessimistic comments on the elusiveness and evanescence of happiness in his novella *Rasselas* and in the *Rambler* essays. He divides pleasure along a spectrum of volition:

PLEA'SURE. *n.f.* [*plaisir*, French.]

1. Delight; gratification of the mind or senses.

2. Loose gratification.

3. Approbation.

4. What the will dictates.

5. Choice, arbitrary will.[12]

His examples of usage are gloomy: 'A cause of men's taking *pleasure* in the sins of others, is, that poor spiritedness that accompanies guilt' (South); 'Now Daphne's dead, and *pleasure* is no more' (Pope). One noteworthy aspect of his definition is the ambiguous way that pleasure stands for both loose gratification, a porous, weak-willed subjectivity, and its opposite, absolute power, domination of one subject over another (surviving in the phrase 'At Her Majesty's Pleasure'). These themes emerge particularly in my reading of Rousseau and Wollstonecraft, as well as in Wordsworth's engagement with power and mastery in *Home at Grasmere* and *The Prelude*.

Diderot and D'Alembert's *Encyclopédie* contains a 3,000-word essay on pleasure (in volume XII, 'Parlement – Polytric', 1765), which has been attributed to Diderot himself. It appears to be influenced by Shaftesbury's *Inquiry concerning Virtue or Merit* (1699), which Diderot translated in 1745, and Lévesque de Pouilly's *Théorie des sentiments agréables* (1749). In the *Encyclopédie*'s definition, pleasure is a force driving human behaviour, analogous to the forces of motion underlying the universe:

Pleasure (Ethics.) Pleasure is a feeling of the soul (*un sentiment de l'âme*) that makes us happy, at least during the time we are experiencing it . . . If there is only one way in which nature manages the material universe, then it is thus only through pleasure that she manages human beings. She has taken care to attach an appeal to those exercises of the organs of the body that do not weaken them, to those occupations of the mind that do not exhaust it by extended and lively disputes.[13]

The stress on motion and movement is particularly interesting, and is witnessed in Rousseau's *Emile* and in Wordsworth's *Prelude*. The entry contains some conventional classifications of pleasure as bodily and mental, but this extract from the beginning resonates strongly with the history of Epicurean and other materialist thought, and in particular with the influence of Spinoza, whose legacy takes us to 'joy'.

Joy

Joy is a Middle English word that comes from Old French and in turn from the Latin *gaudium*; it tends to be thought of as a particularly intense form of pleasure or happiness.[14] Of philosophers, Spinoza most builds on 'joy'; his ethics are centred on *laetitia* (from Latin *laetus*, gladdening, joyful), usually translated as the passion of 'joy'. Joy is meant to represent man's passing from a lower to a higher perfection, and his increase in the power of acting.[15] These ideas later played into Nietzsche's 'gay science' of affirmation, against *ressentiment*. John Locke's definition of joy as 'a delight of the Mind, from the consideration of the present or assured approaching possession of a Good', might also have been influenced by Spinoza, who is increasingly regarded as a central influence on even mainstream eighteenth-century philosophers. Jonathan Israel has argued for the existence of a Spinozist 'radical Enlightenment' (as opposed to a moderate Enlightenment), which, as he puts it, makes Spinoza–Bayle–Diderot supersede the historiographical triumvirate of Hobbes–Locke–Montesquieu.[16] Although Spinoza's place in the period is difficult to analyse for the reason that his very name conjured accusations of heresy and atheism (wittily dramatized in Coleridge's 'Spy Nozy' episode), most of the writers featured in this book had acquaintance with the so-called radical Enlightenment; indeed, to focus on pleasure is to invite that question.

At the same time, attention to pleasure's radical or materialist backdrop does not need to obscure its religious resonances, as they are often intertwined in the texts under discussion. For instance, in one of the most famous Romantic-period poetic uses of the term, Friedrich Schiller's 'An die Freude' ('Ode to Joy', 1785), joy has pagan and Christian connotations, as well as sensual and political ones. The first stanza has a particular resonance for my own arguments about pleasure and community in Enlightenment thought: 'Thy enchantments bind together / What did custom stern divide, / Every man becomes a brother, / Where thy gentle wings abide.'[17] In Coleridge's 'Dejection: An Ode' (1802), 'joy' has a Christian resonance, rescuing it from what Coleridge saw, in the *Opus Maximum*, for instance, as pleasure's sensualist taint. Wordsworth uses the word 'joy' frequently in his poetry, though typically as an intensifier of 'pleasure', not as its opposite, and perhaps partly for prosodic reasons, given its rhyming versatility over pleasure or happiness. The word 'enjoy' is also an important term; one of its meanings (since the fifteenth century) is to have the use or benefit of something, thus 'enjoyment' has intimations of ownership and possession that are evident in Wordsworth's poem *Home at Grasmere.*

Self-interest and self-love

Spinoza's *conatus*, the striving to exist, as well as the idea that pleasure derives from the interaction of bodies, may have influenced Diderot's force-based definition of pleasure. Pleasure is sometimes considered as analogous to self-interest and self-love, and indeed the notion of humans as motivated exclusively by self-interest, usually associated with Hobbes and Mandeville, is often seen as one of the great, controversial Enlightenment ideas bequeathed to modernity. My own reading of eighteenth-century texts cautions against a simplistic identification of pleasure and self-interest and against a hard binary of self-interest and altruism, thus offering a footnote to the great conceptual genealogists, Marx and Nietzsche, and later Albert Hirschman. Marx described how individual interest and common interest were only made contradictory through the historical division of labour.[18] Nietzsche argued 'it is only with the decline of aristocratic value-judgements that this whole opposition between "egoistic" and "unegoistic" comes to impose itself increasingly on the human conscience'.[19] Albert Hirschman showed how the idea of interest drifted over two centuries from a notion of a rational decision-making that could counteract the overwhelming force of the passions and appetites, to a narrower notion of economic advancement. As he summarized it, the seventeenth-century realist political maxim 'Interest will not lie' had become, by the eighteenth century, the crucially broader yet flatter notion 'Interest governs the world.'[20] Hirschman's argument was centrally concerned with how economic activities came to be understood as harmless *doux commerce* as opposed to the context of the violence of the passions out of which interest emerged. It is, however, relevant to my own analysis of how 'pleasure' in the eighteenth century carries a wider range of meanings than simply 'selfishness' or 'individuality'.

Other intellectual historians have recently built on Hirschman's analysis to untangle the semantic web around luxury, self-interest, altruism and 'self-love'.[21] The term 'self-love' in English, 'regard for one's own well-being or happiness' (*OED*), dates from the late seventeenth century. Christian Maurer has shown its growing importance from the 1720s onwards, and identified the various meanings that attached to it: as a hedonistic and egoistic concept; as love of praise; as self-esteem; as excessive pride; and as self-respect.[22] The first is especially important for understanding the history of the concept of pleasure. As Maurer points out, 'hedonistic' desires aiming at pleasure for the agent are now frequently assumed to be a subset of 'egoistic' desires, which benefit the agent more broadly; in terms of power, pleasure, wealth, security, self-preservation, etc. Maurer suggests that in the early eighteenth century, a contrast between hedonistic and egoistic desires was pointed up by Stoic arguments that an infant has a natural impulse to self-preservation but not to pleasure. 'Self-love' is a theme of my reading of Rousseau, which looks at the presence of 'pleasure' in his concepts of *amour de soi* and *amour propre*. Though Maurer does not make this point, the special complexity of pleasure as a 'selfish' feeling in the late eighteenth century is pointed up by the fact that the word 'egoism' appears only in 1800 ('Generous sentiment and affection in France ... was lost in selfishness or according to their new word *Egoism*', *OED*). A certain cultural self-consciousness about new theories of a selfish psychology is also registered in one of the first extended elaborations of the concept of 'disinterest', being William Hazlitt's *Essay on the Principles of Human Action: Being an Argument in Favour of the Natural Disinterestedness of the Human Mind* (1805).[23] One of my aims is to chart a prehistory for this early nineteenth-century articulation of selfish pleasure versus 'disinterestedness'.

Epicureanism and hedonism

The brief mentions of Stoicism, above, reminds us of the long afterlives of ancient theories of pleasure and happiness, which quietly echo throughout my study. Classical Greek philosophy from the pre-Socratics to the Stoics devoted much attention to questions of *aisthesis* and *hedone, euthumia, terpsis, eudaimonia, aponia* and *ataraxia*. Pleasure is a major theme of Plato's *Phaedo, Republic* and *Philebus* and of Aristotle's *Nicomachean Ethics* and *Magna Moralia*. It is, however, Epicureanism that has been remembered as pleasure's great school; a school whose complexity and reception is presently the subject of long-overdue critical attention.[24] Epicurus' focus on pleasure could be said to stem from his premise of cosmic randomness as well as from his legendary gentleness; our *kosmos* is 'just one among indefinitely many which are generated and destroyed in the infinite and everlasting universe simply as a result of the unceasing motion of atoms in the void'.[25] Without teleology or rational design, humans should be free to pursue (albeit thoughtfully and prudently) their own well-being. In the 'Letter to Menoeceus', Epicurus defined pleasure in terms of our perpetual attempts to avoid pain and fear, and to quieten desire:

For we are in need of pleasure only when we are in pain because of the absence of pleasure, and when we are not in pain, then we no longer need pleasure. And this is why we say that pleasure is the starting-point and goal of living blessedly. For we recognized this as our first innate good, and this is our starting point for every choice and avoidance, and we come to this by judging every good by the criterion of feeling.[26]

The ideal state of the soul is *ataraxia*, which consists in 'confident expectation of bodily pleasure and pleasant memory of it'.[27] The absence of any disturbance of mind or stimulation from *ataraxia* suggested to the Cyrenaics onwards that pleasure is something negative, even deathly.[28] Modern literary critics are more likely to associate this argument with Freud or perhaps Derrida, though I frame the problems of *ataraxia* in terms of the work of Rousseau, Wordsworth and Adorno. One of my key arguments is that this model of still, calm pleasure has a politically utopian aspect in these writers, sometimes in opposition to an image of happiness as 'striving' and 'flourishing' (see the discussion of 'happiness' below). Another aspect of the Epicurean notion of pleasure that (I suggest) is relevant to Enlightenment notions concerns the division between pleasures of change (kinetic) and of stable condition (katastematic); i.e. pleasures that arise in the process of satisfying desire, and pleasures that are enjoyed in equilibrium, in the absence of pain. Partly with reference to Jean-Luc Nancy, I argue that the way that pleasure is characterized, the texture of its description, in these eighteenth- and early nineteenth-century texts, has consequences for the political readings we make of it.

Actual references to Epicureanism in the eighteenth century are ambiguous, as they could mean many things, even simply insults. Epicureanism, Epicurism, the Epicure, etc., were terms widely used from the sixteenth century onwards to mean disciples of Epicurus; atheism or irreligion; atomism; materialism; someone who gave himself up to sensual pleasures; gluttony; delicacy of eating preferences. Epicureanism was not necessarily opposed to Christianity: Augustine is sometimes seen as a Christian-Epicurean thinker, and Pierre Gassendi's dissemination of Epicurus was also intended to reconcile him with Christianity.[29] A caution about 'hedonism' and 'atheism' is required. When Leibniz stated that Locke 'is pretty much in agreement with M. Gassendi's system', he was not likely to have been referring primarily to what we now call his 'hedonism', but to his atomism and his cautious claim (in the second edition of the *Essay*) that matter could think.[30] Aside from specialist, now obsolete uses, the words 'hedonist' and 'hedonism', derived from the Greek *hedone* (pleasure), were not used in English until the mid-nineteenth century (*OED*). Amusingly for Romanticists, the *OED* gives Thomas De Quincey the honour of coinage: 'Gentlemen, I am a Hedonist; and if you must know why I take opium, that's the reason why.'

Happiness

In modern everyday usage, happiness is often thought of as a broader, narrative and temporal concept compared with the more fleeting and bodily experience of pleasure; I explore these differences historically in relation to Wordsworth's *Excursion* in Chapter 5. The relation and priority of happiness and pleasure is a longstanding philosophical controversy that may originate in Aristotle's discussion of *eudaimonia* (variously translated as 'happiness', 'flourishing', 'well-being'). In the history of the idea of happiness, as Darrin McMahon has revealed, the Enlightenment was central, as it helped shift what was once a predominantly luck-based or tragic conception (as suggested by the Middle English root of happiness, 'hap', (un)lucky occurrence) to a self-determining and universalizing notion, i.e. the idea that we can find, increase or threaten our own and others' happiness. More recently, much research has been conducted into 'happiness' and 'well-being' in neuroscience, economics and sociology; this has been accompanied by works of popular philosophy and intellectual history, many of which have disparaged 'pleasure' in favour of 'happiness' as a supposedly ethically richer concept.[31] Though I believe that all these terms must be seen as existing in a rich and productive matrix, part of my argument is to defend the basic, Enlightenment notion of 'pleasure', and to question the ethical presuppositions of its dismissal.

Utility and utilitarianism

For Bentham, no fan of poetry or linguistic ambiguity in general, all the terms I have discussed above were completely interchangeable, signifying only pleasurable sensation; nonetheless, he accorded the concept of pleasure absolute priority in his social philosophy. The impact of Bentham's massive yet fragmentary publication *The Introduction to the Principles of Morals and Legislation* (1789) was somewhat lost that year in the din of the French Revolution, and Bentham did not figure prominently in the British cultural imaginary until Mill promulgated his work in the second decade of the nineteenth century. Nonetheless, Bentham stands at the (rationalistic) extreme of a long tradition of thought on pleasure's definition, distribution and maximization: in its attempts to 'spread' pleasure widely and fairly, utilitarianism was one of the most significant destinations of the earlier ideas of pleasure-as-social traced in this book (although within Bentham's strict individualism there could be no such thing as 'communal feeling' or 'community'). Comparisons with Wordsworth's ideas about pleasure are made in Chapters 3 and 5.

Bliss, comfort, delight

The word 'bliss' has an old link with 'blessing', and thus connotes gifts, gratitude and God, all of which I discuss in Chapter 4 in relation to *Home at Grasmere* and *The Prelude*. 'Comfort', on the other hand, appears to lose its primarily religious sense (to strengthen against temptation and affliction) over the course of the eighteenth century, gaining instead a physical, sensual designation (material and physical well-being).[32] Indeed, the *OED* lists the first modern instance of 'comfort' as occurring in Wordsworth's *Excursion*. 'Delight' was originally spelled as 'delite' until the sixteenth century: it comes from the Italian *dilettare* and in turn from the Latin *delectare* (to charm, delight), which is rooted in *lactare*, suckling. Delight has a long link with poetic theory, following Horace's definition of poetry's aim as *aut delectare aut prodesse est* (either to delight or to educate); but as this book shall argue, the specific Enlightenment inflection of this old prescription is to make that delight *shared*.

Contentment, complacency

Content and contentment, distantly linked to 'contain', refer to a state of being stopped or satisfied. Subsequently, perhaps since Nietzsche's extolling of human striving and excess in the mid-nineteenth century, such pleasant containment has tended to be interpreted negatively by modern theorists. I explore this question in my discussion of *Home at Grasmere*. 'Complacency' is a particularly interesting Wordsworthian pleasure-word, which in his poetry carries a positive sense of both mutuality (as in the Latin derivation *complacere*, pleasing-with) and calm content. He might have taken this usage from Milton, credited with the first use of 'complacency' in 1643; the *OED* also cites *Paradise Lost*'s use of the older word 'complacence' with positive connotations of mutuality. (Another Miltonic word with similar communal and Christian inflection, 'congratulation', appears regularly in Wordsworth's poetry, as I discuss in Chapter 4.) But the alternative meaning of 'complacence' as self-satisfaction has now gained a negative prominence: it stands for being apolitical, not mutual.

CRITICAL CONTEXT

These latter terms are particularly interesting for an understanding of the critical history of pleasure, especially Wordsworthian pleasure: they alert us to the significance of 'ordinary' or 'common' pleasure, and to the way that the terms began to accrue 'bad' existential and political connotations, especially in the twentieth century. The strain of shared or common pleasure investigated by this book was described above as 'almost' forgotten. Ideas of plenitude, bliss in nature and existential delight were once considered paradigmatic of Romanticism. Matthew Arnold's 'Preface' to his 1879 selection of Wordsworth provides the classic example of this view:

The cause of its greatness is simple, and may be told quite simply. Wordsworth's poetry is great because of the extraordinary power with which Wordsworth feels the joy offered to us in nature, the joy offered to us in the simple primary affections and duties; and because of the extraordinary power with which, in case after case, he shows us this joy, and renders it so as to make us share it.

The source of joy from which he thus draws is the truest and most unfailing source of joy accessible to man. It is also accessible universally. Wordsworth brings us word, therefore, according to his own strong and characteristic line, he brings us word

'Of joy in widest commonalty spread.'[33]

Arnold's incantatory references to 'joy' (perhaps linked to his longstanding interest in Spinoza) are partly meant to rescue Wordsworth from those admirers who wish to see him as a philosopher, who hanker after a 'system of thought' in his verse. 'Joy', by contrast, is meant to be self-evident, it is 'reality', 'life' and 'power'; philosophy is the 'illusion'.[34] This Victorian view of Wordsworth's poetics as rooted in an essential, healing pleasure – one also emblazoned in John Keble's 1830s lectures on classical poetry, dedicated to Wordsworth – has been a bugbear for twentieth-century critics, who desired to reverse Arnold's emphasis, often using the quotation above as preface and counterpoint to their own readings.[35] The aim of this study is to try to bring pleasure and philosophy back into relation with one another; attempting to redeem the idea of 'joy in widest commonalty spread' as a political core of Enlightenment philosophy and Wordsworth's poetry. But before suggesting how this might be done, a brief history of pleasure's twentieth-century critical career is required.

Modernist critics were often averse to Romanticism's purported emotionalism, and especially to its language of pleasure: hence, perhaps, W.B. Yeats' suspicion that Wordsworth was 'full of a sort of utilitarianism'.[36] The idea that 'contentment' must reflect an affirmation of, or indifference to, political conditions was also prominent. Although his views on hedonism were highly nuanced (and are discussed further in Chapter 4), Adorno gave the strongest formulation of the idea that pleasure supports the status quo in his 1944 'Culture Industry' essay: 'To be pleased means to say Yes. ... Pleasure always means not to think about anything, to forget suffering even where it is shown.'[37] Though historical currents of sexual 'liberation' and the enjoyments of 'mass' culture were part of Adorno's analysis, in the 1960s and 1970s they spurred new accounts of the problem of pleasure for literary criticism. Lionel Trilling's rich 1965 essay 'The Fate of Pleasure' considered the almost 'shocking' assertions of pleasure's significance to Wordsworth and Enlightenment philosophy from the other side of a breach named 'modernity'. For Trilling, modern literature – anticipated in Keats' notion of pleasure 'turning to poison while the bee-mouth sips' ('Ode to Melancholy'), epitomized in Dostoevsky's 1864 novella *Notes from Underground*, and marked by the Freudian death drive – could only represent pleasure as infantilizing and entrapping. This breach also meant a final severance of (existentialist, nihilist) literature from (affirmative) politics.[38] Chapters 1 and 2 discuss some of the late eighteenth-century origins of what we might call this 'liberal' critique, which represents pleasure as at odds with the heroic-tragic striving of the individual.

Emanating from a different political nexus, Roland Barthes' *Le plaisir du texte* (1973) was arguably the most thoughtful and influential attempt to defend pleasure from dour and simplistic 'socio-ideological analyses', and from the 'indifference' of the field of knowledge.[39] A delicate, fragmentary and aphoristic study, treating in particular the reader's pleasure, it has primarily been remembered for its account of (orgasmic, subject-decentring) *jouissance*. Indeed, it is sometimes seen as an attack on 'ordinary' pleasure as conventional, bourgeois and conforming to the status quo, in line with many theoretical suspicions of contentment.[40] But this is to misunderstand its recognition of the dialectic of pleasure and Barthes' constant pressure upon the categories of 'high' and 'low'. Barthes questioned why desire was seen to have 'epistemic dignity' whereas pleasure was 'idle or vain': 'the "populace" does not know Desire – only pleasures'.[41] He showed how pleasure rests on the horns of a dilemma between ideology critique (a 'class notion') and the twentieth-century

French Hegelian tradition (the 'dignity' of 'desire'). Barthes diagnosed the 'entire minor mythology' that makes pleasure a 'rightist notion' as well as the ambivalence of literary critics faced with pleasurable texts and 'bad' ideologies.[42] Barthes' 1977–8 lectures on *The Neutral* at the Collège de France also occasionally lighted on pleasure, and framed it in terms of the irenic (peaceable) desire, the desire for reconciliation in particular of argumentative discourses or ideologies and the evasion of binary positions (active / passive, male / female, subject / object). Pleasure here has connections to quietude and futility (themes that are currently attracting new interest in Romantic studies); Barthes' hints about the ethical and political possibilities of this conjunction are similar to my own considerations of Enlightenment pleasure.[43] In the late 1970s and 1980s, buoyed by feminist and queer politics, questions of the body and sexuality gained increasing prominence in cultural and literary studies. Alongside Barthes, Gilles Deleuze and Michel Foucault contested the meanings and priority of desire, pleasure and *jouissance*, a set of terms that increasingly drew the attention of Anglo-American literary scholarship and cultural studies.[44]

In that context, Barthes' attempt to define pleasure as a space beyond ideological conflict proved controversial. Writing in the early 1980s, Fredric Jameson was suspicious of Barthes' argument in *Le plaisir du texte*, comparing the way that both he and Lionel Trilling appealed to 'individual gratification ... for a repudiation of Left politics', and to an extent confirming Barthes' prediction about the political factionalism that pleasure stirs up.[45] Yet, Jameson concluded his essay with another defence of pleasure, claiming that it stood for 'the reconciliation – momentary as it may be – with the necessity of physical existence in a physical world'; as well as the 'materialization of what had formerly been "idealistic"', including words, images, thought itself.[46] Jameson suggested that Barthes' ideas on pleasure (alongside those of the Italian left thinker Sebastiano Timpanaro, briefly discussed in Chapter 4 of this book) emerged from a sense that Marxism had neglected existential themes.[47] Marxist criticism had often been hostile to a theorization of pleasure, because of its apparent celebration of consumerism, and a feared displacement of labour by affect and sexuality. Pleasure thus presented a quandary to an avowedly materialist criticism: while it might invoke capitalist indulgence and the aesthetic veil of falsely universal feeling, it also gestured towards utopian possibilities represented by the liberated body. The political duality of the aesthetic, brought out in Terry Eagleton's survey, could also be applied to pleasure in general: 'If it offers a generous utopian image of reconciliation between men and women at present divided from one another, it also blocks and mystifies the real political movement towards such historical community.'[48] Drawing from Marx's positive image of human bodily flourishing in the *Economic and Philosophical Manuscripts* and Adorno's *Aesthetic Theory*, Terry Eagleton and other critics have occasionally glimpsed the ethical complexities of the idea of pleasure, but have tended to elaborate only the supposedly ideologically suspect dimension.

This is especially true within modern Wordsworth studies, which (for all the dangers of treating them as synecdochic for literary studies) provide a neat distillation of the critical dialectic of pleasure. The phenomeno-logical and deconstructive work on Wordsworth associated with the Yale School from the late 1960s to 1980s placed emphasis on themes of the body, apperception and intersubjectivity, as for instance in Geoffrey Hartman's work. Yet the tone of much deconstructive work on Words-worth in this period was antithetical to a political engagement with pleasure, shaped rather by a language of asceticism, renunciation and apocalypse.[49] Wordsworth's declarations of shared pleasure were held to be frail or haunted by their impossibility, according with a deconstructive undermining of presence and a stable idea of the subject, and the central-ity of desire, lack and negation in the intellectual framework of Schelling, Schlegel and Hegel. The new historicist and ideology critique work on Wordsworth dating from the 1980s sometimes recognized the political *potential* of Wordsworth's references to common pleasure, but usually treated it as a poetic obfuscation of real (conservative) commitments to be found in Wordsworth's prose writing.[50] To the extent that Wordsworth, especially viewed from the perspective of his political apostasy, was a symbol of Romantic ideology, so too was his version of pleasure corus-cated for being 'bad': transcendentalizing, distracting, disembodied, indi-vidualizing, or not individualizing enough and rather falsely universal.[51] Though they may not have expressed it in exactly this way, one could say that for new historicist critics, Wordsworth's notion of pleasure as 'com-placency' denoted only self-satisfied ignorance of real political conditions.

In trying to rethink the eighteenth-century meanings of pleasure and their political potential, I am not trying merely to dismiss the 'charges' of conservatism or quietism laid at the door of writers like Shaftesbury, Kant and Wordsworth, though it seems clear that critics can no longer avail themselves of that particular prosecutorial persona.[52] I wish to show that their reference to pleasure should not be the evidence by which they are charged, and that it is a resource for many different kinds of ethical and political argument. It has rarely been recognized that pleasure is a histor-ically and theoretically differentiated concept. The sentimental tradition in which modern capitalism developed gave pleasure an important role, both in terms of the idea of pleasurable self-interest that would stimulate economic growth and in terms of sympathetic connection between individuals. Later, diverse, revolutionary and anti-capitalist arguments also imagined alternative forms of society through a notion of pleasure. The questions I try to ask in this study focus on how pleasure is linked to the 'collective' and how it is linked to 'power'. In this sense, it forms part of a wider current in political theory to develop affirmative descriptions of shared life, associated, for instance, with Michael Hardt and Antoni Negri's postmodern, global rethinking of class or proletariat as *multitude*, or, at a more mainstream level, Barbara Ehrenreich's leftist history of 'collective joy', seen in traditions of dancing and other ecstatic celebration.[53]

Returning to scholarly domains, one may witness there a strong and growing interest in the *social* life of philosophy, showing its historical connections with anthropology and putting affect at its heart. So, for instance, intellectual historians and philosophers have done much to shift the image of Kant's 'dry' formalism, focusing instead on the way in which his ideas of reason are embodied and the richness of his discussion of feeling and affect, partly through attention to his late writings including the Anthropology lectures as well as the Third Critique.[54] This newly anthropological attitude to the history of philosophy provides a middle way through theoretical aporia that dominated scholarship in the 1990s: biological determination versus cultural construction; individualism or community; formalism or history. Within other modes of literary theory, continuing the psychoanalytic and feminist projects, subjectivity is often read as inherently social or relational rather than monadic and autonomous. Feeling and affect are sometimes represented as the site of this intersubjectivity or *non*-subjectivity, somewhat surprisingly, given the common tendency to conceive of emotions as primarily private.[55] For any reconsideration of pleasure, timeliness must lie partly in the 'affective' turn that has marked much work in the humanities in the first decade of the twenty-first century. The eighteenth century has been the locus of particularly intensive study of affect and emotion, being a period in which numerous works on feeling were published. Scholars of this period have provided taxonomies of passions and emotion; they have looked at the shifting meaning of individual affects; and cultural history has explored the term 'sensibility', used to describe a generalized cult of strong feelings from around 1740 to the end of the century. The notion of Enlightenment itself implies a refiguration of the relationship between reason and unreason, as Adorno and Horkheimer long ago showed; Enlightenment invites the question of affect in relation to other kinds of experience and knowledge.[56] Interest in affect as well as Frankfurt School influence has shaped contemporary literary criticism's revived sympathy for questions of beauty and the aesthetic: forms of knowing that emerge in pleasure.[57] All of these critical developments – the collective in political theory; the anthropological in the history of philosophy; the social life of affect; and a 'return' to the aesthetic – provide the context for this book's investigation of shared pleasure in the Enlightenment and in Wordsworth. It joins other recent works in Romanticism that recognize new possibilities in the history of pleasure.[58]

OUTLINE OF THE BOOK

This book is organized into two parts. Part I treats Enlightenment thought, focusing on Shaftesbury, Kant, Rousseau and Wollstonecraft and their philosophical legacies; Part II focuses on Wordsworth's prose and poetry. Chapter 1 provides a broad philosophical background to the life and afterlife of one way of thinking about the communal possibilities of pleasure, by focusing on the ancient idea of the *sensus communis* as it resurfaces in the aesthetics of Shaftesbury and Kant. The *sensus communis* originally referred to a sixth, combinatory sense that united the perceptions of the other five senses, and Shaftesbury appears to have been the first to interpret it in terms of pleasure, in order, as I show, to unpick the Hobbesian idea of self-interest. Kant is the other major eighteenth-century figure to draw upon the idea of the *sensus communis* in his consideration of pleasure, a question to which he turned late in his philosophical career and which he described as providing 'material at which to marvel'.[59] This chapter shows how readings of Kant's aesthetics have focused on the politics of the sublime rather than on the collectivity of pleasure described in the *Critique of Judgment*, and looks at modern and postmodern conceptions of the *sensus communis* to consider pleasure's role in political philosophy. Chapter 2 leads on from this by considering how, in Rousseau and Wollstonecraft's political philosophy and novels, pleasure is associated with strength, which has both utopian dimensions (pleasure as the condition for generosity, hope and openness to others) and politically negative ones (pleasure as implicated with mastery and domination). The ambiguous concepts of *amour de soi*, *amour propre* and the sentiment of existence are traced through Rousseau's *Julie* (1760), *Emile* (1762) and the *Rêveries* (1776–8), and contrasted with Wollstonecraft's *Vindication of the Rights of Woman* (1792) and *The Wrongs of Woman, or Maria* (1798). I consider the critical legacies of these texts, particularly for deconstruction and for feminism.

Part II focuses on Wordsworth, refocusing the Enlightenment questions of pleasure raised in Part I through the lens of both canonical and less canonical poems. Chapter 3 explores the status of pleasure in *The Lyrical Ballads*, beginning with a close reading of 'Lines Written in Early Spring' as a poem questioning the natural theological doctrines of the pleasure of the natural world and the naturalness of human happiness. I go on to look at the prose documents that accompanied the *Lyrical Ballads*; well-known texts, but to which the centrality of philosophical accounts of pleasure has not been recognized. I suggest the reasons for Wordsworth's interest in this theme, and the ways in which this topic helps us re-examine the relationship of Wordsworth to utilitarian thought. Chapter 4 focuses on the 1805 *Prelude* and *Home at Grasmere* (*c.* 1806), beginning by charting *The Prelude*'s attempt to define and categorize types of pleasure, and looking at the poem's themes of reciprocity and congratulation. *Home at Grasmere* is premised on hyperbolic joy and satisfaction, recalling Rousseau's bliss on the Ile de Saint-Pierre. Though the poem's images of circularity and enclosure are often viewed as poetic failure or biographical symptom, I read them against Georges Bataille's criticism of a closed bourgeois economy to suggest that the seemingly paradoxical vision of a non-teleological system of pleasure is more theoretically radical than previously recognized. Chapter 5 opens with a discussion of Wordsworth's 'Character of the Happy Warrior' (1807), as a means of opening up the theme of 'happiness', a word that is the subject of a famous crux in 'The Ruined Cottage' and *The Excursion* (1814). In tracing the progression of its central character, the Solitary, from depression to gladness, *The Excursion* stages debates around the nature of pleasure and happiness, drawing on Epicurean, Stoic and Protestant (especially Miltonic) sources. The chapter considers the political problems of sovereignty and normativity raised by *The Excursion*'s attempts to 'spread' more widely the joy celebrated in *The Prelude*.

This book, therefore, spans a period of just over a century, and attests to continuity between the 'Enlightenment' treatment of pleasure represented, broadly, by the major philosophers Shaftesbury, Rousseau, Kant and Wollstonecraft, and the 'Romantic' writing of Wordsworth.[60] Such continuity must be particularly evident when it comes to any discussion of affect in the 'long' eighteenth century, given that Romanticism has often been understood as a discourse of feeling. It is not an influence study; however, there are long-acknowledged lines of influence between its key protagonists. Shaftesbury's philosophy was influential in Germany and France in the mid-eighteenth century; as previously mentioned, Diderot translated Shaftesbury's *Inquiry* in 1745, which Rousseau would probably have known, and Kant was familiar with Shaftesbury from an early stage in his career.[61] Kant was enormously influenced by Rousseau: *Emile* was said to be the only text that kept him from his daily walk. Wollstonecraft read and commented upon much of Rousseau's work, and her *Vindication* was a direct response to *Emile*. Wordsworth, in his turn, read Shaftesbury, Rousseau and Wollstonecraft.[62] If Wordsworth did not read Kant's philosophy in the original, he may have read reviews of it, and introductions; Coleridge's absorption in Kantian thought goes back to 1800.[63] The book gives special prominence to Wordsworth's writing because I believe his poetry offers a uniquely interesting vantage point on, even a high-water mark of, Enlightenment speculations about pleasure as a single yet philosophically suggestive phenomenon.

One way of bringing that singularity into view is to consider the English publishing phenomenon of 'Pleasures Of' poems, which almost constitute a poetic genre in themselves. Between 1700 and 1850, some 330 individual poems based on this formula appeared, many in the wake of Joseph Addison's 1712 essay 'The Pleasures of the Imagination'. Addison's essay, published in *The Spectator* in eleven parts, crowns the sense of Sight as the key facilitator of what would later be termed 'aesthetic' experience. Pleasures of the imagination are good for virtue and for health, offering a perfect mean between the 'gross' pleasures of sense and the 'refined' and 'difficult' pleasures of understanding: 'like a gentle exercise to the faculties, [they] awaken them from sloth and idleness, without putting them upon any labour or difficulty'.[64] The man of taste also experiences a feeling of power (a claim that was subject to ideology critique in the late twentieth century): he gains 'a kind of property in everything he sees, and makes the most rude, uncultivated parts of nature administer to his pleasures'.[65] Addison's essay generated an efflorescence of 'pleasures of' poems over the century, including Thomas Warton's 'Pleasures of Melancholy' in the 1740s, and Samuel Rogers' 'The Pleasures of Memory' and Thomas Campbell's 'The Pleasures of Hope' in the 1790s. Alongside these influential poems appeared countless others detailing all sorts of 'pleasures', from botany, piety and temperance, to oddfellowship and anarchy. Perhaps the most significant was Mark Akenside's precocious philosophical poem, *The Pleasures of Imagination*, of 1744. Akenside's three-part, 2,000-line work expressed an ambition to 'mix the Stoic with Platonic Philosophy', to join empiricist and rationalist doctrines and aspired to the tradition of Lucretius and Pope.[66] The poem operates with various distinctions around pleasure drawn mainly from Addison: first, the 'primary pleasures' of imagination which are derived from the perception of 'greatness', 'novelty' and 'beauty'; second, the 'adventitious' pleasure, usually of sense, which may accompany and enhance the imaginative delights; and third, the 'secondary' pleasure to be gained from art, ridicule and wit. These categories are looser than in Addison's essay, and 'adventitious' pleasure is particularly ambiguous, referring both to sensual pleasure (e.g., smelling a flower), and intellectual pleasure (e.g., the satisfaction of understanding how a rainbow is formed). In this latter discussion, 'pleasure' is generally used in the singular and not the plural; and here the poem approaches the kind of investigation of general, philosophical pleasure with which my book is concerned, and which can be most richly seen in Wordsworth. There are some hints of the egalitarian politics with which pleasure may be aligned in the climax to Book 3, where 'taste' is defined as 'these internal powers ... feelingly alive / To each fine impulse' (515–17), not attainable by wealth or power but imprinted in the individual by God. At the end of day, the 'swain', 'forgetful of his toils / And due repose ... loiters to behold / The sunshine gleaming as through amber clouds, / O'er all the western sky' (528–31). God's justice or generosity is equated with this freely available pleasure in nature: 'Free as the vital breeze or light of heaven' (525).

These passages hint at, but do not get very close to, the vastly expanded engagement with the concept of pleasure that we find in Wordsworth. There are many reasons, historical and poetical, why Wordsworth's poetry might be more philosophically and politically sensitive to 'pleasure' than that of his predecessors. The major shifts in political language brought about in the 1780s and 1790s with the French Revolution and the birth of utilitarianism made available a new utopian and egalitarian register for pleasure. Yet, Wordsworth's poetic-intellectual consideration of pleasure seems to go beyond such a context, amounting to a career-long rumination on pleasure's ethical meanings. One other explanation might lie in Wordsworth's explicit and ongoing attempts to think about the status and social purpose of poetry itself. It is true that poetry has always been associated with pleasure, as far back as Horace's description of the literary function as being to 'instruct and delight'. But the late eighteenth century is sometimes said to be the moment of the definitive fracturing of the modern intellectual 'disciplines' – as Wordsworth put it, into those of 'a lawyer, a physician, a mariner, an astronomer, or a natural philosopher'.[67] At this moment, then, perhaps the question of what 'pleasure' is, and how it might bind or separate people, seemed particularly urgently related to *poetry*. These ideas are further explored in the chapters to follow.

PART I

Pleasure philosophy

CHAPTER I

Aesthetics of pleasure: Shaftesbury, Kant and the sensus communis

In the winter of 1699, at home in St Giles, Dorset, aged 28, Antony Ashley Cooper made an agonized entry entitled 'Familiarity' in his *Askemata*, the philosophical exercises that he privately recorded until his death. His father had just died, making him Lord Cooper, Third Earl of Shaftesbury; friends, his mother, brothers, sisters were gone or changed; lonely and depressed, he had been called 'an untimely plant'; he wondered if he was 'a briar and worse than a briar, a fungus, an excrescence, a disease of the earth?'.[1] Trying with all his might to 'Bear with the regimen, the prescription, the operation', he instructs himself to 'Cut off tenderness of a certain kind; cut off *familiarity*, and that sympathy of a wrong kind. . . . See what thou has got by seeking others.'[2] Incanting Stoic lines from Epictetus and Marcus Aurelius as protection against any more loss, he gives himself a 'terrible' 'condition and law':

> To take pleasure in nothing.
> To do nothing with affection.
> To promise well of nothing.
> To engage for nothing.

Begin, therefore, from this moment and see how thou canst hold up against those other sort of reasonings, those compoundings, extenuations, excuses, self-flatteries, self-bemoanings. *Shall I abandon all my friends?*[3]

This tormented passage gives one example of how, for Shaftesbury, sociability is deeply, even dangerously, connected to pleasure. In a following entry on the 'Passions', the same link is made but the evaluation is reversed: 'sociable' joy, compared to private pleasure, is positive and durable: it is 'soft, still, peaceable, serene, which has no mixture or alloy; of which there is no excess, but the more it is felt, the more perfect and refined it grows'.[4] Much of Shaftesbury's philosophy can be seen as a complex, sometimes contradictory investigation into how feelings of community generate pleasure, and how pleasure may have moral and political consequences. In his writing, pleasure potentially represents selfish voluptuousness; yet, he argues that our unavoidably powerful (and ultimately moral) drive to sociability is ultimately inseparable from pleasure. He goes so far as to suggest that even apparently self-serving hedonism – even the most bodily of pleasures – is grounded in a continual consciousness of others, and a desire for reciprocity.

This chapter offers a philosophical background to the book's key ideas about pleasure and politics by means of a reading of two major figures of eighteenth-century aesthetics: Shaftesbury and Kant. It performs a ground-clearing for Part II's analysis of Wordsworth in several ways. First, concerns Romanticism's critical history: Wordsworth's poetry has often been contextualized within eighteenth-century aesthetics, and his treatment of pleasure has been damned for its traces of 'aesthetic ideology' deemed to stem from that tradition. Returning to that seemingly familiar tradition with a fresh eye and in the light of much recent scholarship (outside English studies) shows us a rich and complex picture, preventing any easy dismissal of Wordsworth's ideas around pleasure and morality as merely or straightforwardly evincing 'Whig ideology' or 'bourgeois self-interest'. Second, I link Shaftesbury and Kant by focusing on their treatment of the *sensus communis*, an ancient concept of a shared or common sense into which Shaftesbury first wove the idea of pleasure. The possibility of this *sensus communis* emerges in Chapter 3 as central to Wordsworth's poetic manifesto. Third, and more implicitly, is the larger question of the relationship of philosophy to poetry, and where pleasure stands in relation to them. One of my larger claims in this chapter and in the book as a whole is that the formal properties of a description of pleasure bear strongly on the political meanings that may emerge from it. Shaftesbury is not a poet nor does he even write very much *about* poetry, but we shall see how his moral and political arguments about pleasure shift along with voice and genre in his work and require a literary analysis. In the case of Kant, my chapter returns to the controversy about whether we can find in his highly formalistic treatment of pleasure any relevance to real communities or politics. Following a number of recent studies, I read the Third Critique alongside his anthropological writings, and look at pleasure as a moment of lingering and openness rather than static closure. Thus, I explore the different political possibilities that may emerge from Kant's eternally suggestive framework for pleasure.

SHAFTESBURY AND THE HISTORY OF THE 'SENSUS COMMUNIS'

The Third Earl of Shaftesbury, the delicate, bookish heir to the earldom, shadowed by his powerful Whig grandfather and his celebrated tutor, John Locke, has often been characterized as somehow weak. Adam Smith wondered if his 'puny and weakly' constitution accounted for his 'pompous' prose style and lack of 'abstract reasoning and deep searches'.[5] From a modern point of view, Shaftesbury's attempt to resist the modernity of Hobbes' and Mandeville's economic individualism, whilst embodying the aristocratic privilege of an earlier era, can easily be seen as hypocritical or doomed. For years regarded as merely a forerunner of Francis Hutcheson's formalized moral sense theory, and of Kantian disinterested aesthetics, his writing has nonetheless begun to be reappraised by intellectual historians.[6] His work provides an interesting vantage on the question of the 'ideological' ramifications of pleasure. Shaftesbury's *Inquiry concerning Virtue or Merit* and *Sensus Communis* present arguments for the natural tendency of humans to socialize, and the pleasure that such sociability entails, which in certain moments is extended to the idea that pleasure is inherently sociable.[7] Yet, as contemporary and later critics have argued, the real existence of this social feeling is provocatively questionable. 'His Notions I confess are generous and refined ... What a Pity it is that they are not true' was Mandeville's excoriating response to the *Characteristicks*.[8] Mandeville set out various arguments against Shaftesbury's belief that men are 'naturally Virtuous', and that virtue may come 'without Self-denial',[9] as well as *ad hominem* attacks on a person of 'Quiet Indolent Nature': passionless, pampered and failing to act either militarily or financially for his country's good. The calm sociable pleasures espoused by Shaftesbury are good only 'to breed Drones'.[10] Mandeville recalls instances of solitary pleasure actually spoiled by society, such as when he was privately enjoying the sight of some shining herring until 'an idle Fellow' came along to chat.[11] 'The Sociableness of Man arises from only these Two things, *viz.* The multiplicity of his Desires and the continual Opposition he meets with in his Endeavours to gratify them.'[12] He concludes that 'what we call Evil in this World ... is the grand Principle that makes us sociable Creatures' and the 'true Origin of all Arts and Sciences'. Our only hope, as his now-famous maxim had it, rests in the possibility that 'Private Vices ... may be turned into Public Benefits'.[13]

The argument about humans' natural selfishness and acquisitiveness seems so familiar to us now that to hear Shaftesbury's claims for pleasure as a source of common interest requires a genealogical sensitivity. Albert

Hirschman's brilliant study showed how in the eighteenth century, self-interest became a general paradigm, even something like a fad. Originally inspired by Machiavelli's account of *interesse* and *ragione di stati*, which advocated a reasoned rather than impassioned approach to princely decision-making, 'interest' gradually acquired in England an exclusively economic cast. Shaftesbury, watching this process at the beginning of the eighteenth century, seems unusually aware of the historical contingency of 'interest':

> You have heard it, my friend, as a common saying that 'interest governs the world'. But, I believe, whoever looks narrowly into the affairs of it, will find that passion, humour, caprice, zeal, faction and a thousand other springs, which are counter to self-interest, have as considerable a part in the movements of this machine. (*Sensus Communis*, 53–4)

Framed in the context of a boisterous dinner party, Shaftesbury's essay *Sensus Communis, an Essay on the Freedom of Wit and Humour* explores different scenarios and cultures for evidence for the existence of non-self-interested feeling. The concept of the *sensus communis* has been prone to widely differing interpretations throughout its long history.[14] This is hardly surprising when one considers that both sense and common are 'complex words' or 'keywords'. As William Empson emphasized, in the very idea of sense is an oscillation between individual and community:

> As to the more doctrinal uses, the man of sense (judging from the direct evidence of his senses) is a good deal of an individualist ... But this is far from making him isolated; for one thing because he agrees with the common man, but also from a more subtle idea that he can handle a complex human situation.[15]

The tension in the word 'common', according to Raymond Williams, is that from an early date it has referred both to 'a whole group or interest or a large specific and subordinate group', i.e. both to humankind and to the low or vulgar.[16] In the classical period, the term *sensus communis* had two main meanings: a body of opinions or knowledge shared by a number of people and a cognitive faculty that allows our separate five senses to work in common. Plato's notion of *doxa*, or common opinion, which is opposed to *episteme* or firm knowledge, comes in the first category; as does Roman common sense, celebrated by Horace and Seneca in their evocations of a kind of ordinary moral wisdom and propriety: the more negative and positive possibilities of this are here apparent. The second meaning is quasi-biological and is associated with Aristotle's *De Anima* in which he discusses an over-riding sixth sense that brings all the individual senses' impressions together. As Daniel Heller-Roazen among others has highlighted, ancient philosophy seems to have hardly used any term corresponding to modern 'consciousness', placing more emphasis on perception and sensation (*aisthesis* in its fullest signification) and particularly on touch.[17] Aristotle presented a doctrine of the five senses, but a question hung over how we compare and differentiate sensations – how do we know something as bright *and* sweet? Rather than suggesting (as modern philosophy would) that we *cognitively* judge our senses, he claimed that we sense our sensing: 'We grasp the common sensible qualities by means of [a] common sensation [or a "common sense"].'[18] Heller-Roazen points out that though Aristotle made only a few scattered comments, other ancient and medieval thinkers 'took the various Aristotelian discussions of common sensation as the starting points for far-reaching theories of a faculty that, in the idioms of Greek, Arabic, Hebrew and Latin philosophical reflection, they consistently called the "common sense" (*koinē aesithēsis, al-h(ḥiss al-mushtarak, (ḥush* or *da'at meshutaf* and *sensus communis*)'.[19]

In his commentary on *De Anima* and the *Summa Theologia*, Thomas Aquinas drew on Aristotle in describing a 'common root sensitivity' that enables us to evaluate and compare our perceptions. Descartes made some use of the term, but it appears over the course of his philosophical career to have progressively slipped from its sensuous Aristotelian meaning. Instead, he turns to the Roman rhetorical ideal of good judgement, *le bon sens*. For Heller-Roazen, this was a regrettable moment in which cogitation and consciousness came to the fore and a barrier was put up between human and animal life; he recovers a half-forgotten path from Campanello, Leibniz and Maine de Biran to Merleau-Ponty. But he does not consider how the idea of the *sensus communis* became defined as pleasurable in British aesthetic theory of the eighteenth century, nor considers the political ramifications of such a shift. Perhaps that Roman rhetorical meaning of *sensus communis* helped give it this tinge of *voluptas*; it certainly lent the concept a more anthropological and cultural signification. For Giambattista Vico, in *On the Study Methods of Our Time* (1709) and *New Science* (1725), the *sensus communis* referred to a kind of practical wisdom that could 'grasp the "circumstances" in their infinite variety' and set them in one, human context.[20]

Written around the same time as Vico's *Study Methods*, Shaftesbury's interpretation of the *sensus communis* oscillated between psychological and cultural-historical possibilities. His essay was written as a response to attacks on his *Letter concerning Enthusiasm* (1708) and published in the *Characteristics* anthology (1711) and begins by defending to a friend the 'raillery' that accompanied discussion of religion and politics during a recent evening. In the debate, appeals to 'common sense' had been made and one guest asked for a definition:

'If, by the word "sense", we were to understand opinion and judgment and, by the word "common" the generality or any considerable part of mankind, it would be hard', he said, 'to discover where the subject of common sense could lie. For that which was according to the sense of one part of mankind was against the sense of another. And if the majority were to determine common sense, it would change as often as men changed. That which was according to common sense today would be the contrary tomorrow, or soon after.' (37)

The guests consider various fields where evidence of common sense might be found – religion, policy, morals – and fail to find any scene of universal consensus: they begin to feel the dread hand of the relativism ascribed to 'our most admired modern philosophers', Locke and Hobbes (38). The author, in the good-humoured spirit of his friends, decides to explore what forms of knowledge may be safe from 'endless scepticism' (39). The second part of the essay roams from the imagined reaction of an Ethiopian to the masked faces at a Venetian Carnival, to how one might have reacted in 521 BC, witnessing the usurpation of the Persian Emperor by the incestuous Zoroastrian Magi. The point seems to be to demonstrate how a humourless fear and hatred of systems of thought may lead to the erection of systems just as prejudiced in their place. This all prepares for an attack on Hobbes, who developed 'such an abhorrence of all popular government and of the very notion of liberty itself that, to extinguish it for ever, he recommends the very extinguishing of Letters' (42). His zealous anti-zealotry leads Shaftesbury to question whether Hobbes' main argument for egotism performatively undoes itself: why should Hobbes take the trouble to 'undeceive us', if he is governed only by private interest (43–4)?

The essay builds upon these hints that natural affection does in fact exist, attempting to counter the neglect of the natural 'love of doing good' in religion and philosophy. The third part opens with a scholarly crux: Juvenal's *Satires* bemusingly claimed of nobility and the court that '*common sense is quite rare in that situation*' (48). The joke is that, under the prevailing meaning of common sense – politeness, wit, verbal skill – the court should be abundant in it. But Shaftesbury continues:

Some of the most ingenious commentators, however, interpret this very differently from what is generally apprehended. They make this common sense of the poet, by a Greek derivation, to signify sense of public weal and of the common interest, love of the community or society, natural affection, humanity, obliging-ness, or that sort of civility which rises from a just sense of the common rights of mankind and the natural equality there is among those of the same species. (48)

Shaftesbury credits four seventeenth-century scholars for interpreting the word in this richer sense, including Salmasius, who defines common sense as 'the moderate, the usual and respected mind of a man, which takes thought for the communal good in some way and does not refer every-thing to its own advantage' (48). There is a double meaning emerging in Shaftesbury's use of Juvenal's, Cicero's and Horace's term: both a feeling *for* others (lacked by a man who demands friends' attention regardless of their needs) and a feeling *shared* by those of the same species. And the former is born of the latter: 'A public spirit can come only from a social feeling or sense of partnership with humankind' (50).

Shaftesbury goes on to establish the links between this social feeling and government and argues – against Hobbes, his chief antagonist – that the obligation to act sociably does not come from the contract of the state; but instead is found in the state of nature. It must be a first principle that '*if anything be natural in any creature or any kind, it is that which is preserva-tive of the kind itself and conducing to its welfare and support*' (51). As Shaftesbury puts it, as much as we naturally eat, drink and reproduce, so do we herd and experience family and kin ties, and the playing out of these natural affections leads to the construction of society, from clan or tribe, to a public. There is not only a pleasure in such social interactions but such apparent necessity that to lack a sense of 'anything in common' would equate to lacking the 'plainest means of self-preservation and most necessary condition of self-enjoyment' (51–2). Shaftesbury argues that in the state of nature there is no clear distinction between actions taken for self and others: all serve the 'interest' of the continued existence of the species; not to feel the *sensus communis* precludes 'self-enjoyment'. It is not quite clear at this stage what the link between *sensus communis* and enjoyment may be, other than that both sex and social interaction are, by Shaftesbury's reading, intrinsically pleasurable and that we must have an innate drive towards them.

Shaftesbury argues that there is clearly evidence of non-self-interested feeling: against the simplistic maxim, 'Interest governs the world', he posits a complex social machine: 'there are more wheels and counterpoises in this engine than are easily imagined' (54). Even Epicurus, the great hero of modern theorists of selfishness, Shaftesbury argues, properly recognized that nature attaches us to lovers, family and society: only by withdrawing completely from these attractions could the self be served. But his modern followers fail to understand this power, merely changing the terminology, so that any social feelings are now considered 'modifications of this universal self-love' (55). In the final section of the essay Shaftesbury considers objections to his arguments on the part of men of taste and refinement. He points out that if they behave immorally, they are inconsistent and contradicting their main principle of pleasure and entertainment (62). Shaftesbury argues that all their enjoyment of the arts – and even of beautiful women – comes from a 'moral part' (63). Poetry, for instance, focuses on human life and the passions, which itself gives pleasure; and not only that but is inspired by 'the love of numbers, decency and proportion and this too, not in a narrow sense or after a selfish way (for who of them composes for himself?), but in a friendly social view for the pleasure and good of others, even down to posterity and future ages' (63). The feeling for beauty is truly common: 'Everyone . . . courts a Venus of one kind or another' (64). Numbers and proportion appeal to us in every part of life, even in interior design and garden planning; try as we might we cannot resist the power of order: 'The *Venestum*, the *Honestum*, the *Decorum* of things will force its way' (64). (The coercive suggestion of that word 'force' will shortly be explored.) Shaftesbury goes on to discuss what a painter's genius should consist in:

[H]is piece, if it be beautiful and carries truth, must be a whole by itself, complete, independent and withal as great and comprehensive as he can make it. So that particulars, on this occasion, must yield to the general design and all things be subservient to that which is principal, in order to form a certain easiness of sight, a simple, clear and united view, which would be broken and disturbed by the expression of any thing peculiar or distinct. (66)

Art must attempt to evoke the whole, without any disrupting particulars, and this gives the visual ease and cognitive relaxation that for Shaftesbury encapsulates aesthetic pleasure. It is clear that Shaftesbury is much less interested in the sublime tradition and its concomitant spectatorial *difficulty*. (In the *Soliloquy*, the sublime – the use of language 'most unlike to humanity or ordinary use' – is presented as a cheap short-cut to raising passions in children and undeveloped mankind, 108–9.) Shaftesbury adds a 'small remark' to Aristotle's theory of the sublime, in fact counter to Aristotle's whole meaning. He adds that artistic error tends to be a result of 'running into the unsizable and gigantic' (66), not of small and delicate work. Works of art must follow the 'natural rules of proportion and truth': 'It must have a body and parts proportionable, or the very vulgar will not fail to criticize the work when "it has neither head nor tail". For so common sense (according to just philosophy) judges of those works which want the justness of a whole' (67). Here, finally, Shaftesbury brings together the two historical meanings of common sense: the combinatory root sense that can grasp the particulars, bringing together all the different sense impressions to get a picture of the whole; and the ordinary, practical wisdom of humans, even of the vulgar, which can see when a painting is off. *Sensus communis* is therefore both the common sense of aesthetic pleasure when experiencing order; and the feeling of humans for community, their natural herd instinct. Because we are creatures that form part of a larger whole and exist relationally, we experience pleasure in perceiving the order to which we belong.

CRITICISMS OF SHAFTESBURIAN PLEASURE

The question of how humans fit into a larger order, and how different individuals may actually connect to one another, was explored in more detail in Shaftesbury's earlier work, the *Inquiry concerning Virtue or Merit*. This text, more formal and sombre than *Sensus Communis*, offers greater detail about the nature of pleasure and how it may connect us to one another. But it is also here that contradictions and hints of disconnection appear in the theory of pleasurable sociability. Even in *Sensus Communis*, Shaftesbury finally admits that common sense does not appear in identical ways in various individuals, but is rather balanced according to the function of that individual:

[I]n every different creature and distinct sex there is a different and distinct order, set or suit of passions, proportionable to the different order of life, the different functions and capacities assigned to each . . . So that where habits or affections are dislodged, misplaced, or changed, where those belonging to one species are intermixed with those belonging to another, there must of necessity be confusion and disturbance within. (215)

How, therefore, can we co-ordinate our pleasures and our common senses in order to build a harmonious and cohesive social order? Given that at the beginning of *Sensus Communis* Shaftesbury had claimed that this feeling 'rises from a just sense of the common rights of mankind and the natural equality there is among those of the same species', a feeling of species-based 'resemblance', then the discovery that there is not actually such resemblance on the level of our inward anatomy suggests that there might not be grounds for social affection at all. At times, it seems as if to bring the proposed community into view induces a rhetorical collapse of the theory of common sense.

In the *Inquiry*, the physiology or economy of pleasure is rooted in ideas about the balance of the mind and the ideal healthy state of the affections, perhaps drawing from pre-Socratic ideas (including those of Alcmaeon and Hippocrates). 'Affection' is the single most frequent word in the text, a word that for Shaftesbury implies both intention (as in the way affections relate to an object: ourselves or another) and feeling. The key task is to define positive and negative forms of affection, which Shaftesbury categorizes as natural affections (aimed at public good), self affections (private good) and unnatural affections (neither public nor private goods) (196). Much of his argument is concerned with blurring the first two categories. He writes that '*to have the natural, kindly, or generous affections strong and powerful towards the good of the public is to have the chief means and power of self-enjoyment and that to want them is certain misery and ill*' and vice versa, 'that *to have the private or self affections too strong or beyond their degree of subordinacy to the kindly and natural is also miserable*', and further that '*to have the unnatural affections . . . is to be miserable in the highest degree*' (200). What Shaftesbury calls 'affection towards self-good' is, and must be, natural. On one level, this fits with the Hobbesian idea that self-love is 'natural', but Shaftesbury reinterprets it as inherently sociable and ultimately benevolent – not because it tends towards the greater good *in spite* of selfishness, but because individual and communal ends cannot be separated. To lack the instincts of self-preservation or heterosexual intercourse – i.e. to lack self-love and self-enjoyment – would be to damage the species (170). Strictly to deny oneself pleasure would also presumably count as demonstrating unnatural affection.

Shaftesbury emphasizes that what we now often describe as aesthetic pleasure is a response to the beautiful harmony of nature (the argument for which he is most well known in the history of philosophy). Beautiful objects and socially beneficial deeds enhance the mind's sense of order, which is equated almost directly with pleasure. Natural philosophers and mathematicians, who contemplate the divine order, enjoy the greatest, most 'irrefragable, solid and durable' kind of pleasure, which is an 'entire affection' for society. This pleasure cannot be self-interested, as it looks beyond the 'private system'; nor is it disinterested ('unnatural'), because despite the seeming lack of natural advantage or interest, it is drawn from 'those numbers, that harmony, proportion and concord' that provide the basis of every structure in the cosmos and make this delight akin to a pleasure in the overall health of the system (203). Although Shaftesbury avows the superiority of academic to sexual pursuits – supported with the weird proof that the love-maker wears a contorted facial expression, unlike the scholar who displays beatific calm (221) – he does at one moment try to recuperate even the most bodily of pleasures for his providential social harmony.[21] He points out that many enjoyments of 'men of pleasure' are not individualist as such, but stem from social feelings of emulation and the company that is part of feasting and drinking. As he puts it, the 'very notion of a debauch . . . carries with it a plain reference to society or fellowship' (212): he who drinks alone can be a sot, but not a debauch (literally, a turning-away from one's duty). Going further, he suggests that even sex is always-already social, because it requires the imaginative possibility of sharing:

> The courtesans and even the commonest of women who live by prostitution know very well how necessary it is that everyone whom they entertain with their beauty should believe that there are satisfactions reciprocal and that pleasures are no less given than received. And were this imagination to be wholly taken away, there would be hardly any of the grosser sort of mankind who would not perceive their remaining pleasure to be of slender estimation. (212)

Working most effectively when they act like their sex-work is all holiday, prostitutes hint at the possibility that the belief in shared pleasure might be at least flimsy, at worst an illusion. Such a pleasure does not give knowledge of the strength of bonds between people but can even be a sign of its lack, of financial and sexual manipulation, fogged with delusion and fantasy. The spectral appearance of work in this account – the work of prostitutes – flags up what for modern commentators is a key political problem for Shaftesbury's account of pleasure. Howard Caygill has argued that the natural 'proportion' which will produce pleasure in the spectator of art or nature is nowhere explained in Shaftesbury's account and that this is because of the absence of a theory of production:

> By regarding the activity of establishing a proportion as a *je ne sais quoi*, Shaftesbury separates production from enjoyment. Pleasure issues from objects which are mysteriously brought forward for discrimination according to unknowable laws. The feeling of pleasure dictates, through an unknowable law, which actions will most contribute to the public good.[22]

For Caygill, Shaftesbury's silence or omission about the source of mental pleasure in taste and in the process by which we are motivated towards socially beneficent action is mirrored in the silence around the pains of the labourers which mysteriously produce the pleasurable luxury of the aristocracy. Caygill's argument is corroborated by other passages in the *Characteristics*, for instance when Shaftesbury casually suggests that 'It happens with mankind that, while some are by necessity confined to labour, others are provided with abundance of all things by the pains and labours of inferiors' (214). According to Caygill, instead of a working pleasure is substituted a passive, spectatorial or consumerist aesthetic, anticipating the economic changes of the eighteenth century. His wider argument traces how an older sense of 'taste' as an experimental and creative practice of 'touching' was lost to a new passive faculty that receives its laws from without. Echoing Mandeville, Caygill writes, 'Pleasure and violence are inseparable, although this inseparability can only be acknowledged in the *je ne sais quoi* or equivocal sense / idea'.[23] He goes on to find in Hutcheson the same 'violent repression of the difference between sense and idea and their analogues, private interest and public good', explicitly echoed in Hutcheson's advocacy of forced labour.[24]

This idea of the inevitable violence involved in pleasure has haunted attempts to think about politics and aesthetics. Shaftesbury's prose contains dark images that may be seen as symptoms of infection in the otherwise harmonious sociable pleasure, for example in his references to 'monsters'. Lorraine Daston and Katharine Park have argued that the meaning of monsters shifted in early modern epistemology, from originally denoting a prodigy or marvel (coming from the verb 'to warn') and being received with both pleasure and horror, to an eighteenth-century redefinition as 'nature's errors' and a considerably cooler 'distaste or repugnance' in their description.[25] In the *Inquiry*, monsters are opposed to beings of healthy affections and enjoyment. Shaftesbury asks us to imagine hearing from a 'historian or traveller' of the existence of a totally 'solitary' creature. The first test for establishing that the creature was not a 'monster' was that he 'enjoyed himself extremely, had a great relish of life' (168). Towards the end of the *Inquiry* Shaftesbury tries to explain the loss of natural affection in terms of creaturely deformation: 'monsters, such as are compounded of different kinds or different sexes'; 'monsters who are misshapen or distorted in an inward part' (215). Shaftesbury's references to monsters fits with the eighteenth-century, neo-Aristotelian paradigm Daston and Park outline, in that they are meant to confirm the impression of an ordered and standard nature.[26] But their multiplying towards the end of the *Inquiry* – along with lengthy accounts of black moods, violent urges and wildness – goes a little beyond that to hint at an intellectual or emotional dissonance with the natural harmony that is the ostensible subject of the book.

There is also a 'monstrous' language in the *Askemata* and similar doubts about the real existence of social pleasure. Shaftesbury writes in the entry entitled 'The End' that 'The perfection of human nature is in that which fits and accommodates to society, for he who wants those natural affections which tend thither, is imperfect and monstrous.'[27] Yet, the tormented notebooks often seem to fear that the author himself is 'monstrous', especially given the strict regimens proposed to guard against 'wantonness' and social dependency. The entry on 'Pleasure and Pain' starts with a series of quotations from Epictetus: 'This weak flesh is sometimes affected by harsh, sometimes by smooth impressions – the door is open.'[28] The idea of the mind as door recurs throughout the discussion, which focuses on the Stoic theme of mental vigilance. Suddenly, the author turns against himself: 'Coward flesh! – Why so? Why blame the flesh? Is not all human flesh the same? ... Say not, therefore, "coward flesh!" but "coward opinion!"' Yet the author cannot stick with the idea that only opinion, or prejudice, is to be 'blamed' rather than the body; he decided to 'throw out pleasure', before suddenly wondering if 'pain be such a business and all of that kind so terrible and hard to bear'. 'Is every soldier less a soldier for having taken of it [pleasure] or yielded to it ever so little? – for having fallen in love, caressed a mistress or a boy with fondness; for having eaten, or lain, or done those other things with too much delicacy?'[29] The same uncertainty about the moral and teleological place of pleasure is apparent in the entry 'Good and Ill', which wonders whether pleasure seems to be too subjective and relative to be defined as 'good to all'.[30]

But the doubts expressed explicitly and implicitly in Shaftesbury's writing about whether pleasure is morally acceptable, and whether it can be harmonized with social existence, should not in fact be seen as showing up the false 'ideology' of his claims. For one thing, whilst we could read the *Askemata* as a biographical 'truth' undercutting the more formal or public discussion, its literary features mark it as a form of Stoic practice of self-questioning, one that is theorized in Shaftesbury's *Soliloquy: Or Advice to an Author*, written in 1710. This long, involuted essay moves over three parts from the question of authority, to politics and the history of civil society, to the definition of philosophy itself and its therapeutic role. It argues that self-dialogue or self-division, which originated in ancient poetry and drama, is the foundational philosophical practice, for it is a means of reordering and subordinating one's passions and establishing a kind of inner plurality and humanity. Shaftesbury does not explicitly associate this process with forms of pleasure: in fact his metaphors are often violent, of military self-invasions and the surgical removal of cancerous growth. 'Interest' and 'pleasure' are nonetheless general themes of the essay. Once we have grown out of school, Shaftesbury writes, we are instructed by the real world and 'prime men' to believe that solely 'interest' governs us (137). But Shaftesbury's self-questioning leads him quickly to unravel such an apparently obvious truth. If fancy governs our interest and our interest is defined as what pleases us, then we follow ever-changing whims; thus we must 'frankly own that pleasure is no rule of good' (138). Here, 'pleasure' is defined negatively as 'interest': but he cannot stop here as his arguments keep running on: 'When I exercise my reason in moral subjects, when I employ my affection in friendly and social actions, I find I can sincerely enjoy myself. If there be a pleasure also of this kind, why not indulge it?' (138). Other kinds of pleasure have negative consequences: the languid will become a drone; the luxurious will end as a sot; the avaricious will end as a miser. But delight in 'honesty' can only have positive consequences ('growing better natured and enjoying more and more the pleasures of society') and is self-reinforcing (because 'good nature and social affection are so essential even to the pleasures of a debauch') (139).

Social pleasure is not only a subject of Shaftesbury's prose but on a certain level also an effect of his writing practice. Thinking aloud through this kind of self-dialogue is meant to strip away a false, delusional autonomy or individuality and recover a more plural, sociable inward self. Shaftesbury complains of France that '[t]he whole writing of this age is become indeed a sort of memoir-writing' (90). Ancient dialogue by contrast had 'neither the "I" nor "thou" throughout the whole work' (90). In dialogue, 'the self-interesting parties both vanish at once' (90). By dividing the self through intellectual questioning and argument, a truer 'humanity' is introduced into our character (162). This raises the question of Shaftesbury's views of the 'human' and what kind of 'plurality' might be implicit in this vision. Daniel Carey has recently revealed the complexity of Shaftesbury's response to the question of cultural diversity, which he suggests posed an increasing moral challenge after Montaigne. Carey points out how Shaftesbury wished to maintain a certain version of universal moral innatism, which would leave space for religious difference, disagreement and thus toleration (a sphere that was actually less important to him than the strictly moral).[31] Whilst Shaftesbury is clearly universalist in his moral vision (Mandeville accused him of looking 'on Virtue and Vice as permanent Realities that must ever be the same in all Countries and all Ages'[32]), the idea of the self as rooted in an interactive sociability leaves some space for our range and variousness *qua* species. And rather than depicting pleasure as an unchanging biological drive (as we might now put it), Shaftesbury suggests at one point that it may have a certain historical variety: 'I *learn* to fancy, to admire, to please, as the subjects themselves are deserving and can bear me out' (*Soliloquy*, 151). Understanding the significance of dialogue to Shaftesbury's concepts of selfhood may make us query Caygill's accusation that Shaftesbury's aesthetics are passive or consumerist and on a larger level help us to question the idea that pleasure is always connected to forms of social violence.

Indeed, the whole procedure of *Sensus Communis* could be said to incorporate a humanist awareness of diversity that generates its own pleasures. In order to counter Hobbes' dogmatic, arrogant scepticism about any other possibility than self-interest, Shaftesbury starts from the point of view of an Ethiopian amused at the sight of masked revellers in a modern European capital, or from within a strange episode of Persian history. The evidence for his argument for a 'sensus communis' is philological and literary as well as anthropological, rather than systematic or biological. Shaftesbury notes that the *Sensus Communis* essay is not a rigidly systematic kind of work and nor should it be: it would be 'out of the genius and compass of a letter such as this to frame a just plan or model by which you might, with an accurate view, observe what proportion the friendly and natural affections seem to bear in this order of architecture' (54). This is quite different from the procedure of his antagonists, 'modern projectors', who want a simple, scientific model: 'They would new-frame the human heart and have a mighty fancy to reduce all its motions, balances and weights to that one principle and foundation of a cool and deliberate selfishness' (54). This suggestion that certain methods may imply not only particular epistemological assumptions but also moral conclusions may be applied to our reading of Shaftesbury. *Sensus Communis* should not merely be seen as a popular version of Shaftesbury's 'serious' aesthetic philosophy, but as presenting those ideas differently through its alternative method of argument.[33] Reading with sensitivity to his miscellaneous literary styles, we may come to think that despite occasional argumentative flaws and political blindspots, Shaftesbury's notion of shared pleasure as a basis for community is more rich and compelling than it has often been regarded.[34]

Before turning to Kant on pleasure and community, we may finally consider Gadamer's arguments about 'humanistic', socially located versions of the *sensus communis*. His *Truth and Method* (1975), an exploration of understanding in the 'field of the human sciences', opens with aesthetics and categorizes the *Sensus Communis* as one of the four 'guiding concepts of humanism', alongside *Bildung*, judgement and taste. Gadamer was particularly interested in the *sensus communis* depicted by Shaftesbury's near-contemporary Vico. Vico's *On the Study Methods of Our Time* (1709) also inflects the concept with Roman models of pedagogy and rhetoric. This is intended as a counter to the Cartesian rationalism that will prevent young men from acquiring 'common sense', crucial for their prudence, eloquence and their interest in politics or in the life of their community.[35] In a fashion analogous to the quasi-biological 'root sense', Vico's *sensus communis* is able to 'grasp the "circumstances" in their infinite variety', to perceive something from a number of different angles and to set it into one, human context.[36] It is attentive to detail, and can cope with contradictory hypotheses; it is expansive, not reductive, unlike abstract knowledge or science.[37] Gadamer approves of Vico's notion of a knowledge based not on 'argumentation', 'but on the probable, the verisimilar', one that, unlike Aquinas' more perceptual, natural *sensus communis*, 'is a sense that is acquired through living in the community and is determined by its structure and aims'.[38] For Gadamer, Vico's deployment of the term keeps alive a 'positive ethical motif' present in the Roman (and to some extent Aristotelian) tradition: 'The grasp and moral control of the concrete situation require subsuming what is given under the universal – that is, the goal that one is pursuing so that the right thing may result. Hence it presupposes a direction of the will.'[39] Gadamer sees some continuation of this form of the *sensus communis* in Shaftesbury's 'intellectual and social virtue of sympathy' on which he built 'an entire aesthetic metaphysics'.[40] He relates this directly to the Scottish philosophy of common sense as a correction of both metaphysics and 'its dissolution in scepticism', which, Gadamer claims, still 'contains the basis of a moral philosophy that really does justice to the life of a society'.[41] It is important for him to claim that Scottish common sense philosophy retains some of this social and moral content because it allows him to set up all the more dramatically the contrast with the destruction of this content in the German appropriation of the *sensus communis*:

The metaphysics of the schools and the popular philosophy of the eighteenth century – however much they studied and imitated the leading countries of the Enlightenment, England and France – could not assimilate an idea for which the social and political conditions were utterly lacking. The concept of *sensus communis* was taken over, but in being emptied of all political content lost its genuine critical significance. *Sensus communis* was understood as a purely theoretical faculty: theoretical judgment, parallel to moral consciousness (conscience) and taste. Thus it was integrated into a scholasticism of the basic faculties.[42]

Thus, Kant's 'scholastic' approach to the *sensus communis* desiccates what had been a thriving and rich theme of humanism. This is the question animating the next section of my chapter, which analyses Kant's use of the term *sensus communis*. Gadamer attends to the passage in §20 of the *Critique of Judgment* where Kant seems to split off 'common human understanding' from what he says deserves to be considered a properly communal sense, aesthetic common sense. He does not focus on the complex, indecisive moments where Kant seems to suggest that common sense is continuous in both cognitive and aesthetic judging. He sees Kant's equation of common sense with taste as not only an empirical 'absurdity' but also as a disastrous 'narrowing' down 'from the whole range of what could be called a sense faculty of judgment', despite his recognition of the importance to Kant of aesthetic judgement in structuring the critical project.[43] Narrowing the sense of community to judgements about the beautiful, for Gadamer, both damages the 'truth claim implicit in the sense of community' and has consequences for 'the self-understanding of the human sciences'.[44] It represents a part of Kant's 'radical subjectivization' of aesthetics that aligns knowledge with natural science and gives the human sciences only terms such as feeling and empathy for their methodological self-descriptions, a poor booby prize.[45] Without going too far into Gadamer's larger argument in *Truth and Method*, we may note that, there, it is not the concept of art or even aesthetic experience that is problematic – indeed, Gadamer theorizes positively the play (*Spiel*) we experience in the encounter with the artwork. But, he perceives Kant to eliminate the fact of our situatedness in the world, in history and in society; to have failed to recognize the finitude, partiality and prejudice that we cannot simply 'correct' in an Enlightened fashion, but which actually enable our understanding.[46] But what about pleasure in Kant's account? Gadamer appears to omit discussion of it almost entirely. Perhaps he takes the driest reading of pleasure in Kant as merely a psychological phenomenon, unconnected to situated human experience, a reading that, as will be shown at the end of this chapter, is increasingly untenable when one links up the critical to the anthropological elements of Kant's project.

KANT ON SHARED PLEASURE

Kant discovered in the 1780s, quite late in his career, that pleasure has been brought up in the wrong family of philosophy. Though Kant had previously thought it 'impossible' to find *a priori* principles – like those for time, space, substance and causality – for the feeling of pleasure and displeasure, he excitedly claimed in a letter to K.L. Reinhold that the 'systematic nature' of his previous analyses of the human mind's ability to rationalize and to desire or will 'allowed him to discover' them: 'I am now at work on the critique of taste, and I have discovered a kind of a priori principle different from those heretofore observed ... giving me ample material for the rest of my life, material at which to marvel, and if possible to explore.'[47]

In the *Critique of Judgment*, published three years after this letter, the discovery of the necessity of judgements of pleasure is hailed explicitly as a recuperative operation, unearthing pleasure's gem-like transcendental qualities from among the dross of empiricist narratives: 'For it is this necessity that reveals an a priori principle in them and lifts them out of [the reach of] empirical psychology, in which they would otherwise remain buried among the feelings of gratification and pain (accompanied only by the empty epithet of being a *more refined* feeling).'[48] As is well known, Kant's Third Critique tries to get beyond the limitations of both empirical and rationalist aesthetics to understand what one might call the logical-linguistic nature or grammar of aesthetic judgements. Kant establishes beauty's disinterestedness, its universality, its purposiveness without purpose and its expression as subjective necessity. In this fourth moment, he asks what kind of 'necessity' means that our judgement of beauty commands that everyone else feel the same way. He states that it can neither be unconditionally necessary nor lacking a principle, but must have a subjective principle. But what is this principle? What *base* is referred to by Kant's claim that 'We solicit everyone else's assent because we have a basis for it that is common to all' (§19: 86)? The movement of Kant's argument up to this point has proceeded in what one critic calls its 'familiar regressive fashion', setting out the conditions for taste, before turning backwards to see what is presupposed in all of them.[49] And, Kant tells us, what is crucial for aesthetics is common sense; we have to 'presuppose' 'that there is a common sense' (§20: 87). 'Common sense' is thus introduced into the *Critique of Judgment* as the necessary source or mechanism of the unique way in which judgements of taste are both entirely subjective and must solicit or woo the assent of others (§19: 86). It is thus a crucial aspect of the subjective universality of aesthetic judgements in which inheres their paradoxical status, and Kant's radical contribution to philosophical aesthetics.[50] But the question over whether it belongs to this fourth moment alone, or rather whether it has a much wider reach, grounding aesthetic judgement and even determinate judgement as well, is a controversial theme in Kant scholarship.[51]

The definitions appear initially clear but then multiply and blur: common sense is described variously by Kant as a principle, an effect, an ideal standard, an ability, a feeling and even the power to judge (§20: 87; §22: 89; §40: 160). At the first appearance of common sense in the Third Critique, Kant makes a distinction between that which is the effect of the harmony of our cognitive powers, and the 'common understanding' that judges by concepts, which is sometimes confused with it. Yet, throughout his discussion the distinction between a logical common sense and aesthetic common sense is frequently blurred. The very possibility of presupposing an aesthetic common sense – that hum of our faculties as they are prepared for cognition – is based on the fact of the communicability of cognition in terms of understanding: 'Cognitions and judgements, along with the conviction that accompanies them, must be universally communicable. For otherwise we could not attribute to them a harmony with the object, but they would one and all be a merely subjective play of the presentational powers, just as scepticism would have it' (§21: 87–8). If, as Kant's *Critique of Pure Reason* had allowed, perceptual judgements are more than random subjective effects, then it is also possible that we can share these judgements with others. Thus, he argues, if we can communicate cognitions, then we must be able to communicate 'the attunement of the cognitive powers that is required for cognition – namely, that proportion [between them which is suitable for turning a presentation] (by which an object is given us) into cognition' (§21: 88). This binding or attuning aspect of the *sensus communis* upon the faculties echoes the Aristotelian and Thomasian description of the root sensitivity of the five senses. Yet, Kant suddenly raises a surprising anxiety: 'But is there in fact such a common sense, as a constitutive principle of the possibility of experience, or is there a still higher principle of reason that makes it only a regulative principle for us, [in order] to bring forth in us, for higher purposes, a common sense in the first place?' (§22: 89–90). He speculates, in this late-added passage whose oddness has been remarked upon by Kant scholars, whether in fact taste is *not* 'an original and natural ability', but rather is a hint or a training-ground for rational sensory agreement, 'only the idea of an ability yet to be acquired' (§22: 90).[52]

Taste starts to look like an elaborate hint 'only that there is a possibility of reaching such agreement' at all (§22: 90).

Later, in the Deduction of Judgements of Taste (§38), Kant returns to the question of how we may feel a pleasure that others must feel. He points out that material sensations cannot be communicable; we do not know whether our friend smells the flower the same way as we do. Our pleasure in moral acts may be communicated, but only through concepts; the same is true of our pleasure in the sublime. But the free, unguided pleasure of the beautiful, where our powers align themselves as if in ordinary cognition but without having to arrive at a determinate concept, is communicable. In the following section, 'On Taste as a Kind of *Sensus Communis*', Kant discriminates between two meanings of *sensus communis*, just as Shaftesbury had done in his own essay. Highlighting the ambiguity of the word common, Kant rejects the meaning of *sensus communis* when it refers merely to that which the vulgar possess everywhere: common human understanding, 'the very least that we are entitled to expect from anyone who lays claim to the name of human being' (§40: 160). Instead, he redefines *sensus communis* as something that we all *share*,

a power to judge that in reflecting takes account (*a priori*), in our thought, of everyone else's way of presenting [something], in order *as it were* to compare our own judgement with human reason in general and thus escape the illusion that arises from the ease of mistaking subjective and private conditions for objective ones, an illusion that would have a prejudicial influence on the judgment. (§40: 160)

We do this by comparing our judgement with an imagined community, by trying to 'put ourselves in the position of everyone else' (§40: 160). Common human understanding, which we expect from everyone, is harder than it first looks, comprising the three maxims of thinking for oneself (allied with understanding); thinking from the standpoint of everyone else (allied with judgement); and thinking consistently (reason, 'the hardest to attain', he suggests). Yet, despite the importance of the extraordinary human ability to think universally, which he then calls the *sensus communis logicus*, Kant asserts that this frail pleasure in the beautiful, the *sensus communis aestheticus*, is still more important, and more shared even than human communication of thoughts. Aesthetic judgement 'deserves to be called a shared sense more than does the intellectual one, if indeed we wish to use the word *sense* to stand for an effect that mere reflection has on the mind, even though we then mean by sense the feeling of pleasure' (§40: 162). 'Even though' it is just pleasure we are talking about, it must take pre-eminence over conceptual communicability because it is free rather than determined.

Yet, despite wishing to separate the two forms out, Kant cannot avoid reminding us of their interplay. He has told us that the pleasure of aesthetic indeterminate harmony 'must of necessity rest on the same conditions in everyone, because they are subjective conditions for the possibility of cognition as such, and because the proportion between these cognitive powers that is required for taste is also required for the sound and common understanding that we may presuppose in everyone' (§39: 159). As throughout the whole text, the separation of the cognitive and social dimensions of common sense from any purely aesthetic one is difficult and undecided. There is a frequent slippage between imagined and actual communities. Kant writes in the General Comment that the fact of judgements of beauty and the sublime being 'universally *communicable*' gives us 'an interest in relation to society (where such communication may take place)' (136). There is a trace of real people, and real arguments, that shadows the seemingly very formal or virtual idea of communication here. This shadow of realness appears in Kant's envisaging of a dispute over beauty in which he might 'stop his ears' (§33: 148), and in his insistence on the direct importance of such debates to how *good we feel*: commanded to agree in beauty, 'we would presumably balk, appealing to our natural right to subject to our own sense, not to that of others, any judgment that rests on the direct feeling of our own well-being' (§29: 140).

De Quincey wrote enviously (and probably fancifully, based on Wasianski's account of Kant) of Kant's own well-being:

> For Kant's health was exquisite; not mere negative health, or the absence of pain, and of irritation, and also of *mal-aise* (either of which, though not 'pain', is often worse to bear) but a state of positive pleasurable sensation and a conscious possession of all his vital activities. Accordingly, when he packed up for the night in the way I have described, he would often ejaculate to himself (as he used to tell us at dinner) – 'Is it possible to conceive a human being with more perfect health than myself?'[53]

This anecdote might remind us to attend more closely to Kant's insistence that the subjective pleasure we find in beauty is 'the direct feeling of our own well-being' (§29: 140).[54] Why should aesthetic pleasure make us feel ourselves to be alive? In Kant's philosophy, the different mental faculties stand for ways that a representation may be related to something else, whether object or subject. The faculty of knowledge deals with that representation's agreement or conformity with the object; the faculty of desire deals with a representation's causal relationship with the object; the faculty of feeling, on the other hand, refers the representation only to the subject.[55] The third power is thus quite different from the other two; what appears to be a tripartite system, as Jean-Luc Nancy has noted, could actually be considered bipartite.[56] Judgement-power may be seen as a supplement for the other two powers; completing, underwriting (and according to some accounts, grounding) and yet complicating the system of reason. The odd action of judgement is emphasized again when Kant explains how in the cognitive pleasure of judgement, 'the presentation is tied wholly to the subject, indeed to the feeling of life itself, under the name of the feeling of pleasure' (§1: 44). Deleuze therefore hardly exaggerates when he describes this third type of relation of the presentation to the cognitive powers as the one that 'affects the subject by intensifying or weakening its vital forces'.[57] Later, Kant writes that the liking we have for the beautiful 'carries with it directly a feeling of life's being furthered' whereas the sublime 'is produced by the feeling of a momentary inhibition of the vital forces followed immediately by an outpouring of them that is all the stronger' (§23: 98).[58]

What remains puzzling, however, is why judgement should be related to the feeling of pleasure and displeasure: 'it is precisely this relation which gives rise to that puzzle regarding judgment's principle', otherwise, Kant writes, this form of judgement would have been a mere appendix (7). As Peter Fenves has recently explained, it is most important for Kant's whole project both that pleasure be linked to judgement and that pleasure has in itself no ethical implications. Despite the lack of any special interest in pleasure prior to the *Critique of Judgment*, Kant must somewhere in his philosophy give an account of pleasure, given his acceptance of it as 'a sheer fact, an indisputable but non-referential *datum* of consciousness'; yet this non-referentiality means for Kant (unlike other moral philosophers such as Aristotle) pleasure can have no connection to the agent's ethical goodness or badness, nor can it be grounded in an expression of good or bad life activities.[59] We have seen Kant's disdain for attempts to demarcate good from bad pleasure (those who use 'the empty epithet of being a *more refined* feeling', §29: 125). Fenves notes that if pleasure were not associated with the cognitive category of judging,

pleasure would have to be mediated by a purpose, and this purpose would bring it into the sphere of practical philosophy, from which it could escape only on the basis of another, much older philosophical proposition that Kant, for his part, could never seriously entertain – the proposition, namely, that the activity of philosophy, understood as the contemplation of things-in-themselves, amounts to the highest pleasure.[60]

(Kant had shown that we cannot contemplate things-in-themselves.) The independence of pleasure is crucial if the faculty of feeling is to be properly distinguished from the other faculties, desire in particular, in order that, through it, understanding and reason can be bridged. Thus, aesthetic judgement is neither regulative nor empirical, but a pleasure as if it were both.

Kant binds up aesthetic and logical judgement, under the form of pleasure, with one important phrase: 'the attainment of an aim is always connected with the feeling of pleasure' (§6: 27; 'Die Erreichung jeder Absicht ist mit dem Gefühle der Lust verbunden'). Fenves gives an alternative translation – 'the attainment of every intention is connected with pleasure', pointing out that Kant offers a stronger and more significant line than commentators have noticed, which both draws from the long-established link between pleasure and desire or will, but also allows pleasure to be broadened beyond practical interest ('aim') to cognitive intentions.[61] The role of pleasure in cognitive judgements is difficult, and controversial. On one level, pleasure is dependent precisely on the fact that these judgements do not become cognitive – because then the harmonious play of imagination and understanding would cease. Kant first suggests that we do not usually find that the fact our perceptions mix up with our concepts has 'the slightest effect upon our feeling of pleasure'; yet then recalls that the natural philosopher regularly gets hits of strong delight in discovering the unity of laws of nature. Rather slyly Kant begins to refine these two positions by suggesting that while 'we no longer feel any noticeable pleasure' from our cognitive interaction with diverse nature, nonetheless 'this pleasure was there at one time, and it is only because even the commonest experience would be impossible without it that we have gradually come to mix it in with mere cognition and no longer take any special notice of it' (§6: 27). This is a tricky assertion, and not simply because of translation difficulties. If experience is 'impossible' without pleasure, is pleasure in some sense a condition for it? Or must pleasure just come alongside it, as in the idea that every determinate judgement implies a corresponding reflective judgement, which would be the same as taking pleasure in that determinate judgement?[62] If the pleasure is 'mixed' in only afterwards, what was its status before? The complexity here may partly be to do with the fact that we can only presuppose, not know, the workings of the laws of nature. Kant's main rhetorical purpose at this moment is to introduce the role of beauty: to remember this pleasure, he says, we need 'something that in our judging of nature makes us pay attention to this purposiveness of nature for our understanding' (§6: 27).[63] That something will be 'the aesthetic presentation of the purposiveness of nature', and here Kant turns decisively to subjectivity and beauty, the main themes of his book.

The odd and seemingly un-Kantian thought that pleasure might be the first step in all cognition is temporarily put out of sight; but as we have seen, it returns through Kant's account of common sense. The critic Jay Bernstein put a striking spin on the connection, and separation, of determinate and reflective judgement in the Third Critique. Highlighting the text's occasional references to loss and grief, Bernstein argued that the split between beauty and truth is experienced as mourning, especially a mourning for the lost or forgotten pleasure of the application of the categories to the manifold of nature. Bernstein speculates that this strange 'pre-critical', almost Edenic epoch was 'a time when the applicability of the categories to experience was sufficiently unsure that their successful employment was experienced with pleasure'.[64] As common sense was replaced with determinate judgement, so the political (communal; intersubjective) was replaced with the objective (the legislation of reason and understanding). Yet, there is a problem here, because, as Bernstein reminds us, Kant argued in *What Is Orientation in Thinking?* that we cannot *think* without communicability, without politics. There, Kant wrote that thought can only be correct when it is communicated or communicable; political repression will necessarily negate man's ability to think as well as his freedom to do so. The critical philosophy thus consumes itself: 'Hence the methodological solipsism of the *Critique of Judgment* becomes self-undermining: it can only have what it seeks, namely, commonality, by turning against its own methodological starting point.'[65] The only way round these aporiae is to consider aesthetic judgement as 'memorial', keeping a 'semblance or trace' of the 'historical suppression'.[66] Common sense does not exist, 'but in so far as "we" remember it (in virtue of serious participation in aesthetic discourse and practice), judge through it, it does exist'.[67]

This is a powerful reading, but it could be argued that this insistence upon 'serious' aesthetics and mourning itself suppresses something important about Kant's text, his suggestion that common sense is marked by, and perhaps identical to, a feeling of *pleasure*. (And Bernstein does not pick up on the political ambiguity of pleasure: to take pleasure in a state that represses us might signify its control over us, *or* the ungovernability of pleasure.) Kant argues that what is communicable when we hear ourselves judge in a universal voice must be a 'mental state', and precisely one in which our powers of imagination and understanding are in 'free play', because not working under a determinate concept. Kant adds 'That the ability to communicate one's mental state, even if this is only the state of one's cognitive powers, carries a pleasure with it, could easily be established (empirically and psychologically) from man's natural propensity to sociability' (§9: 62). Later, in anthropological vein, he calls this concern for universal communication 'an original contract dictated by our very humanity' (§41: 164). Yet, for a transcendental argument such a psychological proof would not do: we are looking for a principle; but nonetheless Kant's own attempt at rigid terminology begins to blur and soften as we read. Though he has rejected an idea that the 'pleasure' could itself be the communicable thing, his analysis does not manage to keep clearly separate the mental state, the relation of the powers, the feeling or sensation (and consciousness) of this relation, the pleasure of it, the play and the harmony that defines this 'state', not to mention the vital quickening of powers involved:

Hence that unity in the relation [between the cognitive powers] in the subject can reveal itself only through sensation. This sensation, whose universal communicability a judgment of taste postulates, is the quickening of the two powers (imagination and understanding) to an activity that is indeterminate but, as a result of the prompting of the given presentation, nonetheless accordant: the activity required for cognition in general. (§9: 63)

A deep shareable pleasure starts to trickle into, and meld, this lively cognitive operation. Then, in the next moment, which considers how purposes and causality might be cognized in relation to beauty, Kant gives a new definition of pleasure as a staying-on, a 'yes' to this state: 'Consciousness of a presentation's causality directed at the subject's state so as to *keep* him in that state, may here designate generally what we call pleasure' (§10: 65); and later adds, 'We *linger* in our contemplation of the beautiful, because this contemplation reinforces and reproduces itself' (§12: 68).[68] There are different political readings one can make of this depiction of pleasure: it can be seen as static and conservative, or as receptive and open; these possibilities shall be explored in the final section of this chapter.

How exactly does Kant describe the pleasure of the beautiful in the *Critique of Judgment*? As we saw earlier, Kant argues that 'Consciousness of a presentation's causality directed at the subject's state so as to *keep* him in that state, may here designate generally what we call pleasure' (§10: 65). Shortly afterwards, he writes that though the pleasure – which is also a 'quickening' of the cognitive powers – has no practicality, it does have a 'causality',

namely, to *keep* us in the state of having the presentation itself, and to keep the cognitive powers engaged [in their occupation] without any further aim. We *linger* in our contemplation of the beautiful, because this contemplation reinforces and reproduces itself. This is analogous to (though not the same as) the way in which we linger over something charming that, as we present an object, repeatedly arouses our attention, [though here] the mind is passive. (§12: 68)

Lingering, dwelling, staying, sojourning (*weilen, Verweilung*): these words do not mean immobilization, transfixion, petrification. A pleasurable tension rather than a final resolution seems to be suggested: the stress on reinforcement and repetition implies an ongoing movement or flickering; thus, Kant's tautologous idea of a passive arousal.[69] Some comparison with Kant's claims about the texture of life are fruitful, because there as well we see a notable openness and tension in his description, again reinforcing the idea that pleasure is *not* closed, soporific and unified for Kant, as some later commentators (discussed in the final section) have implied.[70] Kant points out that not only are all presentations linked to gratification and pain, 'because all of them affect the feeling of life, and none of them can be indifferent insofar as it is a modification of the subject' but that, 'as Epicurus maintained, *gratification* and *pain* are ultimately always of the body' (139). Kant goes on to add:

He maintained this on the ground that, in the absence of [some] feeling of the bodily organ, life is merely consciousness of our existence, and not a feeling of being well or unwell, i.e. of the furtherance or inhibition of the vital forces; for the mind taken by itself is wholly life (the very principle of life), whereas any obstacles or furtherance must be sought outside it and yet still within man himself, and hence in the [mind's] connection with his body. (139)

This is a rather obscure passage, not least in Kant's surprising sympathy for Epicurus. Peter Fenves has interpreted this discussion of the feeling of life as a tension between the living body and the fully alive principle of life that is the mind:

which, as mere consciousness of existence, may be fully aware of itself but cannot be aware of itself *as* life, *as* different from the less-fully-alive internal otherness of its organs. An awareness of this otherness – otherwise known as 'feeling', resides neither in the body nor in the mind but, rather, in the 'binding' (*Verbindung*) of the two.[71]

This powerful interpretation of what 'feeling' is – a bridging of different things that does not eliminate that difference – could also be a useful way of describing pleasure as something alive and responsive to difference.

READING PLEASURE THROUGH KANT'S 'ANTHROPOLOGY'

To some extent, this kind of interest in the body and in life in the Third Critique reflects a move against an exclusively formal view of Kant's critical philosophy and a reconsideration of the significance for it of previously marginal texts including his *Anthropology from a Pragmatic Point of View*. Allen Wood has offered an interpretation of Kant's 'shrewd' and 'bleak' anthropological ethics, whose key statement might be that, for Kant, 'the basic principle of our empirical desires is unsociable *sociability* – social antagonism within the context of mutual need and interdependence'.[72] He develops this by arguing that:

the mistrust of inclination (or natural desire) in Kant's rationalism is not about hostility to anything so innocent as 'finitude' or 'the senses' or 'the emotions' or 'the body'. The focus instead is on the (far from innocent) *social* character natural desires must assume in the natural process through which our rational faculties develop in history.[73]

Rather than focusing on the pure individualism of the categorical imperative, Wood emphasizes Kant's active interest in the way that we are drawn co-operatively and creatively towards fellow humans at the same time that we are repulsed from them by jealousy and competition. When Wood makes reference to common sense in Kant (which he treats more briefly than one might expect), he presses the connection with language as a predisposition to the sharing of ideas and perspectives. 'We can develop our reason only by communicating with others. Our capacity to think at all, and especially to think accurately, depends on our thinking "in community with others to whom we *communicate* our thoughts".'[74] Wood takes Kant's broadest definition of common sense as a 'faculty of feeling', and describes it as 'xenophiliac': '[I]t values and seeks out what is other or different, because without this it would be impossible to find anything having universal validity.'[75] The 'higher end' of common sense to which Kant makes mysterious reference in §22 would be, in Wood's reading, a cosmopolitan community into which are subsumed all the ends of rational beings. Indeed, Kant's other writings argue that this is the peaceful purpose (*Ansicht*) of history.[76] What for Bernstein is a *lost* common world becomes in Wood's reading a potential one, an 'ethical community' without need of hierarchies, laws, constitutions or creeds.[77]

Despite his careful account of the passions, Wood treats pleasure more or less as a simple given, despite Kant's obvious and recurrent interest in the topic evinced in the Anthropology lectures and the Third Critique. Other anthropologically inspired readings of Kant have stressed the 'empirical reinscription of human nature at the basis of "our" cognition'.[78] As we compared Shaftesbury's formal account of pleasure in the *Inquiry* with his more anthropological *Sensus Communis* essay, we might also deepen our understanding of the social forms of pleasure by looking at Kant's *Anthropology* writings.[79] The *Anthropology* textbook is divided into a Didactic, addressing both the interior and exterior of the human being, and a Characteristic, which instructs how to cognize the interior from the exterior of the human being. There are several references to common sense and the *sensus communis* in the first part, but there is no particular stress on the link with pleasure at first. Kant defines common sense in opposition to madness: 'The only universal characteristic of madness is the loss of *common sense* (*sensus communis*) and its replacement with *logical private sense* (*sensus privatus*); for example, a human being in broad daylight sees a light burning on his table, which, however, another person standing nearby does not see, or hears a voice that no one hears' (113). The *sensus communis* is also opposed to dreaming, in which the dreamer is 'abandoned to a play of thought in which he sees, acts and judges, not in a common world, but rather in his own world' (114). Here, one sees the broader, almost ontological character of the *sensus communis* for Kant, which, as the conclusion of this chapter shows, Arendt draws from to argue that our very sense of reality is provided by the intersubjectivity of our judgements.

The second book of the Didactic treats the Feeling of Pleasure and Displeasure. What first strikes the reader is that Kant's general treatment of pleasure and happiness is very negative, particularly in comparison to the more positive role granted to pleasure and its subtle links to morality, life and community in the Third Critique. Kant begins with a traditional distinction between sensuous and intellectual pleasure (one that, as we have seen, is disrupted throughout the Third Critique). Anticipating, but somewhat altering, the discussion of pleasure as lingering that we have seen above, Kant defines pain as that which 'directly (through sense) urges me to *leave* my state'; the agreeable is 'what drives me to *maintain* my state (to remain in it)' (126). But he argues that we can only know what we are leaving (the past state), not what we may come into (the future state); thus, pain gains an epistemic and existential priority. Though life may be a 'continuous play of the antagonism' of the promotion and hindrance of life, Kant emphasizes that because of the temporality implied by the movement between mental states, '*pain must always precede every enjoyment; pain is always first*' (126). This temporal priority is quickly extended in implication to the rather larger claim that *life* is conditional upon pain:

Also, no enjoyment can immediately follow another, rather, between one and another pain must appear. Small inhibitions of the vital force mixed in with advancements of it constitute the state of health that we erroneously consider to be a continuously felt well-being; when in fact it consists only of intermittent pleasant feelings that follow one another (with pain always intervening between them). Pain is the incentive of activity, and in this, above all, we feel our life; without pain lifelessness would set in. (126)

Kant begins the next section on boredom by stating, 'To feel one's life, to enjoy oneself, is thus nothing more than to feel oneself continuously driven to leave the present state' (128). Continuing this depressing theme, Kant points out that we fill our life with activities partly to become weary with it (which is a kind of happiness), and that contentment is unattainable for a human: 'To be (absolutely) contented in life would be idle *rest* and the standstill of all incentives' (130). Kant credits Count Verri for these thoughts on pain, whose *Meditazione sulla felicita* (1763) was translated into German in 1777. Susan Meld Shell has recently argued that reading Verri transformed Kant's attitudes towards pleasure and happiness:

Kant came to reject Rousseau's association of human consciousness with a feeling for the wholeness of our existence. Totality is an idea of reason that cannot be felt (except, perhaps, in the toils of the sublime); and happiness is not the natural end of life (in any but a terminal sense). We can think of happiness 'only in progress' that 'can never be completed'; should it do so, 'happiness would cease'.[80]

One might call this the tragic-liberal view of happiness, which, as we shall see in the next chapter, has frequently been associated with Rousseau himself, especially in Ernst Cassirer's reading of his work. For Meld Shell, Kant goes much further than Rousseau in the pessimistic view of reason's role in disrupting our contentment. She argues that while Rousseau at least seemed to believe that contentment is possible (in the state of nature), Kant believed that we could *never* have a concept of a maximal pleasure.[81] Should we agree with Meld Shell that enjoyment should be characterized as '"conservative" in a most literal sense'?[82]

In fact, we see a slightly different conception of pleasure in the *Anthropology* textbook, which also discusses taste and common sense as Kant moves from the entirely sensuous to the 'partly sensuous, partly intellectual' pleasure of reflective judgement. He states much of the argument that will be presented in the Third Critique, but makes more explicit reference to the forms of (real) sociability it may involve. In its origins, there is not much good about the social condition: it is 'usually *barbaric*, unsociable, and purely competitive' (137). Take cleaning one's house, Kant suggests: we would only bother to do it to impress strangers. (The tone of this is very different from Kant's anthropological remark in the Third Critique, that alone on a desert island, we would not adorn ourselves with flowers, because without sharing there is no pleasure.) Judgements of taste imply something different about sociability, however: 'Taste is, accordingly, a power of making social judgments about external objects as we imagine them. – Here the mind feels its freedom in the play of images (and so of sensibility); for social relations with other men presuppose freedom – and this feeling is pleasure' (137–8). Mary J. Gregor's edition has a footnote on this 'obscure' passage, attempting to understand this analogy between social freedom and aesthetic freedom (an analogy which, as we will see, preoccupied Arendt). She suggests that both taste and social freedom represent a freedom to choose, but under a law of general validity. As social freedom balances individuals' negative *freedom from* (external constraint) and positive *freedom to* (act spontaneously in a way that allows others the same freedom) so aesthetic judgement holds delicately together both our subjectivity with the judgement of others.[83] But how can the feeling of freedom be a pleasure, if Kant has earlier defined enjoyment as 'the ending of a pain and something negative' (126)? Kant, and certainly the more analytical of his commentators, might try to close this difference by saying that it all rests on whether one is talking about the *agreeable* or the particular pleasure of reflective judgement. But just as pleasure seems to escape a clear bodily–intellectual distinction in the Third Critique, there is a difficulty here in the *Anthropology* about the definition of pleasure. This extends to a tension between more and less optimistic views of sociability depending on that definition. This passage also emphasizes how Kant *did* consider the pleasure of taste to have relevance to empirical sociability, whether or not one agrees with Lyotard's pronouncement that Kant merely falls into an occasional mistaken 'temptation' to anthropologize. Kant ends his anthropological discussion of taste with an attempt to explain why modern languages have chosen just one sense, *taste*, to stand for aesthetic judgement, and he gives the example of a dinner party to explain the link between sensory liking and collective experience. A 'good meal in good company' offers a durable, repeatable 'enjoyment' that unites 'sensibility and understanding':

> The aesthetic taste of the host shows itself in his skill in choosing with universal validity, something which he cannot bring about through his own sense of taste, because his guests might choose other foods or drinks, each according to his own private sense. Therefore he sets up his meeting with *variety*, so that everyone will find something that suits his sense, which yields a comparative universal validity. (139–40)

This section is much more optimistic about the possibility of a lasting enjoyment than the earlier discussions, which stressed that pain and boredom were by far the pre-eminent states of existence. There is an amusing congruence with De Quincey's biographical description of Kant as 'a most courteous and liberal host, who had not greater pleasure than in seeing his guests happy and jovial, and rising with exhilarated spirits from the mixed pleasures – intellectual and liberally sensual – of his Platonic banquets'.[84] It places Kant's ideas about taste in line with Shaftesbury's eighteenth-century tradition, in which sociability and pleasure define each other.

In a following section, which declares that taste advances morality, Kant goes even further in anthropologizing the shared pleasure of taste: 'Taste (as a formal sense, so to speak) concerns the *communication* of our feeling of pleasure or displeasure to others, and includes a susceptibility, which this very communication affects pleasurably, to feel a satisfaction (*complacentia*) about it in common with others (sociably)' (141). This statement places an interesting emphasis on the circularity and self-affirming quality of sociable joy: we communicate our pleasure, and this gives our susceptibility or receptivity (*Empfänglichkeit*) an extra pleasure. It has some similarities with what Giorgio Agamben has called the 'ontological basis' for the theory of friendship in Aristotle:

> that there is, namely, a sensation of existence (an *aisthesis* of 'the fact that we exist' and 'the fact that one is alive'); that this sensation, moreover, is a source of joy ('good and pleasant in itself', 'pleasant' and 'desirable'); and that, finally, this sensation is shared, as an irreducibly 'joint perception' (literally, a *sunaisthesis*) between those two selves who 'live together and converse and communicate their thoughts to each other'.[85]

Kant uses a Latin term, pleasing-with, to stress that this 'liking' (*Wohlgefallen*) is *inherently* sociable. (And we shall also discover in Wordsworth

the importance of the term 'complacency'.) In his more negative pro-
nouncements on enjoyment and satisfaction earlier in the *Anthropology*, he
used the Latin *acquiescentia* to explain his use of 'contentment', *Zufrie-
denheit* (130). In modern English, the semantic gap between acquiescence
(literally to become physically quiet, to come to physical repose) and
complacency has narrowed. Kant seems to be suggesting, on the other
hand, that if the quietude of contentment is never possible in this life
(because it would indicate lifelessness and death), what *is* possible, and
does exist, is a peculiarly open kind of shared delight.

COMMON PLEASURE IN TWENTIETH-CENTURY POLITICAL PHILOSOPHY

Howard Caygill has observed that the wide implications of Kant's idea of
the *sensus communis* for his notions of critique, enlightenment and judgement did not begin to be recognized until the twentieth century, at which
point the *sensus communis* made an entrance into the field of political
philosophy.[86] From around the 1960s, the *Critique of Judgment*'s sub-
merged account of the split between art and politics began to be seen as
foreshadowing the crisis of modernity. As David Ingrams has suggested,
both modernists and postmodernists were 'in agreement that Kant's
differentiation of cognitive, practical, and aesthetic domains of rationality
anticipated the fragmentation of modern society into competing if not, as
Weber assumed, opposed lifestyles, activities, and value spheres, and that
this has generated a crisis of *judgment*'.[87] The question was how one could
judge (politically and aesthetically) if one could no longer fall back on
authority nor wished to tumble into relativism. This crisis, and Kant's
mysterious text, preoccupied both modernist critics (Habermas, Arendt,
Adorno, Gadamer, Benjamin) and their postmodern interlocutors (Jean-
François Lyotard and Jean-Luc Nancy). Consequently, several exceptional
engagements with the idea of the *sensus communis* were produced, which
will be examined in light of their relevance for literary-critical views of
Romanticism. My argument is that many of these thinkers have failed to
acknowledge the importance and the complexity of pleasure within eighteenth-century aesthetic traditions, thus limiting the political theories that
they draw from those traditions.

Like Gadamer, Hannah Arendt identified a shift in the conceptual-
isation of the *sensus communis* from a real-world notion to one that was
merely a shared mental faculty, and she likewise saw modernity as a
negative process of the privatization of human life. But unlike Gadamer,

for Arendt it is actually Kant's formulation of common sense that allows a rich expansion of the political possibilities inherent in the theme. Arendt thematizes common sense in almost all of her major works, refracting it through concrete historical experience, the history of philosophy and her own speculation. In *The Origins of Totalitarianism* (1951), common sense is opposed to totalitarianism's procedure of isolating men from one another in the political sphere. Against this transcendental loneliness (at one and the same time, a fundamental aspect of human experience and a recent historical 'weapon'), she sets the Aquinian understanding of common sense as a 'sense of reality' provided by a shared worldly context. Without it, 'each of us would be enclosed in his own particularity of sense data which in themselves are unreliable and treacherous. Only because we have common sense, that is only because not one man, but men in the plural inhabit the earth can we trust our immediate sensual experience.'[88] A common sense is weakened under totalitarianism, the feeling of reality and proximity it lends replaced with a feeling of madness or dreaming. In *The Human Condition* (1958) she maintains this positive account of common sense, but argues that there was a shift from a richer, more worldly account in Aquinas to a more limited, mental concept of rationality in Hobbes and Descartes. She claimed that men now shared 'not the world but the structure of their minds, and this they cannot have in common, strictly speaking'.[89] Here, she seems to be echoing Kant's difference between what we simply expect from others and what we actively *share* (§40). *The Life of the Mind: One/Thinking* (1971) explores in fuller detail the Aquinian, perceptual common sense which fits private sensations into a common shared world, adding that it is the source of identification of common groups, here based on species: 'Though each single object appears in a different perspective to each individual, the context in which it appears is the same for the whole species.'[90] In this volume, she also introduces the idea of 'the intramural warfare between thought and common sense', suggesting that this is responsible for a persistent and 'very curious notion' of 'the affinity between death and philosophy'.[91] As she puts it in *The Life of the Mind*, 'The quest for meaning is meaningless to common sense and common-sense reasoning because it is the sixth sense's function to fit us into the world of appearances and make us at home in the world given by our five senses; there we are and no questions asked.'[92] This makes common sense sound rather passive and conservative, yet it underpins an important distinction between real judgement and speculation. For Arendt (and not for Habermas), political judgement is not based in epistemological issues of proof and validity, nor associated with a universal concept of freedom, but lived through history and particularity.[93]

For Arendt, Kant restores the older notion of common sense, for 'Judging is one, if not the most important, activity in which this sharing with others comes to pass.'[94] In her *Lectures on Kant's Political Philosophy* (published posthumously in 1982), she explores Kant's *sensus communis aestheticus* as the site of his politics, controversially calling the Third Critique Kant's 'unwritten political philosophy'.[95] She layers the terminology of the Greek *polis* upon judgements of taste, which 'share with political opinions that they are persuasive; the judging person – as Kant says quite beautifully – can only "woo the consent of everyone else" in the hope of coming to an agreement with him eventually'.[96] Unlike physical violence but also unlike truth (as she sees it), political and aesthetic negotiation cannot be coercive. She links aesthetics not only with acculturation but also with humanism: 'taste is the political capacity that truly humanizes the beautiful and creates a culture'.[97] She additionally presses upon the connection of language and common sense, arguing that the *sensus communis* is the specifically human sense because communication depends on it.[98] As she puts it in her 'Crisis of Culture' essay, Kant's account of taste stands for 'an anticipated communication with others with whom I know I must finally come to some agreement'.[99] This anticipation is crucial, because the question is one of hope of agreement, rather than actual agreement within existing norms of a community. It allows, as Linda Zerilli has recently shown, openness to the new, to imagination and to 'values that have not yet found expression in the sense of a determinate concept'.[100]

And what of pleasure? We are getting closer to affective values in Zerilli's reference to 'hope'. Zerilli also finds some kind of emphasis on pleasure in Arendt's account of freedom: '*What gives us pleasure is how we judge, that is to say, that we judge objects and events in their freedom.*'[101] Likewise, Ronald Beiner mentions the link between pleasure and the affirmation of freedom in Arendt. He finds in her work the idea that human beings have found '"the awesome responsibility" of freedom to be an insupportable weight', evaded through doctrines of fatalism or historical process. '[B]y eliciting pleasure from the free acts of men by reflecting upon and judging them', human freedom finds a means of affirmation.[102] One other instance of Arendt's use of pleasure in relation to sense is through the ontological security provided by beauty. Arendt approvingly quotes Kant from his posthumously published *Reflections*: 'The fact that man is affected by the sheer beauty of nature proves that he is made for and fits into this world.'[103] Nonetheless, Julia Kristeva has argued that there is an anxiety about or suspicion of the body in Arendt's work, leading to a neglect of certain relevant aspects (psycho-sexual, sadistic) of totalitarianism. Arendt's letters to Karl Jaspers, which insist upon the 'non-political, totally private' nature of bodily sensation, are read by Kristeva as indicating a kind of masochism, and the belief that to be trapped in corporeality is a form of torture. Kristeva writes of Arendt: 'Pleasure is mentioned only so that it can be assimilated into pain', as the body's sensations operate internally, without an object, 'in a sort of autistic closure'.[104] Kristeva finds that although Arendt's turn towards the Third Critique might readmit the body, ultimately the discussion of taste 'spares Kant and Arendt from having to pose the question of pleasure or displeasure in the relationship between the "subject" and the "object of satisfaction", or the Other as a pole of anguish and desire'.[105] More recently, Rei Terada has studied Arendt's 'repulsion' from 'the life process' and her sense of the 'futility of mortal life' expressed in *The Human Condition*. Her analysis (whilst not specifically concerned with pleasure) suggests that meaningless, animal-like pleasure is the negative backdrop against which Arendt's concept of human 'work' is defined.[106]

Arendt's knowledge of the political conditions under which human life might be reduced to its mere bodily needs means that she is not keen to give a strongly affective spin to her reading of Kant. As Simon Swift has recently written, 'Arendt's writing lived in the wreckage of a sentimental mode of identification with others that it kept trying to separate itself from, in ever more tactless ways.'[107] But she found in Kant the idea that we need a certain trust – a trust that there is a common world, and that agreement *might* happen – in order for politics to take place, and her language of trust, affirmation and beauty contains a residue of Kant's central link between pleasure and common sense. Revising our attention to the link between pleasure and commonality in eighteenth-century aesthetics, therefore, adds to Arendt's picture of a political community built on common sense.

The whole project of trying to find politics in Kant's very stripped-down framework in the Third Critique will, however, always be a controversial one. Ronald Beiner argues that Arendt's reading of the Third Critique is mistaken in underplaying the importance of 'autonomy' to Kant's account of both practical reason and aesthetic judgement, an issue which 'places constraints upon how much he can allow relations of community to enter into the formation of judgments'.[108] Further, he argues, she will not accept that 'all her favourite concepts', including

common sense, 'are *transcendental* categories', unconnected to any 'empirical sociability'.[109] Jean-François Lyotard's essay 'Sensus Communis'
sternly rebukes the 'confusion, which is almost the rule in English aesthetics
until Burke, and which will be spread rapidly, after him, by Schiller, right
up to the neo-Kantian and neo-neo-Kantian readings of the *Third Critique*:
it is said that taste prepares, or helps on, sociability'.[110] For him, this
mistake evinces the tendency to anthropologize Kant's transcendental
philosophy, to believe mistakenly that one can find in Kant's discussion
of 'the appeal to the other contained in the beautiful' a reference to actual,
empirical individuals.[111] Lyotard figures this propensity to misread as a
deadly infection and as a temptation: even Kant is at risk, occasionally
letting 'himself get carried away by the anthropological reading of what he
is trying to think'.[112] Lyotard's horror of this plague is based not only in
critical rigour: directly, he asks 'How many illusions or political crimes have
been able to nourish themselves with this pretended immediate sharing of
feelings?'[113] Concluding his essay, he asserts that 'if we claim to have
recourse to' an 'assignable community of feeling, [an] affective consensus',
'we are victims of a transcendental illusion and we are encouraging impos-
tures'.[114] Instead, Lyotard finds in Kant's cryptic account of the *sensus
communis* only a temporary, fleeting and frail subjectivity: 'So what is given
voice in taste is the division of the subject as a division ac(c / h)orded for one
moment, called together in convocation.'[115] Free, momentarily, from being
'mastered by concept and will', this subjectivity 'is a region of resistance to
establishment and institutions'.[116]

Lyotard's reading of Kant exemplifies the postmodern position on the
Third Critique more generally, one that has tended to focus on construc-
tions of frail subjectivity *resistant* to any imposition of community. This is
partly why Kant's seven pages on the sublime – a very small section within
the 250-page-long *Critique of Judgment* – have proved so appealing to
literary theorists.[117] Here, Kant, developing thoughts from his early work
Observations on the Feeling of the Sublime and the Beautiful (1764),
attempted to account for an agitated emotional-aesthetic response to
illimitable and powerful things. Kant wrote, with an apology that to
deconstructive critics (reading by textual blind spots) was irresistible, that
the sublime 'is not nearly as important and rich in implications as that of
the beautiful in nature ... For the beautiful in nature we must seek a basis
outside of ourselves, but for the sublime a basis merely within ourselves'
(§23: 100). Kant's account of the pleasure of the beautiful itself
became marginal in literary-theoretical discourse, if not from the point
of view of analytic philosophers. This neglect was sometimes implicitly

acknowledged, for example when Paul de Man ambiguously justified his focus on the sublime: 'in the section on the beautiful, the difficulties *at least convey the illusion* of being controlled'; 'Contrary to the beautiful, which *at least appears* to be all of a piece, the sublime is shot through with dialectical complication.'[118] Likewise, Frances Ferguson criticized the scholarly tendency to 'present the sublime as functioning in supreme isolation from its companion and counterpoise' (while at the same time partly perpetuating the bias).[119] She claimed, in justification, that this failure of attention was shared by the eighteenth century: Burke 'droop [ed]' in discussing the beautiful, 'as if he could himself marshal little energy for its easy pleasures, and Kant treats the beautiful as a more mixed and confused area of perception than the sublime'.[120]

More recently, political philosophers and literary critics have sometimes distinguished between a bad beautiful community and a good sublime community, in ways that continue to echo Blanchot and Lyotard. Drawing from the First and Third Critiques, as well as from Lyotard, Kath Renark Jones highlights Kant's opposing terms *communio* ('the name of community operating on a principle of unity') and *commercium* ('interactive multiplicity ungoverned by any organizing or binding principle').[121] She compares the epistemological community described in the First Critique – based on the idea of a single human subject, separated from others – to aesthetic community, which by contrast is 'pre-conceptual and pre-schematic', preceding the formation of the subject. But rather than turning as one might expect to the *sensus communis* of the beautiful to find this pre-conceptual, pre-subjective community, Renark Jones finds that 'the sublime can be understood to open on to a being-in-common that is immediate and invokes an ethos for the subject that emerges out of it'.[122] By being-in-common, she means 'a basis for interaction, association and exchange' – *we*, not yet fixed into any one *particular* community – as opposed to the forms of 'humanist identification' epitomized in the term *us*. Thus, the sublime is represented as a purer experience of a dynamic community of multiplicity and disorder, prior to (what she argues is) the determining and unifying *communio* of the beautiful in which a subject emerges. Then, she argues, this more radical common sense is entrapped by Reason in Kant's account: as it tries to bring 'an ethical universality' out of this feeling, the we is turned into a determinate us, and we gain a feeling of the supersensible destination of the species. She makes an analogy between this and the 'modern sense of community', reduced either to mystical 'attunement' or governed by 'dogmatic and authoritarian principle of abstract justice'.[123]

Along similar lines, Vivaswan Soni objects to the fact that the community of the beautiful can only be disclosed as a feeling, which is 'almost mystical', and delivers pleasure, which he renames 'communal narcosis', arising from 'the fiction of the community of harmonious accord'.[124] Awakening from this narcotic pleasure of auto-affection causes '*sublime withdrawal*', and, in effect, Soni implies, a painful awakening to the impossibility of community: 'If there is community, it is not to be discovered in the narcotic euphoria of a common feeling but in the pain of the exposure to the multiplicity of radical alterities who form no community except a finite totality.'[125] Community becomes only mourning for community, he argues, echoing Jay Bernstein. Thus, the *sensus communis* is attacked for being both falsely communal (common substance) and too individual ('the monadic isolation of the self-sufficient individual dreaming of a harmonious community'[126]); the sublime is praised for being more individual ('radical alterities') and more properly communal ('multiplicity'). The deeper presuppositions that underlie Soni's argument include the idea that pleasure is inherently soporific, and may only emanate from an untroubled sense of political identification, and that by contrast pain represents authenticity of experience, even the only true knowledge of reality.[127] Soni also assumes that pleasurable auto-affection must be narcissistic, rather than considering, as certain philosophers have done, that something like auto-affection might *precede* the formation of anything so recognizable as a subject with narcissistic fantasies and relations to others.[128]

Some historical context may help us understand more reasons for the neglect of pleasure in thinking about commonality. Howard Caygill's observation that there are 'two opposed metaphysical conceptions of community' is a useful starting point: 'In the first, the community is a substance or common being; in the second, the individual is substantial and contrives relations with others.'[129] Postmodern philosophies explored formulations of community which would avoid recourse to a model of community-as-substance, a model which for left-wing thought is inexorably tied to the history of fascism as well as the failure of communism. The desire to avoid this substantial image of community, in which certain forms of identification lead to the exclusion of others, led to a refusal of theorizations of community in favour of a focus on subjectivity, or to descriptions of community that built in its own theoretical destruction or impossibility. Georges Bataille's preference for describing *continuity* based on sacrifice and loss has had an abiding influence on postmodern accounts of community: 'The [sacrificial] victim dies, and the spectators share in what his death reveals … This sacredness is the revelation of continuity through the death of a discontinuous being to those who watch it as a solemn rite.'[130]

In death, and in eroticism, our discontinuity (individuation, identity) is dissolved into a formless continuity, or communication: nakedness 'is a state of communication revealing a quest for a possible continuance of being beyond the confines of the self'.[131] Maurice Blanchot, drawing on both Bataille and Levinas, developed the notion of deathly community by introducing the sublime politics of the 'infiniteness of alterity', of 'inexorable finitude'.[132] But he maintains a focus on both ecstasy and communication: 'By itself, ecstasy was nothing if it did not communicate itself and, first, did not give itself as the groundless ground of communication', adding '"ecstasy" itself is communication'.[133] Jean-Luc Nancy has suggested that the association of death and community emerged between the First and Second World Wars, where a philosophy of sociality or intersubjectivity was no longer tenable, and the 'resources of a metaphysics of the subject' ran dry.[134] He argues that there is 'in the thought of community a theoretical excess'.[135] For Nancy, the context is communism's perceived betrayal, and the tendency of communitarian opposition to work from the assumption of the 'immanence of man to man'.[136] He finds in Bataille's communitarian ecstasy a 'clear consciousness' that forms of communal intimacy or immanence based on individuals who produce their own essence in work 'cannot, nor are they ever to be regained'.[137] He represents ecstasy and community as a 'double arealization' and also as 'resistance': 'without this resistance, we would never be in common very long, we would very quickly be "realized" in a unique and total being'.[138]

In a recent essay written to accompany an exhibition of drawings, Jean-Luc Nancy has complicated the concept of pleasure, which may also help us to rethink the politics of the *sensus communis*. Nancy elaborates a fundamental ambiguity in the term 'pleasure' as implying at once contentment and tension, agreeableness and attraction, repletion and seduction.[139] This dichotomy must, he argues, be both distinguished and recombined in our understanding of the term. To the extent that he clearly prioritizes pleasure-as-tension throughout his discussion, his essay appears to retain the older emphasis on *jouissance* and *désir* that preoccupied Bataille in *L'Erotisme* and Deleuze in *L'anti-Oedipe*. Nevertheless, it is the term 'pleasure' that he uses, not dismissing pleasure as bourgeois or limited, and indeed he reminds us that 'l'essence du plaisir ne se laisse pas ranger sous une simple positivité. Le plaisir n'est pas simple' (the essence of pleasure can't be tidied up under a straightforward heading of positivity. Pleasure is not simple, p. 37). He contends that pleasure is fundamentally linked to relationship: 'Le plaisir est dans un rapport qui tend vers sa prolongation ou vers sa répétition, de même que le deplaisir tend à la cessation et au rejet du rapport' (Pleasure exists in a connection which tends towards its prolongation or its repetition, as unpleasure tends towards cessation and rejection of connection, p. 32). Nancy claims that relationship is intrinsic to the subject, making him or her a subject rather than a substance, in that it is the capacity to affect and to be affected which defines the subject. Punning on Sartre's existentialist distinction between being 'for itself' and 'in itself', Nancy writes that pleasure 'gives the fundamental tone or register to the subject', feeling oneself as an object (p. 38). In support of this he cites Kant's mysterious agreement with Epicurus in suggesting that 'all pleasure is of the body', and also paraphrases the Third Critique as the argument that 'L'art est sensualité communiquée' (p. 29). This Kantian theme has long interested Nancy: 'Joy is possible, it has meaning and existence, only through community and as its communication.'[140] Thus, building partly on the definition of pleasure as desiring to stay in a certain state or to repeat an experience that we saw in Kant, Nancy emphasizes the ethical and communal possibilities contained in the experience of pleasure, rather than the impossibility of community and a pessimistically painful conception of subjectivity.

CONCLUSION

Kant's *Critique of Judgment* obviously supports a range of competing and conflicting readings, despite the endless attempts by philosophers to finalize its interpretation. This chapter has summarized some key strands of eighteenth-century aesthetics, and attempted to defend the link that Shaftesbury and Kant make between pleasure and community as more complex and politically significant than twentieth-century critics have recognized. Though many postmodern commentators on Kant's Third Critique have argued that the pleasure of community that he describes is both mystical and sedative, and have allowed only a sublime apprehension of subjectivity to emerge, we should recognize, like Nancy, that pleasure may be described in a range of ways, changing the implied relation between individual and community relation. Nancy's revised description of pleasure not in terms of narcotic closure, but in terms of *opening* and movement, echoes the kinds of possibilities I began to trace in Kant around pleasure as a lingering and a feeling of life. To put this more baldly, pleasure might be a response to forms of community that are diverse; that might be involved with difference and openness as well as homogeneity and closure. The question of pleasure should be considered an open one, rather than valorizing sublime pain or fear as the key affect of the subject or the only appropriate model of community.[141] Eighteenth-century theories of pleasure might resonate with Michael Hardt and Antoni Negri's recent theory of community as 'a process of liberation based on the free expression of difference'; perhaps pleasure might arise from the interplay between 'singularity and commonality at the heart of the multitude'.[142]

How do these different interpretations of the politics of eighteenth-century aesthetics bear on an interpretation of Romanticism, and of Wordsworth's poetry in particular? Previous studies of Shaftesbury's influence on post-1790s writing have focused on the theme of 'regulation'. Jon Mee's important study of the idea of enthusiasm considered how Wordsworth drew from Shaftesbury in 'disciplining' his own poetry to avoid the excesses of feeling linked to political unrest.[143] More recently, Stuart Allen has also claimed that 'Wordsworth's proximity to Shaftesbury is at its greatest when the idea of regulation arises.'[144] Allen argues that Wordsworth's poetry borrows from Shaftesbury, via Mark Akenside, the idea of self-division as self-mastery, and also, ultimately, Shaftesbury's Whig ideology around taste and class privilege. My own reading is much closer to Chris Jones' earlier argument in *Radical Sensibility* that it is not regulation, or even reason, that is the key idea carried through to Wordsworth, but outward-directed feeling. Jones argues that a particularly Shaftesburian idea of benevolence influenced 1790s writers more than Adam Smith's and David Hume's mid-century descriptions of sensibility, and had its high-water mark in Wordsworth's poetics. Like Jones, I have attended to the way that Shaftesbury reacts against his contemporaries' 'selfish' definition of the passions, but I have intensified the consideration of the political meanings of pleasure, both historically and philosophically. Wordsworth elaborates these ethical and political meanings through the *Lyrical Ballads* and in the long *Recluse* poems. I shall suggest that Wordsworth's ideas, for instance, about poetic pleasure deriving from 'the perception of similitude in dissimilitude' and 'dissimilitude in similitude' can be linked back to the eighteenth-century treatment of the *sensus communis*, and possess similar political ambiguity. There are many analogies between Kant's and Wordsworth's discussions of pleasure, including the tautological descriptions of a state of pleasure in *Home at Grasmere* and the metaphor of pleasurable 'fitting' in the world that we found in Kant and Arendt. The crucial difference, of course, is that the context –

and frequently the substance – of Wordsworth's philosophical exploration of pleasure is poetry itself. Before turning to Wordsworth, however, we shall consider the political philosophy of Rousseau and Wollstonecraft. In the foregoing discussions of Shaftesbury and Kant, pleasure has been described mainly in terms of general ethical ideas of sociability and communication. The embodied, strength-based image of pleasure in Rousseau and Wollstonecraft fleshes out the individual's delight and places it in a more directly political context. The anthropological framework that underlies eighteenth-century accounts of the *sensus communis* comes to life, as we turn to the power-struggles of actual people and the way pleasure mediates both competition and collaboration.

CHAPTER 2

Powers of pleasure: Rousseau and Wollstonecraft

Aged sixteen, a pretty, awkward boy with bad teeth, Jean-Jacques Rousseau had run away from his apprenticeship to an engraver, and met an attractive older woman (his type, as one biographer wittily put it: 'a lot of heart in a lot of *poitrine*'[1]), who, for reasons both pious and politic, sent him to be converted to Catholicism in Turin. It was a three-week coach adventure in the company of a married couple who produced mysterious noises in the night; Rousseau gazed at the countryside and day-dreamed of the lovely Mme de Warens. He later recalled it as the 'most fortunate situation of body and mind' he ever experienced: 'Young, vigorous, full of health, security, confidence in myself and in others, I was in that short but precious moment of life in which its expansive fullness extends our being through all our sensations so to speak, and in our eyes embellishes all of nature with the charm of our existence.'[2] This retrospective glance of bliss may be filtered through memory and writing; but it is a compressed statement of the themes that are crucial to Rousseau's theory of pleasure. Key aspects include the social dimension of well-being ('confidence in myself and in others'); a physiological basis for pleasure in corporeal strength ('vigorous, full of health'); the idea of striving ('its expansive fullness extends our being'); as well as a link to the Rousseauian notion often considered central to his oeuvre, that of the sentiment of existence ('the charm of our existence'). Though Rousseau felt his own moments of bliss were rare and short – and his documented sufferings have encouraged a view of him as a tragic thinker – his account of pleasure and its place within his philosophy merits a full attention.[3] The importance he himself placed on this theme is indicated by the existence of manuscript fragments for an intended work, rarely mentioned in Rousseau scholarship, entitled *The Art of Enjoyment*.[4]

Deconstructive and liberal readings of Rousseau have often downplayed the meaning of pleasure in his work, stressing a drive towards 'asceticism' in his writing, and, in a connected move, have often regarded his portrait of the individual's relation to the community as inherently tragic. Liberal interpretations have defined the Rousseauian individual in terms of the attempt to overcome vulnerability, lonely, striving, but free. According to this way of thinking, pleasure is antithetical to freedom; sensuality is a form of slavery, limiting our rational self-determination and possibilities for perfection. These ideas were not formerly associated with Rousseau. At the start of the twentieth century, Irving Babbitt derided Rousseau's 'indulgence of infinite indeterminate desire', in which all serious values were dissolved.[5] Rousseau's defenders, most importantly Ernst Cassirer writing in the 1930s, made their case for him partly by sidelining pleasure and reading him as the prophet of Kantian disinterest-edness and as the ultimate anti-utilitarian.[6] Cassirer drew from Rousseau a rational (perhaps also Stoic) conception of individual freedom that prom-ised the transcendence of animal existence. Here, freedom was submission to the law of the general will and to a State that concerned itself not with welfare but only with rights and duties. Cassirer wrote that Rousseau 'did not found the human community on mere instinctual life: he regarded neither the pleasure instinct nor the natural instinct of sympathy as a sufficient and adequate foundation'.[7] He demanded 'the power of renunciation' of men.[8] Likewise, George Armstrong Kelly has written of Rousseau that 'for one who believed as he did in the positive and indwell-ing corruption in the human heart, a simple hedonism could not suffice. For one thing, it could not sustain that sometimes gruesome heroism in which he periodically sets so much store.'[9] Paul de Man traced in Rousseau's *Julie* an 'ethic of renunciation', which is 'not to be equated with a puritanical denial of the world of the senses'.[10] He finds in Julie's 'Elysium' garden echoes of the Puritan writing of Bunyan and Defoe, and 'the triumph of a controlled and lucid renunciation of the values associ-ated with a cult of the moment'.[11] His key argument is that allegory recognizes its own 'time lag' or differentiation from the thing that it allegorizes, unlike the symbol, which pretends to a temporally simul-taneous connection. Allegorical language has serious ontological implica-tions: 'it prevents the self from an illusory identification with the non-self, which is now fully, though painfully, recognized as a non-self. It is this painful knowledge that we perceive at the moments when early romantic literature finds its true voice.'[12] The idea of Rousseau's 'asceti-cism' stands therefore for the painful recognition of the impossibility of community.

These issues were also raised in Derrida's reading of Rousseau in *Of Grammatology*, in which he argued 'presence is always determined as pleasure, for Rousseau'.[13] He relentlessly attacked both the bad philosophical reasoning of Rousseau's claims for a pure and authentic enjoyment and the power implications of his fantasy of sovereignty. Derrida exploits the etymological overlap between enjoying and possessing in Rousseau's phrases like *jouissance de soi*, arguing that pleasure for Rousseau is ultimately a form of auto-affection, an 'idealizing' operation by which we imagine that all our interaction with the world is actually self-generated, self-enclosed and self-sufficient. Derrida writes: 'Here idealization is the movement by which sensory exteriority, that which affects me or serves me as signifier, submits itself to my power of repetition, to what thenceforward appears to me as my spontaneity and escapes me less and less.'[14] Taking cues in particular from the *Reveries'* description of a happiness 'in which the present lasts forever without, however, making its duration noticed and without any trace of time's passage',[15] Derrida suggests that what ostensibly interrupts or destroys pleasure for Rousseau is language and temporality: 'The present is always the present of a pleasure; and pleasure is always a receiving of presence. What dislocates presence introduces différance and delay, spacing between desire and pleasure. Articulated language, knowledge and work, the anxious research of learning, are nothing but the spacing between two pleasures.'[16] The dark irony that Derrida discovers throughout (especially in Rousseau's prohibition of the 'supplement' of masturbation) is the link between pleasure and death: 'Pleasure *itself*, without symbol or suppletory, that which would accord us (to) pure presence itself, if such a thing were possible, would be only another name for death.'[17] Derrida finds a kind of shadowy knowledge in Rousseau that there cannot be pleasure without desire and imagination, which are both related to the master-signifier of death, because they are forms of non-presence and loss. Derrida asserts: 'Rousseau knew that death is not the simple outside of life', and that without that non-presence and loss, we could not even want anything like 'pleasure': 'Without the possibility of différance, the desire of presence as such would not find its breathing-space. That means by the same token that this desire carries in itself the destiny of its non-satisfaction.'[18] The very pleasure with which presence is entwined is created by the 'abyss' of representation.[19] Derrida suggests that 'writing' (which stands in the chain of signifiers with 'imagination' and 'death' against the chain of signifiers including 'presence' and 'voice') is 'the greatest sacrifice aiming at the greatest symbolic reappropriation of presence'.[20] This idea of sacrifice could be supported with the *Reveries'* example of the man who 'digs in the bowels of the earth. He goes to its center, at the risk of his life and the expense of his health, to seek imaginary goods in place of the real goods it freely offered him when he knew how to enjoy them' (62). Derrida's account does not therefore relinquish the ideal of pleasure for Rousseau, but asserts the inseparability of any organic or bodily experience from its association with writing and the figure of death. Derrida's reading saves the symbolic status of pleasure in Rousseau's texts, but undermines the actuality of a lived experience of pleasure, which would be able to carry the ethical and even ontological implications that, as I shall show, Rousseau wants to give them.

The question of the relation of power and pleasure is central to this chapter. Derrida could be said to find *only* a negative meaning of power in pleasure, with Rousseau's *jouissance de soi* standing only for sovereign self-possession. Foucault, on the other hand (though without specific reference to Rousseau), arguably recognized more ambiguity in what he called '*perpetual spirals of power and pleasure*'.[21] In *The History of Sexuality*, he contrasted a pleasure in domination and surveillance with a pleasure of resistance: 'the pleasure that comes of exercising a power that questions, monitors, watches, spies, searches out, palpates, brings to light; and on the other hand, the pleasure that kindles at having to evade this power, flee from it, fool it, or travesty it'.[22] In analysing what he called the 'repressive hypothesis', that is to say, the idea that since the nineteenth century sexuality has been repressed by institutions of power, and comparing it to the psychoanalytic (especially Lacanian) idea that power is constitutive of desire, Foucault noted the antimony around the relation of power and pleasure. As he put it, in these accounts power can only produce absences and gaps, or say 'no' to sexuality, and he challenged, instead, that 'We must at the same time conceive of sex without the law, and power without the king.'[23]

This is a challenge with which, I suggest, Rousseau and Wollstonecraft are also grappling. In their work, one can find the idea that pleasure as a form of natural power and strength might also be the very undoing of sovereign self-possession, *contra* Derrida. This chapter shows that pleasure is represented in the work of Rousseau and Wollstonecraft as something that makes possible our relations with other people, creating the generosity and hope which must underlie any kind of community. It aims to trace the power dynamics of pleasure through their novels and their formal political philosophy. Power is a complex word: the word first meant 'ability (to do something)', and from 1300 had dual senses of 'physical strength' and 'authority (over others)' (*OED*). As the Introduction described, there is a longstanding semantic link between the ideas of pleasure, joy and power. A simple way of stating the disturbing implications of the connection may be as follows: if pleasures are conceived of as inherently selfish, individuals may experience pleasure sometimes – perhaps always – at the expense of another. According to this account, the violence of an individual's pleasure-drive will necessarily disrupt forms of community. In a sense, de Sade's pornography could be seen as the ultimate test of the Enlightenment connection between pleasure and sociability. The focus here, however, is on the moderate, yet arguably more fraught, negotiation of this tension in Rousseau and Wollstonecraft's work, aiming to deepen the consideration of the politics of pleasure sketched in relation to eighteenth-century aesthetics in the previous chapter. Against a more cognitive description of pleasure (linked to the unconscious, fantasy, desire or attention), Rousseau and Wollstonecraft often prefer an account of pleasure as inherently bodily or material, linked to strength and power and associated with the life-force. They suggest that this natural, healthy pleasure is the basis for co-operation and non-violent sociability. Yet, within individual texts, this argument comes under pressure, both in the way that the positive metaphor of pleasure as power transforms into empirical, negative examples of pleasure as domination, and in the difficulty of keeping pleasure 'pure' of imagination and fantasy. Formal and generic aspects of pleasure's representation appear, once again, to alter the political ideas that may be built around pleasure.

This chapter first offers a discussion of Rousseau's novel *Julie* (1760), contrasting the erotic, imaginative passion of St Preux and the harmonious enjoyment that supposedly supplants it. Thus, in Clarens, the life of Julie and the Baron de Wolmar represents an ideal philosophy of simple material pleasure, which promises to not only be free of lack or loss, but also to generate an ordered social world. However, as I demonstrate, a closer look at certain aspects of the novel reveals social conflict over servants' pleasure, and ultimately a question over whether St Preux's desiring-pleasure has in fact more potential in creating forms of community. Next, I explore Rousseau's key distinction between *amour de soi* and *amour propre* in considering the status of pleasure in Rousseau's account of the development of the individual in *Emile* (1762). *Emile* argues that the experience of pure, bodily delight is necessary to the kind of generous and non-jealous subjectivity on which good interpersonal relationships, and ultimately community, may be built. But it excludes women from this form of pleasure, in suggesting that women must be *for* the pleasure of men, thereby reintroducing the possibility of social domination that the pleasure-education was meant to eradicate.

This quandary is deepened by considering the role of imagination in Rousseauian pleasure and in the gender politics that attend it. Here, I turn to Wollstonecraft, and the critique of the eighteenth-century association between pleasure and power presented in the *Vindication of the Rights of Woman*. But I find a different notion of pleasure in Wollstonecraft's use of the term 'social enjoyment' in *The Wrongs of Woman, or Maria*. In conclusion, I return to Rousseau's autobiographical writings, especially the *Reveries*, to consider their relevance to Romanticism and to Wordsworth's poetry in particular.

'JULIE', PLEASURE AND COMMUNITY

Julie, ou la nouvelle Héloïse: lettres de deux amans, habitans d'une petite ville au pied des Alpes is a legendarily pleasurable book. Rousseau's *Confessions* boasts of the story of the Princess of Talmont who, awaiting her servants to prepare horses to take her to a ball at the Opera, became so absorbed in the 'new Novel' that all night long she kept sending them back, before luxuriantly giving up on departing in order to continue reading into the new day. *Julie* was the shortened title frequently used by Rousseau and his early fans, one that was 'disconcertingly lightweight' and 'unconventional' for the period.[24] But the book's long title broadens that focus on a single outstanding individual to the literary past, the couple and the small community, and it seeks to explore how an individual's pleasures may be relational. It is a *roman à these*, packed with arguments and ideas, yet also full of contradictions and different voices, not least through its epistolary structure (Rousseau referred to the book in the 'Preface' only as 'these letters'). My reading focuses on the different definitions of enjoyment and pleasure in the book, and their moral and political implications. As we saw at the end of the previous chapter, Jean-Luc Nancy has recently elaborated the fundamental ambiguity of pleasure, as signifying both contentment and tension, repletion and seduction.[25] This dichotomy runs all the way through Rousseau's philosophical novel, and is interwoven with its very formal features as well as its ethical statements.

The novel sets up a set of major contrasts: between the two worlds of Julie's girlhood (Vevey) and marriage (Clarens), and Julie's two lovers, St Preux and Wolmar. These worlds also encapsulate different meanings of pleasure. In the early letters, pleasure has mainly a romantic and erotic connotation, and is often framed in the context of loss, both that of the short duration of pleasure and its costs. Julie opposes it to 'happiness' after the couple have sex and destroy the 'virtue' of their love: 'we pursued pleasure, and happiness has fled far from us' (83). Pleasure stands below other ethical goods: Julie asks St Preux to 'sacrifice a day's pleasure to the duties of humanity' (97). St Preux talks about pleasure as 'time out of time', presenting an almost unbearable, untimely intensity: 'Days of pleasure and glory, no, you were not for a mortal! ... A sweet ecstasy absorbed your whole duration ... There was for me neither past nor future, and I tasted all at one time the delights of a thousand centuries' (260). Having lost the bliss of Julie's love, St Preux finds that life stretches out in an unbearable tedium. Pleasure is redefined in the second part of the novel. The explicit moral is that the lovers' passion is effectively selfish; it disrupts the wider social order, and thus St Preux must be re-educated by Julie de Wolmar to enjoy civil pleasures ('such sweet and pure pleasures as I am learning to enjoy', 363). These civil pleasures may also be read as forming part of a new economy of pleasure; one that is not predicated upon an endless gap between desire and its satisfaction. They aspire to secure pleasure so that it is durable, perhaps even permanent. The loss of a romantic paradise through sexual knowledge (recalling that Julie and St Preux are forced apart after her pregnancy and miscarriage) leads to a postlapsarian world-building of laborious, but supposedly truer and better, delight. This new order is not simply a monastic kind of joy, where rational delights are preferred to those of the body. Julie is a perfect hedonist, acutely sensitive to delight – 'She was made to know and taste all pleasures' (443) – and her great skill is the creation of a multitude of tiny, simple yet refined comforts and enjoyments. The description of her table, below, is a good example both of these prudent delights – crucially *local* as shall shortly be discussed – and of the prose style of the second half of the book: 'Rare game? Saltwater fish? Foreign foods? Better than all that. Some excellent local vegetable, some one of the savory greens that grows in our gardens, certain lake fish prepared in a certain manner, certain cheeses from our mountains, some German-style pastry, to which is added some piece of game brought in by the household servants' (444–5). The descriptions of Clarens life are slowly paced and paratactic, encouraging a cognitive pleasure on the part of the reader that is different from the high drama and erotic suspense of the first part. Instead, these passages give fascinatingly intricate detail that promotes a slower, more absorbed reading style.[26] One order is predicated on expenditure; the other predicated on conservation. Julie and Baron de Wolmar's life on their estate at Clarens represents comfort, austere hedonism, authentic as opposed to false, consumerist pleasures, and above all efficiency and a lack of waste. As St Preux notes to his friend Edward (as Rousseau's translators render Édouard), Julie and Wolmar have an understanding of happiness as 'the art of living':

> not in the sense which that word is given in France, which is to have with one's neighbor certain manners established by fashion; but with the life of man, and for which he is born; with that life you tell me of, the example of which you set for me, which lasts beyond itself, and which one does not hold as lost the day one dies. (433)

In this immortal practice, there will no longer be an opposition between pleasure and happiness, between desire and contentment; instead, pleasures, rightly managed, can be transmuted into happiness. The metaphor of expenditure becomes literalized in the miraculous profitability of Clarens, where there is seemingly a complete absence of loss at every level: agricultural, financial, libidinal. St Preux reports Wolmar's contention that 'land produces in proportion to the number of hands that till it', leading to an inexorable spiral of profit: 'better tilled it yields more; this excess production furnishes the means of tilling it better still; the more men and beasts you put on it, the more surplus it supplies over and above their subsistence. It is not known, he says, where this continual and reciprocal increase in product and laborers might end' (364). Likewise, Wolmar arranges his funds so that he is always living 'ahead' on his capital (434). Wolmar accepts that some might initially be challenged by this very laborious management of pleasure, but even this cognition delivers further pleasure into the system: 'Upon reflection contentment increases, because one sees that the source is inexhaustible and that the art of savoring life's happiness further serves to prolong it' (451). Julie practises the same art upon her own body and psyche: 'the privations she imposes on herself through that temperate sensuality I have mentioned are at the same time new means of pleasure and new opportunities to economize' (451). She is like an endless fount of joy: 'The happiness she enjoys multiplies and extends about her' (437).

How have they achieved this miraculous sustainability of enjoyment? One feature is that the Clarens estate is money-free, to prevent 'intermediary exchanges between the product and its use ... Transportation of our revenues is avoided by using them on the premises' (449). At every level, usage is preferred to exchange, and Wolmar explains that 'Only the order and discipline that multiply and perpetuate the usage of goods can transform pleasure into happiness' (383). He describes the 'paterfamilias' who takes pleasure in his house in this way: 'Alone among mortals, he is master of his own felicity, because he is happy like God himself, without desiring anything more than what he already has: like that immense Being he does not worry about expanding his possessions but of making them truly his own through the most perfect relations and the shrewdest direction' (384). Of course, there are 'real' economic resonances of this notion of the difference between mere possession and 'genuine ownership', but it is also relevant to an affective economy.[27] The idea of developing happiness by removing any possibility of 'lack' or desire through dependency on other people is developed in *Emile* and in the *Reveries*. The psycho-physiological economy of happiness in *Emile* consists in 'diminishing the excess of the desires over the faculties and putting power and will in perfect equality. It is only then that, with all the powers in action, the soul will nevertheless remain peaceful and that man will be well ordered'.[28] This stands for the prevention of excessive, unsatisfiable desires, but also the prevention of an unused 'excess' of faculties over and above our desires. We must use the full extent or range of our human abilities in order to enjoy our 'whole being', echoing Wolmar's idea of the perfectly efficient use of one's estate.

To modern readers, the powerful, impermeable happiness of Wolmar may not seem at all attractive; he deliberately resists sympathy and sentiment. As he puts it, 'My only active principle is a natural taste for order, and the right concurrence of the play of fortune and of men's acts pleases me exactly like a beautiful symmetry in a tableau' (402–3). He lacks what Rousseau calls 'inner conviction' (486): he believes in no moral values and no God. He 'carries deep in his heart the horrible peace of the wicked' (481), though paradoxically it is this cold atheism that makes him an almost godlike patriarch over Clarens: all-seeing, all-managing. Perhaps there must be no God beyond the enclosure of Wolmar's estate, for this would mean that its borders could be transcended, introducing a lack or an escape route for energy that would negate its pleasurable self-sufficiency. Wolmar is something like the first mover in the system of pleasure that Clarens represents: from his mirthless control over the domestic and libidinal economy emanate all the enjoyments of Julie and her servants, with their greater constitutional sensibility. But from another perspective, Wolmar exemplifies the Stoic ideal, the calm, ordered and rational enjoyment that we also saw in Shaftesbury. Modern discomfort at his coldness shows up the way in which the novel as a whole is so dialogic and at times discordant, crossing ancient paradigms and modern moral frameworks. Perhaps it is also inevitable in an eighteenth-century text that a theme like pleasure activates the ancient–modern conflict so acutely; it is a topic that speaks to progress and modernity as well as to the long-distant past.

Another discordance for a modern reader lies in the discussion of the estate's servants. The novel's enchanting political economy lectures reveal the barely concealed tyranny on which the apparently joyful Clarens household runs. The servants' own interests are channelled to serve the ends of their masters, a practice which has been anticipated in the emotional mechanisms and tests designed to manage St Preux's desire for Julie. Almost *bred* as ideal workers – 'They are chosen young, of good constitution, in good health and of pleasant physiognomy' (366) – the servants' 'occupations, habits, tastes, pleasures' (370) are carefully shaped so that any mismatch between their desires and their labour duties is eradicated. As St Preux notes, 'The master's whole art consists in hiding this coercion under the veil of pleasure or interest, so that they think they desire all they are obliged to do' (373). Something similar could be said of the tutor's art in *Emile*, or that of the legislator in *The Social Contract*. In *Julie*, it extends to the prevention of relationships between the servants through psychological conditioning and the prevention of any separate leisure experience off the grounds of the estate that might in any way impair the ability to work. Further, any infraction, including that of failing to inform on their colleagues, results in ruthlessly swift dismissal. Under Clarens' regime of 'transparency', the servants are allowed no private communication or reflection, contrasting vividly with the masters' rich emotional lives. All the servants' own attachments, pleasures and interests are made to fall in line with the increase of the Clarens estate. St Preux draws a distinction between the way a Republic controls its citizens by 'morals, principles, virtue' and how 'domestics, mercenaries' can only be contained by perfect affective coercion (373). This relationship of servants to masters is allegorized in Julie's aviary, the idea of which discomfits St Preux until he discovers with relief that the birds are 'guests and not prisoners' (391). Providing abundant food and nesting materials, and protecting the spot from intruders, Julie has with much 'patience and time' managed to get a huge assortment of birds to 'choose' to nest in one spot in her garden. Nonetheless, the verbal interplay between hosting and imprisoning, between kindness and control, continues to resonate, as in St Preux's report: 'Thus, I said to her, lest your birds be your slaves you have become theirs. Now that, she replied, is what a tyrant would say, who thinks he is enjoying his freedom only insofar as it disturbs that of others' (392). Julie's implication is that St Preux can still only think of a scenario where there is a winner and a loser, one who gains enjoyment only at the cost to the other one. Despite Julie's morally authoritative answers, St Preux's questions about inequality continue to resonate. He argues with Julie over the question of people's station and their talents. Julie is strongly averse to social mobility from a 'happiness' principle: her 'great maxim is therefore not to favor changes of condition, but to contribute to making each one happy in his own' (439). The most naturally happy state, Julie argues, is that of 'a villager in a free State', a situation that offers simple and gratifiable desires: 'The peaceable dweller of the fields in order to feel his happiness needs only to understand it' (439, 438). St Preux still argues that men may have 'sundry talents' irrespective of 'the condition in which they were born' (439). Julie's reasoned answer finally arrives at a point of plain utility: 'if we took away from that work all those who are better suited to another, there would not remain enough labourers to till it [the land] and provide us sustenance' (441).

The ending of the novel again complicates the relation between desire, contentment and power. The shoring up of pleasure against loss that has been presented as the aim of the Clarens economy becomes to Julie so complete and decisive that her life actually cannot continue; she feels she is going to 'die of happiness': 'there is nothing left for my imagination to do, there is nothing for me to desire; to feel and to enjoy are to me one and the same thing; I live at once in all those I love, I am sated with happiness and life: O death, come when thou wilt!' (566). This is reiterated in a grimmer key a few pages into her letter to St Preux, where she admits that to 'live without pain is not a human condition; to live thus is to be dead' (570). Deprived of the 'pleasure of desiring', she is being slowly consumed with a 'secret languor', a peculiar 'affliction': 'I am too happy; I am weary of happiness' (570). Whilst Rousseau's editorial footnote accuses her of being contradictory and melodramatic ('this letter looks to me like the swan's song', 570), her death-wish can be interpreted in various ways. The least suspicious or ironic reading available would be that she has reached what we might call a 'higher plane' of happiness, pointing her towards the spiritual realm. Her sense of readiness for death is, on this reading, a search for the 'source of sentiment and being' (570). She takes a new, rarefied delight in piety: 'I do not contend that this taste is wise, I merely contend that it is sweet' (571). Julie, ultra-hedonist, finds a new level of pleasure in the satisfactions of a soul merging with God. The more ironic reading sees this gloom as a possible undercutting of the pleasure-economy that the novel celebrates; that it is not, in fact, possible to secure a 'wholesome' form of pleasure free of desire, imagination and freedom. The permanent forms of contentment that Clarens aims to achieve – everyone 'goes to bed content with a day spent in labor, merriment, innocence, which one would not be unhappy to begin anew the next day, the day after, and his whole life long' (499) – could be read as a deathly repetitiveness. Again, we have the question of what pleasure really is; whether it may be separated from desire in this way. Julie's ultimately fatal leap into the river to save her child might thus look like an escape-attempt, a line of flight.

Her depression also makes possible a reconsideration of the kind of desiring-pleasure that characterized the affair with St Preux in Vevey, that which the novel has ostensibly reformed. Julie comments to St Preux that though the passionate wanting of things leads to pain and disappointment, it also lends the huge uplift of hope and illusion. Unexpectedly desire, perhaps more than gratification, turns out to offer the self-sufficiency that seems key to Rousseau's ontology: 'As long as one desires one can do without happiness; one expects to achieve it; if happiness fails to come, hope persists, and the charm of illusion lasts as long as the passion that causes it. Thus this condition suffices to itself, and the anxiety it inflicts is a sort of enjoyment that compensates for reality' (569). To possess the desired thing, to 'enjoy' it, is to lose the 'spell', the 'embellishment', the 'fantasy': 'illusion ends where enjoyment begins' (569). She has begun to realize that the land of illusions and imagination is 'on this earth the only one worth living in, and such is the void of things human that, with the exception of the Being who exists in himself, the only beauty to be found is in things that are not' (569). Thus the appeal of her religious enthusiasm and piety; they are the extension of her passionate sexual hopes for and fantasy of St Preux. Both forms of eros offer the same structure of frustrated hope that is the best a mortal can hope for. The energy of the sexual desire and imagination of Julie and Wolmar cannot be completely sublimated into gardening and interior design, which is why the novel finally returns to desire: 'The virtue that separated us on earth shall unite us in the eternal abode. I die in this flattering expectation. Only too happy to pay with my life the right to love thee still without crime, and to tell thee so one more time' (610). In this shift back to eros and fantasy, we should also note Julie's desire to *tell* her love again. On her deathbed, she declares: 'I was happy, I am happy, I am going to be happy: my happiness is fixed, I snatch it from fortune' (596). This verbal recollection and reiteration points up the pleasures of representation itself, in a novel so much about the enjoyment generated by letters and reading.

So the book proposes a reformation of pleasure, from a concept associated with desire and lack, to a pleasure that is both more socially oriented and more philosophically stable. But, as my reading has tried to show, the perfected form of pleasure cannot entirely conceal social injustices that support it. This leaves open the possibility, which Julie's doubts at the end of the novel seem to support, that the wild imaginative desires experienced by the younger lovers do in fact enable hope and social change. One might argue that through his romantic idealization of Julie, St Preux ends up with a stronger power of empathy for humankind than Wolmar, who experiences only 'weakly that sentiment of interest and humanity that causes us to assimilate the affections of others' (402). In these various ways, the novel encapsulates the tensions between a pleasure-focused ethics and a liberalism of freedom and imagination to which I alluded at the beginning of this chapter. In *Emile*, published shortly after *Julie*, Rousseau explored in a different form the role of individual pleasure in creating forms of community.

'EMILE' AND 'AMOUR DE SOI'

Emile's answer to the question of how to find happiness within a social order that threatens our sense of self – and how to find pleasures that do not come at another's cost – is different in certain respects from *Julie*'s. If St Preux's natural sources of enjoyment must be transformed into 'civil pleasures' more suited to the wider community, *Emile* holds out the hope that if natural man could be brought up in the fullest expression of his natural pleasures, he would be able to experience the pleasure of being without domination. Pleasure is central to Rousseau's account of human existence and its ideal or flourishing condition; but it is ethically and politically ambiguous. In particular, there is a question over whether the natural needs of individuals can ever be aligned, and whether pleasure might always be inherently involved with the desire to dominate. The quasi-physiological understanding of pleasure as a force or motion (seen in de Pouilly and Diderot, and discussed in the Introduction) can thus be seen to merge with the political consequences of pleasure *as* power. This section will examine self-pleasure in *Emile* and its implications for modes of community as well as its gender contradictions.

The crucial distinction in Rousseau's philosophy between two, hard-to-translate, kinds of love, *amour de soi* and *amour propre*, has been much discussed by scholars; I argue that is another way of framing the question of the 'selfish' and 'utopian' dimensions of pleasure.[29] In simple terms, *amour de soi* is associated with natural and instinctual life, the securing of self-preservation and well-being, whereas *amour propre* is associated with social life, opinion and reputation and our desire to compete with and dominate others. *Amour de soi* is sometimes seen as affectively neutral, or even fearful and defensive, something comparable to the early modern description of the drive for self-preservation. But in numerous passages, Rousseau links *amour de soi* to the expansion of enjoyments rather than merely the avoidance of pain and danger. Likewise, though some scholars see *amour de soi* as an essentially individual, non-communal feeling, contingent on isolation – we are good in the state of nature because we encounter no one towards whom to be bad – N.J.H. Dent has argued that *amour de soi* also incorporates human relationships and our work and action; it is not a merely 'animal' sense of preservation.[30]

Initially, at least, Rousseau's *Emile* appears to offer the possibility of separating pleasure from the exercise of power over others: Emile's peaceableness is a consequence of his 'education which, having not fomented *amour propre* and a high opinion of himself, has diverted him from seeking his pleasures in domination and in another's unhappiness' (251). The key aims of Emile's education are to strip imagination away from desire, returning man's wants to his natural needs, and to ensure that the satisfactions of these needs are not derived from the domination of others. These two related moves foster the individual's happiness and the general good, by training the individual not to desire things that are out of his power to obtain, and by undermining the sources of social evil: competitiveness, anger and envy. Rousseau's *Emile* represents pleasure in terms of physical power and vitality. In summary, there appears to be a desire to define pleasure as purely physical in order to keep it untainted by the imagination and social emulation that he sees as threatening to all possibility of human happiness and non-violent community. This can be witnessed in his idea that a preverbal infant is not only 'unconscious of his own life', but, more surprisingly, cannot truly be said to enjoy his existence, or to experience the sentiment of existence. The baby can, for sure, feel pleasure and pain, as basic or primary perceptions: 'Children's first sensations are purely affective; they perceive only pleasure and pain' (62). His account of pleasure at this point seems to be quite Lockean (and in fact Epicurean): that pleasure is a simple idea, a form of perception one cognitive step up from bare sensation. But Rousseau immediately exceeds this Lockean framework by suggesting that as the toddler gains both consciousness and physical strength, she will be able to 'sense the pleasure of being', to 'taste life'. He implies that there is a turn in the child's early development where either a new kind of pleasure develops or where what is merely a physiological response to stimuli is transformed into this existential awareness.

Rousseau has to press this point because he wants to link the ability to experience the pleasure of being not to the child's cognitive development, as we might otherwise imagine, but to the child's physical growth and increasing strength: only once the child has 'strength' does his 'life' and 'consciousness' begin (78). The tutor exhorts his readers to be 'humane' in encouraging childhood enjoyments: 'As soon as they can sense the pleasure of being, arrange it so that they can enjoy it, arrange it so that at whatever hour God summons them they do not die without having tasted life' (79). Here, we can see that life, strength and enjoyment are to some extent coterminous. In the young child, the 'active principle' 'is superabundant and extends outward; he senses within himself, so to speak, enough life to animate everything surrounding him' (67). Thus, a little child should be forgiven for a mindless killing of a bird: he has such a powerful sense of energy that he simply wants to make a physical impression on the world. The child should be allowed the risk of injury in order to gain 'the well-being of freedom': 'My pupil will often have bruises. But, in compensation, he will always be gay' (78). Only with strength comes a full enjoyment of being, and only by being encouraged to experience the bodily pleasures of selfhood can one grow into a moral, and sociable, being such as Emile will become.

This brief sketch leaves a host of questions: namely, what exactly is it to enjoy fully one's being, and how can this pure childish pleasure be sustained into adulthood? And can *amour de soi* really be considered as a social feeling? The late autobiographical work *Rousseau, Judge of Jean-Jacques* offers a fuller exploration of the social dimensions of *amour de soi* and *amour propre*.[31] Here, the character 'Rousseau' imagines a parallel world, similar to our own but one whose inhabitants are driven by strong and good natural passions, the kind that *Emile* celebrated. Inevitably, obstacles arise, but because the passions are strong, they are not easily deflected and the true aim remains in sight. The lives of these creatures are full of enjoyments, but not competitive, status-oriented ones; and they quickly abandon efforts towards impossible desires. Later in the same work, Rousseau is invited to describe his view of sensitivity, in response to a book supposedly called 'Research on the Soul' (Helvétius' *De L'esprit*), which claims that there is no soul because one cannot find anything like a soul at the base of the nerves in the brain (111).[32] First, he presents a 'purely passive and organic sensitivity which seems to have as its end only the preservation of our bodies and of our species through the direction of pleasure and pain'. This is distinguished from another kind, 'active and moral . . . nothing other than the faculty of attaching our affections to beings who are foreign to us' (112). This kind, the soul's sensitivity – 'about which study of nerve pairs teaches nothing' – can be compared to the magnetism of bodies, sometimes attracting, sometimes repulsing (112). Rousseau notes that '[i]ts strength is in proportion to the relationships we feel between ourselves and other beings': this claim is crucial because it posits an inherent sociability, or intersubjectivity, to affect (112). Nonetheless, there are good and bad forms of our social feeling: 'The positive or attracting action is the simple work of nature, which seeks to extend and reinforce the feeling of our being; the negative or repelling action, which compresses and diminishes the being of another, is a combination produced by reflection' (112). Kind, 'loving and gentle passions' come from nature, and this natural tendency to extend our own being; 'cruel passions' come from reflection, which brings about the desire to squash others. As soon as our self-love degenerates into habits of comparison with others, 'it is impossible not to develop an aversion for everything that surpasses us, everything that lowers our standing, everything that diminishes us, everything that by being something prevents from being everything' (112). Here, the distinction between *amour de soi* and *amour propre* and their social dimensions becomes increasingly complex. Positive feelings of *amour de soi* do derive from relationships with other people, suggesting that pleasure may be sociable instead of selfish; yet, triggered by our perceived lack of recognition, relationships turn into 'comparisons', thus corrupting the pleasure of sociability into the violence of competition.

Emile contains one crux, however, that calls into question the utopian possibilities of its account of healthy pleasures and their role in an ideal society: female experience. What could be called ordinary sensual pleasures, the pleasures of touch and movement in particular, are crucial to Emile's education, but conspicuous by their absence from that of little Sophie, his counterpart and future partner. Rousseau implies that boys experience sensual pleasure readily, and indeed Emile's tutor repeatedly exploits this to bring Emile towards knowledge, including ethical knowledge, in the process of what one critic has called Emile's 'sensual-physical education'.[33] All the boy-child's *genuine* demands for pleasure must be met: 'So, as far as possible, grant them everything that can give them a real pleasure; always refuse them what they ask for only due to whim or in order to assert their authority' (89). By contrast, Rousseau's account of young girls implies that they have a far more alienated experience of their bodies, concerned only with how they look and not with how they feel. The pleasures of *amour propre* – exactly what Emile's education is designed to eradicate, for the sake of his happiness – which at best might include social approbation and at worst delight in domination, are represented as central to young girls' experience.

The text oscillates between presenting girls as *naturally* focused on the secondary pleasures of approbation, and as girls having to *learn* such habits. In one vignette, a young girl learning to write who loves forming the letter 'O' catches herself in a mirror and, disliking the way she looked, 'she threw away the pen' (369). Her brother hates writing too, 'but what irritated him was the discomfort and not the appearance it gave him', Rousseau adds, to underline the difference between sensuality and self-consciousness (369). His sister only returns to writing when she is given the incentive of monogramming her own linen underwear, appealing to her vanity and possessiveness. Little Sophie, a natural glutton, steals handfuls of sugarplums and bonbons from the cupboard, for which her mother scolds her in order to persuade her that sweets will ruin her teeth and figure. For the simple pleasure of sugarplums is substituted the pleasure in imagining herself attractive to men: 'In growing up, she acquired other tastes which diverted her from this base sensuality' (395). These examples suggest that girls do have something of a 'base sensuality' after all, it seems, but they must be taught, quickly, to suppress it for the sake of their natural desire for the approval of the man who can assure them their biological and social survival. The relentless drive of man-catching requires that women learn pleasure only in the transitive form, 'pleasing'.[34] From early years, they must follow the logic of delayed gratification and self-command. Naturally weaker than and dependent on men, the only power women can obtain is through controlling men's desires, and the only pleasures they can obtain are those of vanity and competition.

Many readers have been startled by Rousseau's recommendations for women's education in the final book of *Emile*, and feminist readers have pressed on the contradiction between his egalitarianism and sexism.[35] Famously, it greatly dismayed Wollstonecraft whose important critique will be discussed shortly. Rousseau argues that men and women are identical in all respects apart from the sexual ones, which leads to a striking chain of argument: 'One ought to be active and strong, the other passive and weak. One must necessarily will and be able; it suffices that the other put up a little resistance. Once this principle is established, it follows that woman is made specially to please man' (358). On this link between the unequal physical strength of men and women and their unequal relation to pleasure hang almost all of the subsequent claims about female subservience and limitation. Beyond the historical misogyny, there is something puzzling in the metaphor of pleasure as power. Rousseau argues that women's weakness, and their need to please men, entails the use of modesty by turns to dampen and inflame male desire. The woman's resistance allows the man to feel the sense of conquest of difficulty, adding an extra pleasure to that of sexual gratification. Surprisingly, however, the role of female modesty is based on the principle not of overwhelming *male* sexual desire, but on the unlimited nature of *female* desire. In Rousseau's history of humanity, women first became reliant on men for their survival (and forced to cohabit with them) when increased human contact led to more frequent pregnancies, and growing populations put pressure on resources. Then, Rousseau argues, women had to learn to use modesty both in order to arouse men into giving them the sex they wanted, and also in order that men were not depleted, perhaps even extinguished, by the force of women's desire. Sex presents a risk to life and limb – not, as one might imagine, because of pregnancy, but through the expense of man's vital force. Rousseau writes that if 'reserve did not impose on one sex the moderation which nature imposes on the other, the result would soon be the ruin of both, and mankind would perish by the means established for preserving it' (358–9). In a lurid apocalypse, he imagines men being 'dragged to their death' by sexually ravenous women (359). This brief sketch of Rousseau's views of gender difference, and its use of the ideas of pleasure and power, again shows that desire, for Rousseau, is a dangerous and anti-social force. It requires education, yet differently so for men and for women. For boys, physical pleasures must be cultivated to give them the fullest possible healthy sense of self, *amour de soi*, which will protect them from the violent unhappy ravages of *amour propre*, and its social consequences of domination. This concept is, however, built on the idea that girls must follow the reverse move, learning to repress their natural enjoyments for the delayed gratifications of *amour propre* that will enable them to entrap and 'please' men, with the further advantage that by limiting their sexuality, they can help prevent men, supposedly strong, but potentially weak, from being wiped out from sheer sexual exhaustion.

PLEASURE, GENDER AND THE IMAGINATION

Rousseau generally links imagination to lack and the creation of impossible desires, and therefore to unhappiness; thus, as we have seen, his insistence on describing the 'pleasure of being' in terms of corporeality. In the fifth book of *Emile*, Sophie appears to temporarily lose herself to imagination. Having been told by her parents that she is free to choose her own husband, she falls in love with a fictional figure, Fénelon's Telemachus. Rousseau seems to acknowledge that an *imaginative* Sophie threatens his theory of women's role, because it shows that 'in spite of the prejudices born of the morals of our age, enthusiasm for the decent and the fine is no more foreign to women than to men, and that there is nothing that can be obtained under nature's direction from women as well as from men' (405). However, as Barbara Taylor has wittily noted, this 'Sophie Two' is made to vanish as quickly as she appeared: Rousseau writes, 'Let us resuscitate this lovable girl to give her a less lively imagination and a happier destiny' (405).[36] Taylor hints that this imaginative outburst is a return of the repressed – the repressed being Sophie's 'entire intellectual and ethical subjectivity' which has been 'lodged in her male partner'.[37] The vanquishing of Sophie's imaginative alter-ego is, to some extent, consistent with Rousseau's advice that imagination is the enemy of happiness. But what is she being turned *back* into, if not into the self-consciousness and scheming of the *amour propre* in which she has been schooled? Imagination fits uneasily into Rousseau's schema of men and women's identities, for he wants to insist that men have the sublime intellects of speculative reason, whereas women have pragmatic and teleological desires. As a consequence of their vulnerability in a state of nature, he argues, women are focused on getting a single mate: this changes the nature of their imagination. Susan Meld Shell writes that '[m]ale desire, more readily directable toward fantastic goods, is the easy ally of imagination, fuelling the latter even as it is sustained by it'.[38] She paraphrases Rousseau as arguing that male desire is 'weaker than women's and more free-wheeling or, alternatively, more open to perversions (from its immediate natural object) of all kinds'.[39] For the purposes of humanity and society, men must be taught to direct their diffuse eroticism on to one idealized figure, to attach their energy to an idea of beauty and virtue that will enable them to learn from it a sense of citizenship. One interpretation of the strange appearance and disappearance of the imaginative Sophie is that Rousseau is hereby insisting that modern life *is* a compromise, *is* a construction; and women's self-sacrificing, compromised personalities epitomize a chaste feminine rule that is the ideal model for civilization. Barbara Taylor has read *Emile* as suggesting that Sophie One actually possesses the 'requisite civic personality', and that the destiny of men is 'to be "women"'.[40] In a similar vein, Shell has suggested that women's practical craftiness can be read as a form of freedom from natural determination, adding a liberal-feminist slant to the view she ascribes to Rousseau, that 'mankind is defined essentially by our perfectibility or our freedom'.[41]

First, however, we might consider Wollstonecraft's contemporary response to *Emile. A Vindication of the Rights of Woman* has long been recognized as a multi-faceted text: as an insightful philosophical response to some of the quandaries presented by Enlightenment theories of sensibility, as a hastily written political tract of the 1790s, as well, of course, as the ur-text of feminism.[42] It is also a text preoccupied with pleasure and hedonism. Memorably, the *Vindication* argues that women are reduced to the state of infants or animals by their addiction to sensual enjoyment. As if in a 'seraglio' or like an 'epicure', women 'supinely dream life away in the lap of pleasure' (98). This is the basis of Wollstonecraft's trenchant attacks on contemporary culture and her abomination of her otherwise adored forerunner Rousseau for providing fodder for what she calls a 'philosophy of lasciviousness' (121). Her images of gluttony, sex and fashion, her pleasure-seeking characters – idle natives, aroused men and, above all, enervated, sensitized, hedonistic women – show the deep conscious impact of a widespread cultural discourse of pleasure and the urgent necessity that Wollstonecraft feels to respond to and reform it. She sees it as extending from intellectual to economic spheres, referencing sugar as the ultimate pleasure-as-commodity, the true price of which is violence and inequality: 'Is sugar always to be produced by vital blood?' (235).[43] Philosophical hedonism is a crucial tool in justifying and enabling both forms of violence. Women 'become in the same proportion the slaves of pleasure as they are the slaves of man' (270). She asks if half of humanity, like 'the poor African slaves', should be brutalized 'only to sweeten the cup of man?' (235). She questions whether the story of Eve being created from Adam's rib was a patriarchal 'invention to shew that she ought to have her neck bent under the yoke, because the whole creation was only created for his convenience or pleasure' (95).

In an important article, Cora Kaplan argued that the radical tenet of *Emile* – the creation of a self-determining ideal bourgeois man – depended upon the control of passion, which in turn required the repression of woman as the object of that passion. In this way, Rousseau, friend of radicals, coincided in crucial points with a hardening conservative attitude towards gender in the period. Against these two factors, Wollstonecraft needed all her rhetorical force. Kaplan famously concluded that '[b]y tampering with the site of degrading sexuality without challenging the moralising description of sexuality itself, Wollstonecraft sets up heartbreaking conditions for women's liberation – a little death, the death of desire, the death of female pleasure'.[44] Drawing partly on this analysis, Thomas Pfau has noted that the *Vindication* targets pleasure as a 'meta-feeling', 'since "pleasure" functions as an affective substratum underlying any particular conscious experience to begin with (as is also the case in Kant)'. According to Pfau, Wollstonecraft proscribes pleasure because it represents 'narcissistic self-awareness', is 'unproductive', 'self-replicating' and part of a 'wasteful aristocratic *habitus*'.[45] But Pfau's analysis leaves open the question of how the phenomenological priority of pleasure and the need to proscribe it can be reconciled in Wollstonecraft's thought. Does she think that it is possible to be a subject without pleasure?

Certain passages of the *Vindication* seem obviously to contribute to Wollstonecraft's reputation for asceticism. She castigates physical intimacy between girls at boarding school and is bothered about cleanliness as much as chastity, in a way which comes close to a misogynist dislike of female fleshliness. Some critics have viewed this purported anxiety in terms of the 'eruption' of a repressed female body, or in terms of the threat to the integrity of the borders of the female body.[46] Yet such passages, which discomfit a modern feminism, have perhaps obscured others in which positive references to bodily life appear. A powerful example is Wollstonecraft's emphasis on the development of female physical strength, especially near the end of the *Vindication* in the chapter 'On National Education'. Wollstonecraft criticizes schools which force girls to walk in rigid postures, preventing the release of youthful energy: 'The pure animal spirits, which make both mind and body shoot out, and unfold the tender blossoms of hope, are turned sour, and vented in vain wishes or pert repinings, that contract the faculties and spoil the temper' (259). She argues that girls should exercise and strengthen their bodies rather than follow the dictates of a culture that valorizes languid frailty as a mark of cultivated femininity. Female exercise might actually undermine some longstanding assumptions: 'Let us then, by being allowed to take the same exercise as boys, not only during infancy, but youth, arrive at perfection of body, that we may know how far the natural superiority of man extends' (165). This quotation both suggests an idea of the body as far less determined and determining than we tend to expect; it echoes Spinoza's surmise that 'no one has yet determined what the body can do', and Rousseau, who notes that 'we do not know what our nature permits us to be' and, of men and women, that 'we do not know the extent of these relations' (*Emile*, 62, 361).[47] Though, for Wollstonecraft, 'power' usually carries the negative sense of mastery, she occasionally refers to human 'powers' more positively, in a way suggestive of the philosophical notion of becoming: 'I see the sons and daughters of men pursuing shadows, and anxiously wasting their powers to feed passions which have no adequate object' (193–4). As Adriana Craciun has noted, the word 'strength' is ambiguous in the *Vindication*: '"strength" and "weakness" oscillate between these long-standing masculine and feminine connotations so that a curious subtext of women's possible physical reformation emerges. Because strength refers simultaneously to masculine force and feminine forbearance, the term endows strong women with an ambiguity extending to their biology.'[48]

Craciun's useful insight about the ambiguity of strength can be developed by considering that power–pleasure spiral with which this chapter began. Wollstonecraft alludes frequently to a line from Pope's poem 'Of the Characters of Women' (1735):

> In Men, we various Ruling Passions find,
> In Women, two almost divide the Kind,
> Those, only fix'd, they first or last obey;
> The Love of Pleasures, and the Love of Sway.[49]

Examples of Pope's jokey analogy between pleasure and sway in the *Vindication* include the following: 'a love of pleasure or sway seems to divide mankind' (150); 'it is indolence and vanity – the love of pleasure and the love of sway, that will reign paramount in an empty mind' (265); 'still we hear of nothing but their fondness of pleasure and sway' (262); 'an immoderate fondness for dress, for pleasure, and for sway, are the passions of savages' (286). The word 'sway', from Old Norse 'sweigr' for switch or twig, carries from the sixteenth century meanings of prevailing influence and sovereign power (*OED*). As with the semantic link between pleasure and will, the association between pleasure and sway hints both at the inconstant mind that is easily bent by pleasurable impulses, and the taking of pleasure in influencing or dominating others. Wollstonecraft abjures the female desire to 'reign' over men, like 'short-lived queens' (130), rather: 'I do not wish them to have power over men; but over themselves' (138); 'Why are women to be thus bred up with a desire of conquest? The very word, used in this sense, gives me a sickly qualm!' (176); 'It is not empire, – but equality, that they should contend for' (186). Where Rousseau's *Emile* could be said to present a situation where girls sacrifice the healthy pleasures of *amour de soi* for the sake of some power in the battle of the sexes, Wollstonecraft appears to present women as simultaneously addicted to pleasure *and* power.

We could thus take Wollstonecraft to be rejecting Rousseau's avowed distinction between good and bad forms of self-love: to claim that all forms of pleasure are tied up with forms of domination. Rather than giving an account of subjectivity as based in the experience of pleasure, and, to this extent, somewhat porous or receptive, she appears to aspire to a form of highly rational selfhood: self-controlled, self-contained, maintaining an essential reserve from others, yet willing to expend its energies for their sake. Developing from her ethical critique is the religious mistrust of pleasure for its 'presentism', as she repeatedly puts it (101). If there were no afterlife, she points out, a prudential hedonism would be perfectly justified, but given our hopes for heaven, virtue must be practised, perhaps to the cost of pleasure (192). This idea strongly inflects her feminism, one point of which is the claim (echoed much later by Simone de Beauvoir) that women in present conditions cannot transcend the ordinary routine of life. Wollstonecraft argues that given no grander ends than vanity and control, women's understandings have shrunk, and supposed female virtue has become no more than prudence, based on the false principles of selfishness and self-preservation. Wollstonecraft at this point seems to be a theorist of desire, imagination and transcendence rather than gratification, arguing that desire, with its concomitant lack and pain, is what unfolds our mental faculties and stretches us to our maximum capacity for virtuous behaviour. This side of Wollstonecraft's thought, especially her tropes of imagination, desire and modesty, have been emphasized in recent criticism, especially that which seeks to represent her as an Enlightenment philosopher rather than 'only' a feminist philosopher.[50] Rather than being an 'ascetic' thinker who neglected affect and the body (as earlier readings such as Kaplan's suggested), Wollstonecraft is now hailed for her nuanced perspective on the relation of reason and affect, in which passion is a necessary stage in the individual's ethical and spiritual growth. Implicitly or explicitly, Wollstonecraft is thus presented as essentially a thinker of freedom and perfectibility.

WOLLSTONECRAFT AND SOCIAL ENJOYMENT

Despite the seriousness of Wollstonecraft's critique of an Enlightenment pleasure culture, and the recent scholarly view that she should be considered a thinker of *desire* rather than gratification, there are moments in her work where she is positive about pleasure, even according it an ethical status. Even the *Vindication* has a reflex of eighteenth-century hedonism, perhaps derived from natural theology and utilitarianism, in that its manifesto for the reformation of women promises 'new sources of enjoyment' (103). Women could choose, she suggests, to labour for 'the sober pleasures that arise from equality', rather than be 'short-lived queens' (130). The reward of virtue is a kind of calm satisfaction or rational delight, a subtle, low-lighting of our experience unlike the vigorous sensations of our animal bodies. The *Hints* towards the planned, unwritten second part of the *Vindication* are particularly interesting in revealing the complexity and ambivalence of her thinking on pleasure, especially in relation to Rousseau.[51] She notes, for instance, that though men experience 'physical love' more strongly than women, it is women's 'confined education' that makes jealousy predominate, confirming the Rousseauian idea of the corruption of natural physical affects into comparative emotions. She also seems to admit the limits of the mild content that she lauds in place of stronger pleasures throughout the *Vindication*. She notes that whilst the 'calm satisfaction' generated by the appreciation of Greek architecture may be 'lasting', it is not a 'great' feeling (302). Her final hint is to wonder whether 'some principle prior to self-love must have existed: the feeling which produced the pleasure, must have existed before the experience' (303). This is a curious fragment, because it seems to suggest that the question of pleasure, sensation and selfishness – presented here, as in Kant, in the context of the place and priority of perceptions and apperception – was both puzzling and important to Wollstonecraft.

Ordinary phenomenological delights from breast-feeding to the breeze on one's face are, in fact, important to Wollstonecraft's conception of subjectivity. Drawing from the social possibility generated by Rousseau's accounts of *amour de soi* and the sentiment of existence, there are traces in her work of an account of affect as intersubjective; even as a basis for ethics. Wollstonecraft's personal experiences after the publication of the *Vindication* in 1792 – her love-affair with Gilbert Imlay, the birth of Fanny Imlay and, later, her relationship with William Godwin – are sometimes seen to have made possible the revised view of intimacy and sexuality witnessed in the *Letters Written during a Short Residence in Sweden, Norway, and Denmark* (1796) and *The Wrongs of Woman, or Maria* (published posthumously in 1798).[52] The *Letters* have been read as a statement of the intersubjective basis of our being, of the fact of our dependence on and vulnerability to others. Nancy Yousef has looked at the representation of solitary natural experience in the *Letters* and shown how it is always interlaced or inscribed with 'social disaffections'; there is a disharmony between the calm of nature and the author's restless, grieving human mind: 'because the meaning of aloneness itself has been learned in the experience of social life'.[53] She argues that Wollstonecraft takes from Rousseau's *Reveries* (to be discussed in the final section of this chapter) an idea that solitary pleasure stands for isolation and death; thus Wollstonecraft denies 'the solace of nature and solitude' in a 'rejection of an illusory ideal of autonomy that both challenges and corrects a (perhaps particularly male) ideal of self'.[54] However, it is also possible to look at this claim the other way around, and to see in *Maria* an interlacing of ruminations on social experience with natural *enjoyment*. One can find in the accounts of *pleasure* – rather than pained loneliness – a stress on what we might now call intersubjectivity.

The key phrases Wollstonecraft uses are 'social enjoyment' and 'social pleasure', which are each used twice in *Maria*. In *Maria*, Jemima, the unloved woman of the underclass, has the fullest experience of social pleasure as she is for the first time 'acknowledged' as a 'fellow-creature' (119). When Maria and Darnford fall in love, we hear that 'every sense was harmonized to joy and social extacy' (106), but it is Jemima who sheds a tear, 'the first tear that social enjoyment had ever drawn from her. She seemed indeed to breathe more freely' (106). Whilst social pleasure is, on one level, another word for sympathy, it has a basis in physicality as well: Jemima can *breathe*. At the end of the novel, an opposition is created between 'substantial happiness' and the 'reveries of a feverish imagination', making an analogy with a walk in the countryside compared to roving in an artificial garden. Isolated and miserable, Maria's fantasy life does not allow her to exist in the 'wild ease' of ordinary happiness, one that allows her to enjoy 'social pleasure' and the 'soft touches of humanity' (176–7). The energetic language of 'bursting forth, branching out, enlarging, roving and inhaling' points to the association, for Wollstonecraft, between physical freedom and enjoyment, hope and sociality (177).

These associations echo Rousseau's *Emile*. The character Maria subscribes to several of that book's sentiments when she recalls her own childhood in her memoir for her infant daughter, when the 'varying charms of nature' gave her the formative 'first consciousness of pleasure'.[55] Thus, she highlights exercise and the full use of the body's capacities: 'But the healthy breeze of a neighbouring heath, on which we bounded at pleasure, volatilized the humours that improper food might have generated. And to enjoy open air and freedom, was paradise, after the unnatural restraints of our fire-side' (124–5). Returning to her home village, Maria remarks – with hedonism seemingly alien to the *Vindication* – that 'The first scent of wild flowers from the heath, thrilled through my veins, awakening every sense to pleasure' (143). Upon receiving a copy of Rousseau's *Julie* in her cell, Maria opens her window, and feels the 'voluptuous freshness' of the night breeze on her cheek (95): '[a]bsorbed by the sublime sensibility which renders the consciousness of existence felicity, Maria was happy' (96). The most positive instance of social and natural joy is when Maria decides that she is effectively free from the marriage that had 'bastilled' her. 'I rose, and shook myself, and methought the air never smelled so sweet' (152). Her feeling of liberty allows an intensely pleasurable disruption of subjective autonomy: 'I was all soul, and (wild as it may appear) felt as if I could have dissolved in the soft balmy gale that kissed my cheek, or have glided below the horizon on the glowing, descending beams' (152–3). Despite the bleak view of women's futures presented by the novel's vignettes, Maria insists that her daughter should pursue pleasure *and* happiness, warning against letting 'the spring-tide of your existence pass away, unimproved, unenjoyed' (123), and that 'to fly from pleasure is not to avoid pain!' (125). Spring is linked to hope, buds and pleasure in this passage, recalling the *Vindication*'s description of the 'pure animal spirits, which make both mind and body shoot out, and unfold the tender blossoms of hope' (*Vindication*, 259).

Yet, the novel also asks some questions of a Rousseauian hedonist philosophy. Wollstonecraft suggests that an overdeveloped sense of life can come from isolation: '[i]n a life of such seclusion, the passions gain undue force' (98). The pessimistic developments of the novel sometimes undermine the enthusiasm for life and sensuality that is presented. Maria's joyful confidence – '[e]very bird that twittered in a bush, every flower that enlivened the hedge, seemed placed there to awaken me to rapture – yes; to rapture. The present moment was full fraught with happiness' (130) – is quickly dashed. Several critics have pointed out the complex, possibly even parodic, aspect of the novel's treatment of Maria's enthusiasm and passion: Anne K. Mellor writes that, 'For Wollstonecraft, genuine sensibility does *not* consist of the imaginative enthusiasm and passionate love felt by Maria.'[56] One proposal for interpreting Wollstonecraft's ambiguous representation of passion in *Maria*, and its contrast with the *Vindication*, has been to suggest that she sees dangerous passions as educative. 'Mistakes of conduct' in a young person, she writes in a passage that has drawn much recent attention, prove 'strength of mind' (104). Young men and women must not rest satisfied with 'the ordinary pleasures of life' (103), because they need the challenge to their understanding that comes from desire and the idealizing of objects of love. Taylor points out that Maria's 'painful education' leads not to a transvaluation, where her passion becomes devotion to God, but instead provides 'courage realistically to evaluate herself and others'.[57] Simon Swift reads this passage on Maria's 'mistakes of conduct' in relation to Kant's interest in literary or symbolic 'mistakes' before reason; both show how 'reason is enabled through emotion, it takes on an expressive capability that allows it to be responsive to the embodied particularity of its context'.[58]

These readings revise the earlier view of Wollstonecraft as an 'ascetic' to show how, in her writing, passion and affect are necessary training grounds for civic virtue; imaginative desire for fantastical objects (whether political utopias or unsuitable lovers) helps stretch our capacity to imagine better futures, and the needs of others.[59] Indeed, they may help us reconsider the very idea of ascesis: perhaps we should see it not merely as pleasure-renouncing but more in line with Pierre Hadot's idea of self-transformation. Yet, we must note the extent to which Wollstonecraft also retains an eighteenth-century hedonist idiom, witnessed especially in her concept of *social* pleasure, which may well draw from Shaftesbury.[60] *Maria* also raises questions around who is *able* to enjoy; at points it suggests that freedom and social justice are the preconditions for the taking of pleasure. The character Darnford comments on the political conservatism of the argument that the poor may be perfectly 'happy': 'though riches may fail to produce proportionate happiness, poverty most commonly excludes it, by shutting up all the avenues to improvement'; Jemima, who is a poor woman, responds, 'Of the happiness to be enjoyed over a washing-tub I need not comment' (116). Maria loses all hope in her capacity for pleasure when she is entrapped in marriage: 'I discovered in myself a capacity for the enjoyment of the various pleasures existence affords; yet, fettered by the partial laws of society, this fair globe was to me an universal blank' (146). One could read these back against the *Vindication* and Rousseau's *Emile* to suggest that Wollstonecraft hints at the reformation of pleasure itself – not only in the way that such a reformation is usually read, i.e. in terms of a shift away from selfish, vain and immoral enjoyments towards only religious and altruistic forms, but also in terms of a utopian re-visioning of the *capacity* for pleasure. Women's access to pleasure would be different in a future state of freedom and equality from that possible within the sexist culture of the eighteenth century, and perhaps even the link between pleasure and dominion would be broken, or their meanings altered. In *The Female Reader* (1789), Wollstonecraft quotes one of Hester Chapone's moral lessons from the *Letters on the Improvement of the Mind, Addressed to a Young Lady*, one of the most famous conduct books of the 1770s and an important source for the *Vindication*, especially in its discussion of female sensuality. The extract on 'The Government of the Temper' describes how the smallest disappointments spoil the pleasure of immature people, exemplified by a girl who gets in a rage over her appearance before a party that she would otherwise have enjoyed. Those who 'crave' too much will be foiled in their pleasure; the 'meek and humble', by contrast, get more than expected pleasure from an event that they could just as mildly have passed over. But beyond the simple moralism here presented is a subtext relevant to the wider questions around power explored in this chapter. Chapone notes: 'There is a degree of resignation necessary even to the enjoyment of pleasure; we must be ready and willing to give up some part of what we wish for before we can enjoy that which is indulged to us.'[61] To be able to resign some of what we wish for is not only a position of 'humility'; it is also a position of power, in which one has enough to throw something away. Can powerless women thus truly 'enjoy' anything? This is what Adorno asks in *Minima Moralia*, in one of his rare discussions of gender, which strangely echoes Chapone's comments on temper. Adorno identifies an 'archaic frigidity' in women, reminding us that society can entrap women in biological constraint that dampens their sexual enjoyment: 'The experience of pleasure presupposes a limitless readiness to throw oneself away, which is as much beyond women in their fear as men in their arrogance. Not merely the objective possibility, but also the subjective capacity for happiness, can only be achieved in freedom.'[62]

CONCLUSION: ROUSSEAU'S 'REVERIES' AND ROMANTICISM

This idea of freedom as a precondition for true forms of pleasure might help to resolve some of the quandaries set out at the start of this chapter about the 'tragic' side of liberalism. Perhaps we could understand Rousseau and Wollstonecraft as being pessimistic about the pleasures obtainable under actual power relations, but optimistic or utopian about how pleasure and power might be refigured in different social conditions. Certainly, Rousseau does sometimes seem to suggest that pleasure is impossible because it is always tainted by desire and lack. He writes in *Emile*: 'Every feeling of pain is inseparable from the desire to be delivered from it; every idea of pleasure is inseparable from the desire to enjoy it; every desire supposes privation, and all sensed privations are painful' (*Emile*, 80). From here we may get the idea that the pain of desire is the only thing spurring human existence; pleasure represents merely idle docility. A version of this idea was seen in Kant's thought in the previous chapter, and it is also present in Wollstonecraft. At one point, she approvingly quotes Rousseau's sad claim for the inherent self-destructiveness of gratification: 'The habitual state of the affections always loses by their gratification. The imagination, which decks the object of our desires, is lost in fruition' (*Vindication*, 169). But straight after the claim that pleasure is always tainted by lack, Rousseau writes:

In what, then, consists human wisdom or the road of true happiness? It is not precisely in diminishing our desires, for if they were beneath our power, a part of our faculties would remain idle, and we would not *enjoy our whole being.* Neither is it in extending our faculties, for if, proportionate to them, our desires were more extended, we would as a result only become unhappier. But it is in diminishing the excess of the desires over the faculties and putting power and will in perfect equality. It is only then that, with all the powers in action, the soul will nevertheless remain peaceful and that man will be well ordered. (80, my italics)

Thus, Rousseau's own answer to the problem that pleasure is weaker than desire is not actively to diminish desire, as one might expect for instance on a Stoic account. He introduces a curious notion of enjoying our whole being, one that we also saw in Kant's Third Critique. It is perhaps meant to recall Aristotle's teleological model of *eudaimonia*, the plenitude of performing all one's activities with virtue, though it is rather more bodily or vital than Aristotle's notion. If our desires are so limited that some of our powers – our intelligence, strength, creativity, sexuality for instance – remain slack and unused, we cannot fully enjoy our existence. So, then, both Sophie in *Emile*, and the servants in *Julie*, are not given the opportunity to use their capacities fully, which are rather deliberately limited; pleasure as 'enjoying our whole being' has implications for the political themes of equality in Rousseau's work. As he adds in *Emile*, the idea of enjoying one's whole being overlaps with a broad conception of 'life': 'To live is not to breathe; it is to act, it is to make use of our organs, our senses, our faculties, of all the parts of ourselves which give us the sentiment of existence. The man who has lived the most is not he who has counted the most years but he who has most felt life' (42). Some of the strongest claims for the sentiment of existence and the full enjoyment of our being occur in Rousseau's late work, *Les rêveries du promeneur solitaire*. The central role of enjoyment in this text emerges partly out of the author's avowed aim of defeating his persecutors by finding happiness in solitude: 'I learnt from my own experience that the source of true happiness is within us, and that it is not in the power of men to make anyone truly miserable' (36). In the Second Walk, the author famously awakens from being knocked down by 'a huge Great Dane' (12). He experiences a delirious joy in 'existence' that occurs before self-awareness: 'I felt neither injury, fear, nor worry. I watched my blood flow as I would have watched a brook flow . . . I felt a rapturous calm in my whole being; and each time I remember it, I find nothing comparable to it in all the activity of known pleasures' (12). This pleasure in the 'whole being' receives its fullest elaboration in the Fifth Walk, where Rousseau describes his happiest existence on the Ile de Saint-Pierre (Lake Bienne, Switzerland). Here, he describes a superior state of pleasure that can last indefinitely and is not punctuated with unpleasure or lack, but is rather a passionless delight without object or content: 'without any other sentiment of deprivation or of enjoyment, pleasure or pain, desire or fear, except that alone of our existence' (46). Rousseau's example is the perfect pleasure of sitting beside a lake: 'The ebb and flow of this water and its noise, continual but magnified at intervals . . . was enough to make me feel my existence with pleasure and without taking the trouble to think' (45). It is contrasted to intense enjoyments, 'moments of delirium and passion', which are overwhelming to our sensibility and cannot be long borne (45). This pleasure is non-bodily and non-appetitive: 'I never found true charm in the pleasures of my mind except when concern for my body was completely lost from sight' (61).

Some readers may feel that this account of 'pure movement', stripped of content, of strong affect, of time and of lack, has a curiously deathly and inhuman note. It is almost as if in getting to something purely bodily we lose everything that makes bodies *feel* 'bodily'. It could be argued that there is an inherent potential for a non-teleological account of desire to resemble a rather inhuman force. A comparison might be made with the force of creativity or life in Deleuze. Peter Hallward has argued that, for Deleuze, life is alienated and restricted by the bodies and organisms that it is driven to create: 'The actual or the lived organism is thus itself the first and deepest obstacle to the virtual power of living, to the powerful, non-organic Life which grips the world.'[63] In similar vein, Laurence Cooper has described Rousseau's account of the desire for existence as 'an intrinsically directionless, non-teleological *push*, a kind of inchoate expansiveness or overflowing'.[64] He sees the sentiment of existence as a good prior to any 'content' or object, and goes on to suggest that for Rousseau 'happiness depends not so much on pleasure or on any other positive thing but on the relative absence of pain and psychic conflict'.[65] If there is no distinctive affective colouring to the desire to exist, could unhappy things or the experience of pain be seen as furthering *felt* existence?

Eve Grace has also argued that the sentiment of existence is a form of restless striving rather than perfect plenitude, though she finds two visions of it in Rousseau's work. One, based chiefly on *Emile*, involves the feeling of power and activity; the other, based mainly on the *Reveries*, is a sentiment of existence generated by passive quiescence, at the minimum threshold for human activity. Grace concludes that rather than offering an ideal statement of perfect independent delight, the Fifth Walk represents for Grace a kind of negative version of the sentiment of existence described in *Emile*, as 'Rousseau's last eloquent statement regarding the pains and difficulties to which we are subject through the activity of our expansive self-love and the imagination'.[66] To be free of the energy of desire is godlike, yet 'a rather more austere or almost inhuman experience' than readers have wanted to acknowledge.[67] But, interestingly, she tries to make space for *history* in the sentiment of existence. She points out that Rousseau's discussion seems to imply the necessity of 'activating' our powers, a process in which reason and imagination – directed by historical circumstance – play an important role.[68] Our desires are shaped by historically located existence, which may alter the strength of our feeling of existence. Grace also places the sentiment of existence in relation to hope: 'it begets desires as particular forms of the more general desire to animate, to affect, to have a domain'.[69] Our very excess strength and the pleasure in our abundance, not our poverty or weakness, is what encourages us to 'increase our being and our pleasures'; yet, at the same time, they expose us to disappointment and unhappiness.[70]

So, the pleasures described at the Ile de Saint-Pierre seem on the one hand to encapsulate the most utopian and redemptive dream of pleasure that could be imagined, a real high-point of Enlightenment speculation on pleasure as an end in itself. Clearly, however, the image of subjectivity presented there is ambiguous with respect to Rousseau's arguments elsewhere about equality and community. For one thing, the *Reveries* are certainly solitary: Rousseau appears to have abandoned the intersubjective dimension of pleasure that appeared so strongly in *Emile* and in the *Dialogues*. In the *Dialogues*, Rousseau stresses that the most intense pleasure of existence involves, in some way, escaping the confines of the self, of self-consciousness and *amour propre*, into communality: 'Our sweetest existence is relative and collective, and our true *self* is not entirely within us' (118). Likewise, the intense happiness described by Rousseau on his coach journey to Turin with which this chapter began also explicitly depends on social trust ('confidence in myself and in others'). Rousseau does claim that the pleasure of the *Reveries* is a 'compensation for all the human felicities' for one who is finally excluded from society and can offer it nothing further (47). The walks could be seen to have the quality of a Stoic spiritual exercise, similar in intention to Shaftesbury's self-exhortations in the *Askemata* to divest himself of his reliance on friends. The *Reveries* are about solitude, yet they exist against a backdrop of human sociality, and represent Rousseau's key consideration of the way pleasure mediates between the individual and others.

Pleasure has politically utopian dimensions, and a close reading of Rousseau and Wollstonecraft shows how much it matters to political philosophy to understand whether mankind is defined by pleasure in being alive, or if freedom is feeling one's existence to the full. Against the almost dogmatic account of pleasure presented by Derrida in *Of Grammatology*, where he declares what pleasure 'really' means, the preceding analyses have tried to retrieve in these eighteenth-century writings a complex and occasionally optimistic account of pleasure in its relation to problems of power and equality. The question that remains is how the philosophical debates seen first in Shaftesbury and Kant, and second in Rousseau and Wollstonecraft, are altered by Wordsworth's central question around the function and future of poetry. The multiple meanings of an economy of pleasure explored in this chapter in relation to *Julie* and *Emile* recur in Wordsworth's 'Lines Written in Early Spring' and *Home at Grasmere*. *Home at Grasmere*, like *Julie*, has an overall pattern of a contrast between desire and contentment, whilst *The Excursion* could be seen as a companion text to *Julie* and *Emile*, in that it seeks a cure for unhappiness within a larger vision of social destiny, and that its exploration of the nature of pleasure plays out many conflicts between Stoic, Epicurean and modern economic ideas. But the most important point of connection between Wordsworth and the ideas set out in this chapter lies in the image of still, unproductive bliss portrayed in the Fifth Walk of the *Reveries*. As I show in Chapter 4, drawing partly from Adorno, this scene of intense pleasure – epitomized in a description like 'when from excess / Of happiness my blood appeared to flow / With its own pleasure, and I breathed with joy' (*Prelude*, II. 191–3) – can be seen as a negative counter-image to a certain 'capitalist' image of happiness. Of course, depictions of pleasure in Wordsworth are at times just as ambiguous and even anti-social or anti-communitarian as certain moments of Rousseau's *Reveries*; nonetheless, we should attend seriously to the trust, hope and community that, according to Wordsworth, is generated by poetry's cognitive-sensual delight.

PART II

Wordsworth's common pleasure

CHAPTER 3

Poetics of pleasure in Lyrical Ballads

The *Lyrical Ballads* are often remembered for their focus on sad, even desolate, situations. Yet, the celebration of physical sensation and the joy of the natural world appear in a clutch of ballads, from the 'sweet' life of the narrator of 'Expostulation and Reply' to the 'blithe' birds in 'The Tables Turned', and the 'sense of joy' of the air in 'Lines Written at a Small Distance from my House'. 'Tintern Abbey' and Coleridge's 'The Nightingale' might also be seen as profound considerations of pleasure. And pleasure was a repeated theme of correspondence with friends and reviewers. Charles Lamb found that his ambivalent response to the *Lyrical Ballads* generated

almost instantaneously a long letter of four sweating pages from my Reluctant Letter-Writer, the purpose of which was, that he was sorry his 2d vol. had not given me more pleasure (Devil a hint did I give that it had *not pleased me*), and 'was compelled to wish that my range of sensibility was more extended, being obliged to believe that I should receive large influxes of happiness and Happy Thoughts' (I suppose from the L.B.).[1]

Thomas De Quincey, in a letter written three years before meeting Wordsworth, but soaked in the language of the 'Preface', claimed that the *Lyrical Ballads* saved him from a dizzy pleasure of self-regard ('delirious & lawless pleasure which I drew from the hope of elevating my name') and brought him to an obscurely moral, definitely Wordsworthian delight ('a confused feeling of purer & more permanent pleasure flowing from other sources').[2] John Wilson thanked Wordsworth for the 'pleasure', 'happiness' and 'enjoyment' that the poems had given him, again directly echoing the 'Preface'. Wilson firmly concurred that '[n]o feeling, no State of mind, ought in my opinion to become the Subject of Poetry, that does not please'. But whilst '[p]leasure may indeed be produced in many ways', Wilson found that readers had a universal 'inability to receive pleasure from descriptions such as that of the Idiot boy', a principle set out in 'Smiths Theory of moral Sentiments' (*sic*).[3] Wordsworth's long reply returns to the problem of pleasure repeatedly. He first of all approves Wilson's achievement of a pleasure from the *Lyrical Ballads* which is not 'blind or unthinking', 'cheap or vulgar', but will not let his young interlocutor's complaint pass: 'You begin what you say upon the Idiot Boy with this observation, that nothing is a fit subject for poetry which does not please. But here follows a question, Does not please whom? ... I return to [the] question, please whom? Or what? I answer human nature, as it has been [and eve]r will be.'[4] Wordsworth's answer focuses on the fact that he has associated 'habitually' with people of 'cottages and fields, and children', giving him a better grasp than Wilson on the sympathies and pleasures of humans in general; but finally his insistence comes from something more like the inarguable position of subjective universality: 'I wrote the poem with exceeding delight and pleasure, and whenever I read it I read it with pleasure.'[5] Pleasure is the lynchpin in his argument about the hope of agreement and the possibility of community: 'it is not enough for me as a Poet, to delineate merely such feelings as all men *do* sympathise with; but it is also highly desirable to add to these others, such as all men *may* sympathise with'.[6]

This chapter focuses on the 'grand elementary principle of pleasure' that is both theme and purpose of the *Lyrical Ballads*, and it aims to show how for Wordsworth pleasure is a term of 'infinite complexity' (as he describes it) in relation to social and moral life, as we saw in different ways in Shaftesbury, Kant, Rousseau and Wollstonecraft.[7] My aim is partly to dislodge what was once a regularly hostile and dismissive reading of pleasure in the 'Prefaces' as parasitic on a culture of sensibility yet nervously resisting some of its implications, and founded only in his aspiration for elite recognition.[8] His idea of moderate pleasure has been read as bad faith: afraid of the vivid enjoyments of the working class, yet not fully separable from the empiricist, associationist and utilitarian tradition which would, ultimately, give equal credence to the delights of sport, dance and drink as to those of poetry.[9] Instead, I want to show the philosophical richness of Wordsworth's treatment, though without disavowing the difficulty that the poet evidently found in trying to analyse this theme. Pleasure in the 'Preface' documents evinces a weird difficulty: apparently simple, resounding and politically and spiritually urgent (pleasure is everything, the *primum mobile*, our essence), yet also slippery, abstract and general. Rather than presenting pleasure as one of a set of aesthetic effects, or as one form of emotional response, or even as simply the basic affect alongside pain, Wordsworth insists that pleasure is the condition of our existence.

This chapter begins with a reading of the theme of pleasure in 'Lines Written in Early Spring', before going on to discuss the way that pleasure becomes increasingly central to Wordsworth's successive versions of the 'Preface'. I discuss a range of ways that Wordsworth's poetic theory of pleasure might be understood, with reference both back to earlier texts and forward to the twentieth and twenty-first centuries.

'LINES WRITTEN IN EARLY SPRING' — A READING

> I heard a thousand blended notes,
> While in a grove I sate reclined,
> In that sweet mood when pleasant thoughts
> Bring sad thoughts to the mind.
>
> To her fair works did nature link
> The human soul that through me ran;
> And much it griev'd my heart to think
> What man has made of man.
>
> Through primrose tufts, in that sweet bower,
> The periwinkle trailed its wreaths,
> And 'tis my faith that every flower
> Enjoys the air it breathes.
>
> The birds around me hopp'd and play'd,
> Their thoughts I cannot measure: -
> But the least motion which they made,
> It seemed a thrill of pleasure.
>
> The budding twigs spread out their fan,
> To catch the breezy air;
> And I must think, do all I can,
> That there was pleasure there.
>
> If I these thoughts may not prevent,
> If such be of my creed the plan,
> Have I not reason to lament
> What man has made of man?[10]

Despite its ostensibly simple logic, there are several odd things about 'Early Spring'. The speaker experiences aesthetic pleasure in nature; he feels a sense of connection to the natural world around him, but this brings in consciousness of the violence and poverty of human interaction. He observes the flowers, birds and twigs seemingly enjoying their existence; and asks again why men in society are so cruel. The first oddity is the way that the objection to human life – 'what man has made of man' – is restated in the second and sixth stanzas: we are led, as so often in

Wordsworth's lyrics, to expect a turn or revelation in the intervening passage, but it is not clear if one has taken place, especially with the repetition of the same phrase, and its reiteration as a (rhetorical?) question. The opening, with its no-place, no-time tale of idly observant relaxation in a verdant nook, appears at first glance to promise a hyper-real scene of Wordsworthian natural ecstasy. But the end of the first stanza quickly interlays these 'pleasant thoughts' with 'sad thoughts', introducing an oscillation between superlative claims for general pleasure and a set of negative emotions and actions: sadness, grief, scepticism, effort and lamenting. The sad thoughts of contemporary society lead to three uncannily repetitive stanzas, each a description of natural activity: periwinkle trailing, birds hopping, twigs fanning, followed by a couplet which states an interpretive position; and the stanzas show an odd (lack of) argumentative progression. First, we hear that it is the speaker's 'faith' that the flowers are enjoying themselves; secondly that it 'seemed' that they thrill with pleasure; thirdly that he 'must think', despite the oddness of it, that there *was* pleasure. The register shifts from the theological, to the phenomenal-empirical ('measure'; 'thrill'), to an issue of rationality and will; at the same time, the tense changes from the present, to the past, to the present looking back at or revising the past. It is uncertain what epistemological priority these modes of proof have or why they are ordered as they are, an uncertainty that is continued in the poem's linking of thoughts to pleasure.

Pleasure and thinking are mutually explored in this poem, as they are in Kant's Third Critique. Initially, pleasure seems just the affective shading of thoughts, in the philosophical domain of mood: 'pleasant thoughts' and 'sad thoughts'. But then, watching the birds, the speaker acknowledges that he can identify only their likely pleasures but not their thoughts: here, pleasure seems an entire aspect of existence that can be separated from representation; one that is available generally to all creatures even where consciousness or rationality cannot be ascribed with certainty ('their thoughts I cannot measure'). In any case, how can pleasant thoughts 'bring' sad thoughts to mind; how can a grove lead to grieving? The 'feeling of inclusion in the natural world' segues straight into a feeling of exclusion from mankind. In an analysis of Wollstonecraft's writing, one critic has suggested with respect to Wollstonecraft that 'the meaning of aloneness itself has been learned in the experience of social life', so solitude always implies 'being or remaining without others'.[11] To read 'Early Spring' this way would argue that human social interaction is ultimately the main deal; to some extent, it would undermine the poem's attempts to generalize beyond human life certain characteristics considered to be uniquely human; i.e. pleasure, enjoyment. Rather, the poem seems to want to displace an anthropocentric model, to argue against the idea that man may have dominion (possession; enjoyment) over 'every creeping thing that creepeth upon the earth' (Genesis 1.26).

Wordsworth's choice of a periwinkle in a poem about pleasure and interconnection may not be accidental. The periwinkle has an intriguing etymological, folkloric and literary history. Its Latin genus is *Vinca* (thus the Old English *peruenke* and *paruink*), from *vincio*, to bind, presumably referring to the plant's trailing and binding tendencies. The flower has long associations with marriage, friendship and sex, perhaps because of that binding, or the virginal blue of the flowers which inspired the French common name of *Pucellage*. In early modern England, it was sometimes known as 'Joy on the Ground'.[12] In the *Confessions*, Rousseau recalls Mme de Warens pointing out some blooming periwinkle in a hedge, of which the young Rousseau takes no notice. Thirty years later, whilst 'herbalizing', he shouts for joy as he sees some, transported back in memory.[13] Hazlitt picks up on the periwinkle in his contrast of Rousseau and Wordsworth:

Rousseau, in a word, interests you in certain objects by interesting you in himself: Mr. Wordsworth would persuade you that the most insignificant objects are interesting in themselves, because he is interested in them. If he had met with Rousseau's favourite periwinkle, he would have translated it into the most beautiful of flowers. This is not imagination, but want of sense.[14]

Perhaps Hazlitt has forgotten 'Early Spring', and the poet's use of a periwinkle in a poetic attempt to think beyond the 'egotism' of which Hazlitt accused Wordsworth. The periwinkle is also, surprisingly, an image that occurs in William Paley's natural theology. The *Principles of Moral and Political Philosophy* (1785) had a long presence in Wordsworth's life: the standard examination for the BA at St John's College, Cambridge, in 1791 involved near-memorization of it (it was a standard text in Cambridge moral philosophy), and there was a copy in Wordsworth's Rydal Mount library in 1829.[15] Paley deploys a 'periwinkle' in the chapter on Happiness – intending the mollusc rather than the starry blue flower – but with reference to the same idea that even the most humble species feels pleasure. The notion of the happy bivalve actually goes back a very long way: Chrysippus discussed the Pinna mussel's and its Pinna-guard's sense of existence and sociability; they appeared to 'collaborate with each other in virtue of the good and enjoyment, since they could not subsist individually'.[16] Both Wordsworth's and Paley's periwinkles are said to take pleasure in their own physiological functioning, breathing and living, and this irreducible pleasure is the condition of everything ('Health, in this sense, is the one thing needful' writes Paley); it is a pleasure that is neither interested nor disinterested ('independent of any particular outward gratification'), and it is superfluously 'annexed to life':

When we are in perfect health and spirits, we feel in ourselves a happiness independent of any particular outward gratification whatever, and of which we can give no account. This is an enjoyment which the Deity has annexed to life; and it probably constitutes, in a great measure, the happiness of infants and brutes, especially of the lower and sedentary orders of animals, as of oysters, periwinkles and the like; for which I have sometimes been at a loss to find out amusement.[17]

The three stanzas where Wordsworth has *faith*, then *perceives*, then *wills* that there is pleasure in the natural world appear as a strange, inconclusive debate around Paley's propositions, just as the author at university would have defended similar Paleyan theses in verbal (Latin) combat with an Opponent and Moderator. Wordsworth's ambiguous line ''tis my faith' plays on the contortions of Paley's argument in this passage regarding evidence and benevolence: Paley's theological voluntarism decrees that God wills general happiness, but Paley is unsure ('I have sometimes been at a loss') as to how generally applied or 'spread' this happiness is, beyond sentient adults. Wordsworth's 'faith' seems to carry two senses: first, a trust or confidence, stemming from authority or testimony but not empirical evidence, that flowers enjoy the air; secondly, it hints at a spiritual belief in joy, like the faith in the pleasure-stream in *Home at Grasmere* (discussed in the next chapter) which approaches pantheism. Various critics have linked this idea of the faith in flowers' pleasure to Erasmus Darwin's *Zoonomia* that Wordsworth borrowed from Cottle in 1798.[18] Although this may be another important intertext, it seems to me that the moral and political questions raised by pleasure in 'Early Spring' present a more overt dialogue with Paley, especially given the charged word 'reason' in the poem. Immediately after mentioning periwinkles, Paley concludes that his investigation into happiness has provided 'reasons' to support the following claims:

FIRST, that happiness is pretty equally distributed amongst the different orders of civil society:

SECONDLY, that vice has no advantage over virtue even with respect to this world's happiness.[19]

Thus, for Paley, general pleasure provides 'reasons' for maintaining the socio-economic and the moral-religious status quo. These conservative outcomes hardened in Paley's pamphlet *Reasons for Contentment: Addressed to the Labouring Classes of Great Britain* (1792), which deployed the utilitarian doctrine of pleasure to claim that if the British poor reasoned well enough (in contrast to the Revolutionary French), they would recognize how good was their lot compared to the richer portions of society. First, Paley argues that as individual happiness is felt in comparison with our close peers, we should pity the wealthiest and most eminent man, for he has no peers above whom he can enjoy his superiority. Secondly, he claims that nourishment and repose are actively enjoyed by those who hunger and labour, whereas to the idle rich they offer no diversion: 'Being without work is one thing; reposing from work is another. The one is as tiresome and insipid, as the other is sweet and soothing.'[20] Contradictorily, after basing these arguments on the relativity of pleasure, he argues that pleasure is a basic, irreducible force which all experience. Because God is benevolent and wills the 'general' happiness, the general distribution of pleasure *must* be just and equal. In a sophistical twist, this can only be argued by converting the social and physical ills of the poor into their boons: thus the *universality* of pleasure; thus the enjoyment of periwinkles. Wordsworth's poem, however, amplifies the tension around the evidence: 'do all I can'; despite his attempts at undeceiving himself, despite the evidence of misery and the unlikeliness of natural happiness, it seems that there 'was pleasure there'.

Wordsworth noted in his fragmentary *Essay on Morals* (1798) that both Paley's *Moral and Political Philosophy* and Godwin's *Political Justice* are 'impotent [?in or ?to] all their intended good purposes; to which I wish I could add that they were equally impotent to all bad one[s]'.[21] His bracketing of the two authors reminds us that utilitarian ethics could ground conservative and radical texts.[22] Whilst Paley borrows the discussion of happiness from *Moral and Political Philosophy* for the conservative purposes of *Reasons for Contentment*, often quoting directly, he makes some significant adjustments which in themselves point to the political and conceptual complexities of pleasure. In place of the active, restless subject described in the *Moral and Political Philosophy*, who is constantly comparing his position to that of others, and taking pleasure in novelties, including profitable increases, *Reasons for Contentment* poses quite a different subject. He is a calm spectator of his own daily struggle of life, barely noticing the improved situations of those around him, and he has become highly change-averse: 'An alteration of circumstances, which breaks up a man's habit of life, deprives him of his occupation, removes him from his acquaintance, may be called an elevation of fortune, but hardly ever brings with it an addition of enjoyment.'[23] As was detailed in Chapter 1, the *form* of pleasure, and particularly the role of movement and openness within it, here changes the political implications that are drawn from it. The topoi of habit and novelty, stasis and change, recur in 'Early Spring'. The speaker begins in a physical and perhaps intellectual position of repose: 'in a grove I sate reclined'; but this ease leads to restlessness as sad thoughts are stirred. The easeful, immediate connection of soul to nature (smoothly 'ran') in the next stanza again leads conjunctively to negation: 'it griev'd my heart'. The flowers, birds and twigs are all in an active state of pleasure – trailing, breathing, hopping, playing, making motion, thrilling, budding, spreading, catching – not a passive one of physiological equilibrium. Does this 'teach' the speaker to *move*? His responses change from a relatively comfortable 'faith' which exists in the present moment, to a more active empirical mode of perception which involves doubt and the passing of time ('It seemed'), to the most physically and temporally active account which urges forward into a future intellectual perspective and back into memory and history.

As I mentioned, Wordsworth puts pressure on the word 'reason'. In *Reasons for Contentment*, Paley points out that for the poor to think themselves hard done by would be quite 'ill founded and *unreasonable*'.[24] The first and prime 'reason' for the good fortune of bad circumstances is that 'it is an inestimable blessing of such situations, that they supply a constant train of employment both to body and mind'.[25] Paley revises inequality and suffering into narratives of happiness: what are taken to be the pains of a subsistence existence are 'not hardships but pleasures. Frugality itself is a pleasure.'[26] Here, we have some echoes of the ordered hedonic economy of Julie's estate in Rousseau's novel. By contrast, Wordsworth wonders if the evidence of natural joy presents a different 'reason', the reason to 'lament' the state of society. But as suggested earlier, the restatement of 'what man has made of man' is somewhat ambiguous: is it merely emphatic, or, given the argumentative stasis implied by the repetition, does it undermine our expectation that something has changed in the speaker's understanding? It is also unclear what the cryptic or naïve phrase 'what man has made of man' actually means. It could be taken along the lines of Rousseauian developmental history; that man was originally pure and pleasure-loving, living in nature, but that over time he has self-corrupted. Or it could be taken to suggest that man has made *things* of other men, as means and not ends; in which case we could interpret the poem as offering a subtle, divided response to utilitarianism, separating out that tradition's positive focus on pleasure from its negative instrumentalism. The idea of how we use other people and things for our pleasure is at stake in the way the poem revises the idea that nature is something from which humans merely suck out their own subjective pleasure ('in a grove . . . In that sweet mood'). It posits instead an aspiration for a connective 'thrill of pleasure' that is not ascribed to birds or speaker but shared or spread between them. For the birds' hopping 'seemed a thrill of pleasure': it hints that the pleasure may have thrilled into the very sensorium of the speaker; but it scrupulously maintains an ambiguity about the evidence presented and how it should be interpreted. A very similar doubt is displayed in 'The Barberry-Tree', a manuscript poem attributed to Wordsworth since its discovery in 1962 and dated around 1802; it describes walking out on a breezy evening, and witnessing the most 'blithesome blossoms e'er displayed'.[27] The blossoms and breeze and boughs and onlooker may, or may not, share a transmissible delight:

> But whether it be thus or no,
> That while they danced upon the wind
> They felt a joy like humankind,
> That this blithe breeze which cheerly sung
> While the merry boughs he swung
> Did in that moment while the bough
> Whispered to his gladsome singing
> Feel the pleasures that even now
> In my breast are springing (ll. 16–24)

One might conjecture that Wordsworth worked up some of these ideas about reciprocal natural pleasure for the breeze image that opens the second version of *The Prelude*, which will be discussed in the next chapter. In any case, the theory of pleasure was strongly on his mind in 1802, as the revisions to the 'Prefaces' make abundantly clear.

THE 'PREFACES' TO THE 'LYRICAL BALLADS'

When one turns to the 'Preface' documents, a simple word count reveals the extent to which Wordsworth increasingly focused his discussions of poetry around that theme. We can see this shift from the 1798 'Advertisement' which mentions 'pleasure' only once, to the 1800 'Preface' which uses 'pleasure' 25 times, and to the 1802 'Preface' which has 43 instances of 'pleasure' and 'pleasures'. Hence 'pleasure' follows only narrowly in frequency behind the words that tend to be thought of as the text's main subjects: 'language' (53 instances) and 'Poet' / 'Poets' (47 instances).[28] Thus, pleasure begins as an occasional topic of his poems at the beginning of the 'great decade' and gradually swells to become a central feature of his poetics. Wordsworth's philosophical language of pleasure begins in empirical vein, alluding to 'experiments', 'types' and 'quantities', but gradually becomes more grandiose. By the 1802 version, pleasure is daringly made analogous with God; it is by 'pleasure' that man 'knows, and feels, and lives, and moves', echoing Acts 17.18: 'For in him we live, and move, and have our being.' In particular, Wordsworth links the operations of metre to pleasure: but it is striking that he seems to feel his arguments all rest upon a missing 'systematic' explanation of how pleasure is produced. I hope to show how in these documents Wordsworth appears intellectually *agitated* by the question of pleasure – a fact backed up by Crabb Robinson's claim that in 1808 Wordsworth apparently intended to write an essay called 'Why bad poetry pleases', adding 'He never wrote it – a loss to our literature.'[29] Drawing on W.J.B. Owen and Jane Worthington Smyser's editorial work, I will discuss possible intellectual sources for Wordsworth's discussion of pleasure, but I also suggest that he goes far beyond those sources. In particular, Wordsworth begins to link pleasure to the social claims of his poetic manifesto. This is hinted at the end of the 1800 'Preface', where Wordsworth comments that the 'purer' pleasure of his 'genuine poetry' will be important in 'the multiplicity and quality of its moral relations'. In what follows, I will work through the several steps of his arguments and revisions.

The 1800 'Preface'

The short Advertisement of 1798 mentions the word 'pleasure' only once, in the context of the 'experiment' to see how far middle- and lower-class language can be adapted 'to the purposes of poetic pleasure'. In the 1800 'Preface', the quasi-empirical language suggested by 'experiment' is developed from the outset, where Wordsworth alludes to types and quantities of readerly pleasure. He does not return to the topic for another 200 or so lines, where he adds that he intends to produce a different kind of pleasure from that which is usually supposed to be present (220). A little further on, around halfway through the text, Wordsworth reintroduces pleasure into the discussion when he comments that poetic history confirms that rhyme and metre only 'heighten and improve the pleasure' which can be found in the imagery or passion (306). Wordsworth elaborates the idea that metre gives pleasure (and is agreed to do so 'by all nations'; a power which some contemporary voices 'greatly under-rate', 318, 328). A confirmation of this is that simple poems have for a long time generated pleasure through metre. Wordsworth then goes on to explain why it is that 'words metrically arranged' have this effect, beginning the exposition of his theory with the claim that 'The end of Poetry is to produce excitement in coexistence with an overbalance of pleasure' (341–3). Metre is importantly, yet complexly, related to the pleasure that poetry generates: it is meant to calm excitation by virtue of its familiarity, and add pleasure by virtue of surprise. Metre both offers a 'co-presence of something regular' and 'ordinary feeling' to offset the extremities of passion; yet, it also offers 'small, but continual and regular impulses of pleasurable surprise from the metrical arrangement' (349, 352, 357–9), a pleasure which stops us from getting too upset by, for instance, a Shakespearean tragedy. How may this metre both calm and surprise?

His answer is never quite presented. Wordsworth admits that a 'systematic defence of the theory' of poetic pleasure would require an explanation 'of the various causes upon which the pleasure received from metrical language depends' (369–72). The guess he hazards is that the main cause is 'the pleasure which the mind derives from the perception of similitude in dissimilitude' (374–5). This 'principle' is 'the great spring of the activity of our minds, and their chief feeder': from this comes 'the direction of our sexual appetite' and the 'life' of ordinary conversation; judging it is the basis of our 'taste and our moral feelings' (376–81). But Wordsworth hesitates about explaining in full detail how exactly metrical pleasure derives from this principle: 'It would not have been a useless employment to have applied this principle to the consideration of metre ... But my limits will not permit to enter upon this subject' (381–5). The evasion of something rather important is only strengthened by the fact that in the 1802 version Wordsworth capitalizes the missing 'SYSTEMATIC defence of the theory' (610). Wordsworth goes on to offer a strange summary of the way that the pleasure experienced by the poet during composition is transferred to the reader. Nature is careful to ensure that the poet experiences an overall feeling of enjoyment in the stages of composition, whatever emotions are recollected; therefore the poet should aim to do the same for the reader. This pleasure takes a 'complex' form, composed of the 'music' of metre, the 'sense of difficulty overcome' and the 'blind association of pleasure' from familiar metrical works (402–6). Wordsworth returns to the problem of his missing theory of pleasure at the end of the 1800 version, in which he admits that his argument would be much stronger could he properly explain why the kind of poetry he recommends gives a particular kind of pleasure than other kinds. He admits his argument based in pleasure-poetics meets trouble in the *fact* that people already get pleasure from the kinds of poetry he wants to overturn: 'for the Reader will say that he has been pleased by such composition and what can I do more for him?' (528–9). If he did not suffer 'limits' in being able to give a systematic theory of pleasure, Wordsworth could explain how we would not have to unlearn our habitual pleasures or give up our old friends, but could discover different enjoyments, 'of a purer, more lasting, and more exquisite nature' – a kind of poetry that could 'interest mankind permanently' (546–54). Lacking space or skills for this, Wordsworth ends by turning that question back on to the reader, inviting us to find our own pleasure.

Thus the 'Preface' sets out the following claims: that pleasure is the end of poetry; it is connected to metre in both calming our passions and surprising us; pleasure derives from a perception of similitude in dissimilitude; it is associated with overcoming difficulty, and it is also associative and habit-based; there is a special kind of pleasure that would endure longer than other kinds of pleasure. According to Owen and Smyser's commentary, the main sources for these ideas lie in Hartley, Beattie, Coleridge and Priestley. For Wordsworth's comments that 'words metrically arranged' will long impart 'pleasure', and that poetry's aim is to produce excitement and an 'overbalance of pleasure', they point to Hartley. The statement on the natural agreeableness of metre is linked to Beattie's *Essays on Poetry and Music* (1779) and to the *Monthly Magazine* of 1796. Coleridge is credited for the comments about the 'co-presence of something regular' which calms the passion. Coleridge's *Notebooks*, which describe two key impulses of mankind as the pleasure taken in 'variety' and the pleasure taken in 'uniformity', are given as a possible analogue for 'small, but continual and regular impulses of pleasurable surprise from the metrical arrangement'. The editors connect Wordsworth's discussion of why we can enjoy otherwise distressing scenes in verse to Priestley's *Course of Lectures on Oratory*, particularly the idea that painful emotions are diminished by our awareness of their fictionality; since pleasure comes from 'moderately vigorous' sensations, artificiality draws tragedy within the enjoyable range of feeling. The idea of 'difficulty overcome', which according to Wordsworth forms one of the main strands of that 'complex feeling of delight' provided by verse, is aligned again with Priestley's *Oratory*, where the extra pleasure of verse comes from its being more difficult to compose.[30]

Arguably, the editors' understandable impulse to source-hunt, and perhaps their elevation of 'real' philosophers over poets, means they underestimate the freshness of Wordsworth's synthesis of his close and more distant intellectual antecedents; certainly, they are not particularly sensitive to the term 'pleasure'. For instance, Wordsworth's notion of the 'perception of similitude in dissimilitude' is described by Owen and Smyser as merely a 'commonplace of eighteenth-century aesthetics', derived from Hutcheson, Kames and Adam Smith. But, as a recent study of Wordsworth's relation to figures such as Burke and Shaftesbury has noted: 'he only takes ... what he pleases, coaxing the critical potential from eighteenth-century aesthetics'.[31] The idea of 'similitude in dissimilitude' has been criticized in recent years as heterosexist and for implying a sovereign overcoming of difference, the false imposition of homogeneity on real heterogeneity.[32] But Wordsworth goes on to stress that it is not only the perception of 'similitude in dissimilitude' but 'dissimilitude in similitude' which is our source of pleasure. As the pleasure of metre derives from both the fulfilment of expectation and the experience of novelty, so too does this key principle of pleasure flicker between stasis and kinesis. Wordsworth's precision here reminds us of the need to contextualize his poetics not only in aesthetic history but also within his poetry; at the end of the chapter, I shall draw out some of the larger possibilities of his language of pleasure and its implications for ideas around 'difference' and soporific 'closure'.

The 1802 'Preface'

Broader ethical and political ideas about pleasure blossom in Wordsworth's 1802 revisions of the 'Preface'. They included a 225-line insertion into the middle, nine paragraphs which have been described as Wordsworth's shift from a mimetic theory of art to an expressive one, in so doing 'substituting *himself*... for the class of rural workers on which his arguments were founded in 1800'.[33] This acerbic description has some truth, but it misses a crucial extra component: that Wordsworth amplified the discussion of pleasure in every way. The passage begins with the question of how to differentiate prose from poetry, a key topic, for poetic pleasure depends upon it, and this pleasure in turn 'is in itself of high importance to our taste and moral feelings' (306–7). Wordsworth begins with first principles, the definition of a 'Poet'. This has often been read in terms of the special sensibility the poet possesses (and has often been attacked for elitism), but less often for the comment that the Poet is a figure with stronger than usual joy. He is 'a man pleased with his own passions and volitions, and who rejoices more than other men in the spirit of life that is in him; delighting to contemplate similar volitions and passions as manifested in the goings-on of the Universe' (324–7). Wordsworth describes how the Poet must fall into a trance of sympathy with the passions he traces, his only conscious modification being to select the right language for the 'particular purpose' of 'giving pleasure' (356). Those who think that this 'selection' means fancy diction are those 'who talk of Poetry as of a matter of amusement and idle pleasure; who will converse with us as gravely about a *taste* for Poetry, as they express it, as if it were a thing as indifferent as a taste for rope-dancing, or Frontiniac, or Sherry' (374–7). This bold defence of aesthetic seriousness has frequently been castigated by modern critics as snobbish about popular culture and fearful of the body and appetite; though the emphasis should surely be seen as falling on consumer fads, given the deliberately capitalized commodities and the centrality of bodily pleasures to *The Prelude*, as the next chapter shall show. These ideas about selecting language for pleasure introduce Wordsworth's passionate defence of the philosophic nature of poetry, as offering 'general and operative truth', the 'image of man and nature', quoted here at length:

The Poet writes under one restriction only, namely, the necessity of giving immediate pleasure to a human Being possessed of that information which may be expected from him, not as a lawyer, a physician, a mariner, an astronomer, or a natural philosopher, but as a Man ... Nor let this necessity of producing immediate pleasure be considered as a degradation of the Poet's art. It is far otherwise. It is an acknowledgment of the beauty of the universe, an acknowledgment the more sincere, because not formal, but indirect; it is a task light and easy to him who looks at the world in the spirit of love: further it is a homage paid to the native and naked dignity of man, to the great elementary principle of pleasure by which he knows, and feels, and lives, and moves. We have no sympathy but what is propagated by pleasure. I would not be misunderstood; but wherever we sympathise with pain, it will be found that the sympathy is produced and carried on by subtle combinations with pleasure. We have no knowledge, that is, no general principles drawn from the contemplation of particular facts, but what has been built up by pleasure, and exists in us by pleasure alone. (387–406)

As Coleridge wrote, the 1802 additions have a sort of 'Verulamian Power & Majesty', alluding presumably to Francis Bacon's compact moral force in the *Essays*, though Coleridge's private compliment of Sara's 'acuteness, that she wished all that Part of the Preface to have been in Blank Verse' is interesting, with its implication that poetic pleasure should be dealt with *in poetry*.[34] Whatever we think about the successfulness of Wordsworth's argument, it is still startling that Wordsworth should insist that both natural philosophy and poetry share an epistemological ground of pleasure. There is, of course, a longstanding historiographical controversy about the origin of what C.P. Snow called the 'two cultures' split, where arts and feeling went on one side of discourse, and science and insensitive 'objectivity' on the other.[35] Nonetheless, given that even in De Quincey's near-contemporary writing such a split is evident, it is very strange that Wordsworth writes as if it were *obvious* that scientific epistemology must be grounded in enjoyment. He seems to be pointing towards an epistemology of analogy, where what we know comes only from what is pleasurably 'connected' in our minds, and, at the same time, what we enjoy solicits our (scholarly) attention. Hartley's associationism may have provided some basis for such an epistemology; this pleasure-inflected treatment of analogy also appears in Joseph Priestley's science.[36] But the pleasures of knowledge are the pivot around which Wordsworth first links poetics and science, and then sunders them: by the end of this section, scientific knowledge lacks 'flesh and blood', and is not an 'inmate of the household of man' (468, 470). The crucial turn is when Wordsworth withdraws from science the communicative, sociable and sympathetic potential of man's active principle of pleasure, and unexpectedly attributes private, subjective, incommunicable pleasure in its place. Why?

One reason may lie in the new cultural imagining of the 'scientist' in the early nineteenth century, a figure of fascination and perhaps perceived threat to the cultural position of writers.[37] The language of professional specialization (mineralogist, mariner, lawyer, botanist) is particularly marked in the passage.[38] Scientific knowledge is a lonely endeavour, 'by no habitual and direct sympathy connecting us with our fellow beings' (436–7); this line might be aligned with the new cultural imagining of the 'scientist'. The lecture given to the Royal Institution in January 1802 by Humphry Davy, part-time collaborator on *Lyrical Ballads*, could have goaded Wordsworth into some of these statements. Davy's broadranging, entrancing *Discourse Introductory to a Course of Lectures on Chemistry* treats the history of the world, progressive politics and the nature of human existence in its celebration of chemistry. It also places a heavy stress on pleasure, both in terms of new luxuries that may be manufactured and in terms of the pleasure involved in studying chemistry. He is concerned with the quantity of pleasure and sources of enjoyment currently available to man, and the kinds of 'simple pleasure' and 'permanent and placid enjoyment' that experimental research and contemplation of phenomena may provide.[39] It is plausible that his conversations with Wordsworth and Coleridge about poetic pleasure may have contributed to his thinking in the 'Discourse Introductory', and that what Wordsworth heard about Davy's lecture may have likewise fed into the second version of the 'Preface'.

Whilst Wordsworth grants that both poetic and scientific knowledge 'is pleasure', he nonetheless insists that one 'cleaves to us as a necessary part of our existence, our natural and unalienable inheritance'; 'the other is a personal and individual acquisition' (434–7). Here, Wordsworth begins to try to multiply and redefine the kinds of property and ownership applicable to pleasure. The half-logic of this passage runs as follows: the poet is special because he takes special pleasure in observing the pleasurable knowledge, that all men intuitively possess, that the world is pleasurable. Thus, he writes that the Poet views 'man and the objects that surround him as acting and re-acting upon each other, so as to produce an infinite complexity of pain and pleasure' (412–14). The Poet sees man in ordinary life as having a deep, intuitive knowledge of this fact, which also generates pleasure ('an overbalance of enjoyment', 420–1). Wordsworth restates this claim again, stressing the absolute ordinariness of this daily knowledge and pleasure, sympathies in which 'we are fitted to take delight' (424). Next, in a very influential sentence, Wordsworth writes that the Poet considers man and nature as 'essentially adapted to each other'; the mind is a 'mirror of the fairest and most interesting properties of nature' (425–7). Finally, the Poet, 'prompted' by pleasure, 'converses' with nature, with 'affections' similar to those of the Man of Science, but the scientist has taken longer and laboured harder to achieve the same epistemological joy.

CONCLUSION: PLEASURE, HABIT AND THE 'CLINAMEN'

These are difficult arguments that merit more philosophical attention than has usually been given them, certainly more than casting them as aesthetic commonplaces. The pleasure of poetry for Wordsworth is not a simple, unitary phenomenon, but a 'complex', mixed one, involving 'music', the overcoming of 'difficulty' and habituation (642–8).[40] He insists that there are different qualities of pleasure; that his work might be able to impart a *particular* pleasure. But he struggles with this idea, because one thing that he recognizes about pleasure is that we all own our *own* pleasures: he cannot disagree that readers may have taken real enjoyment in other kinds of poetry. Indeed, the conclusion notes that his aim has *not* been to prove that other enjoyments are 'less vivid, and less worthy', but rather to suggest that there *could* be poetry significant for its 'moral relations' (780–5).

On a simple level, this begins to reveal the complexity of Words-worth's interaction with contemporary utilitarian thinking, because he both agrees about the centrality of pleasure and yet wants to admit more differentiation than would the Benthamites. The relationship of Roman-ticism and utilitarianism, long considered a self-evident and frosty opposition, has begun to be reviewed by literary critics over the past decade. Philip Connell has drawn attention to the 'close, complex and often ambivalent relationship that existed between Malthusian argument and the politics of the Lake school during the late 1790s and early 1800s'.[41] He argues that the poets found some surprisingly congenial social and political claims in Malthus, but that they were chiefly reacting against Paley; my chapter has, I hope, brought out some of the shading of Wordsworth's response to natural theology. Frances Ferguson has suggested that Wordsworth shares with Smith, Bentham, Malthus and Godwin the 'utilitarian conviction that happiness provided the only true measure of the value of actions'; yet, that at the same time he 'recognized the kinds of self-deception and superstition that made it difficult for pleasure simply to make its way directly and uncomplicatedly in the world'.[42] She sees Wordsworth as a true 'liberal', between Bentham and Burke, who sees that pleasures are *not* comparable; fundamental differ-ences between individuals' desires and feelings *cannot* be permanently resolved: 'Poetic knowledge, by contrast, involves us in recognizing the commonality of the inalienability of individual emotion – the way in which the "primary laws of our nature" express themselves in emotional connections.'[43] And, according to her reading, we are not therefore resigned to a set of private emotional reactions that determine our (lonely) outcomes, because moral and aesthetic judgement (for Words-worth as in the liberal tradition of Rousseau and Kant) 'requires indi-viduals to imagine an ideal that includes differences from their own particular situations and that recognizes the limitations of even their own strengths'.[44]

A 'liberal' view of pleasure is also enabled by a consideration of the important metaphor of 'fitting': it is a notion unexpectedly shared with Kant, and one that helps us to think about the political implications that we might draw from particular descriptions of pleasure.[45] Wordsworth says that we are fitted to take delight in sympathies, and we also gain pleasure from the 'fitting to metrical arrangement a selection of the real language of men in a state of vivid sensation' (16–17). Blake was probably the first reader to react badly to this word, seeing a coercive, normative strain within Wordsworth's talk of pleasurable fitting in the Verse Prospectus, which will be discussed in Chapter 5.[46] Brendan O'Donnell, on the other hand, sees 'fitting' as a 'continuous process ... not so much the accomplishment of a single and determining fit', making it less of a normative or restrictive political metaphor and more one of negotiation and tolerance:[47] 'Poetic pleasure comes not through the poet's fulfilment of a preordained conception of any one kind of relationship between meter and language but through artful confrontation and reformation of deeply ingrained habits of association, including those habits that inform the reader's experience at the most minute levels of the physical impulses of the verse.'[48] If pleasure is an ongoing fitting rather than a final *fit*, we find, as with Kant, a kind of openness and indeterminacy that alters the concomitant forms of subjectivity and community. Further ideas about the political status of pleasure are yielded by considering the question of habit. The 'Preface' states (contrary to the Wordsworth caricature) that good poetry is *not* merely the 'spontaneous overflow of powerful feelings' but involves long and deep thought about those feelings. 'For our continued influxes of feeling are modified and directed by our thoughts, which are indeed the representatives of all our past feelings'; relating these histories of feeling to one another, the poet discovers 'what is really important to men', until finally he acquires such 'habits of mind' that his descriptions cannot fail to have a powerful and improving effect on the reader (133–40). This constant, repetitive interaction of feeling and thought that may 'incorporate itself with the blood & vital juices of our minds' stands against any idea that there is a purely concrete, bodily pleasure separable from our history and our imagination.[49] Thus, Wordsworth can remind us that 'we not only wish to be pleased, but to be pleased in that particular way in which we have been accustomed to be pleased': our 'habitual gratitude' for our favourite poems lends its own delight. The circularity of our pleasurable, *habitual* gratitude is important to the argument of *The Prelude* and *Home at Grasmere*, but here the point is that our pleasures are linked to our history, rather than being a plain sensation (if such a thing were indeed possible). Perhaps this historical dimension accounts for the way that Wordsworth thinks that poetic pleasure can 'bind' the community of man. Habit, rather than being associated with custom and conservatism, may be viewed as a bridging of biology and history, more creative and productive than deadening and restrictive.

The apparently simple problem of poetics that Wordsworth faces in the 'Preface' – that his belief in a utopian, truer kind of pleasure must be set against the fact that people *do* take pleasure in the kind of poetry he wants to overturn – opens a larger problem around imposing affective norms on other people. And yet, Wordsworth still holds fast to the universality of pleasure; its human commonness as an experience; and the fact that it is also generated by our sense of this commonness with others: this circularity is its own proof. This recalls the *sensus communis* as we saw it in Chapter 1. Kant's claim that the *sensus communis* is the pleasure of the 'attunement' of our faculties with each other, and with the universe, offering an affirmation of community, that communication *is possible*, seems echoed in Wordsworth's notion that this pleasure 'binds together by passion and knowledge the vast empire of human society, as it is spread over the whole earth, and over all time' (440–50). Further, there is a structural echo in the circularity of Kant's and Wordsworth's arguments about pleasure. Stanley Corngold has framed the key question of the Third Critique as follows: 'is the feeling of pleasure posterior to judging the object? And the answer, for Kant, in §9, is yes, the feeling of pleasure is posterior, although this posteriority, as we shall see, is at bottom circular (though by no means meaningless).'[50] Drawing on Heidegger, Corngold suggests that the seeming paradox about whether pleasure comes before or after judgement can be understood to suggest that '[a]esthetic feeling constitutes a circle, producing by means of *its own narrative* an "*unabsehbarer* [visually indeterminate, unsurveyable]" space.'[51] Our pleasure is more like points on a circle than a sequence; Corngold finds that the temporality of aesthetic pleasure looks like Rousseau's *sentiment de l'existence*: 'where the consciousness of consecutive wave motion gives way to a "play" of the mind with itself, a play without consciousness of serial time, an intensification of self-affectivity without awareness of regular sequence'.[52] For Corngold, this bliss is 'relief from the sober labor of the concept'.[53] But Kant, and Wordsworth, refuse to break the link between pleasure and knowledge, and insist that community is spoken by this pleasurable circularity. Furthermore, Wordsworth's varied accounts of pleasure do not focus on this kind of self-reflection, but rather on the interactions between humans and other forms of life, even other non-living objects and forces.

The interest of 'Lines Written in Early Spring' lies partly in the commonness of pleasure between humans, birds, twigs and breezes.

Wordsworth's thoughts here may be involved not only with the natural theology that dominated his education, but also with ancient debates, such as Aristotle's development of Eudoxus' view that pleasure must be good because all creatures follow it. At moments, his ideas come closer to Spinozist and Epicurean models than a Kantian one. We can see this in his account of pleasure as an *elementary* principle, which hints at ancient atomism, as does his stress on forms of connection and interaction in his descriptions of a cosmos defined by affect. Thus, Wordsworth describes the 'volitions and passions as manifested in the goings-on of the Universe' (326–7), and a vision of a world where all objects are 'acting and re-acting upon each other', producing an 'infinite complexity' (412–14) and a 'complex scene of ideas and sensations' (418). The idea of fitting, connections and collisions repeatedly generating an (*uneconomic*) 'overbalance' of pleasure reaches its fullest expression in the central motif of *Home at Grasmere*, where the birds swoop up to the boundary of the skyline and down again.

The idea that we pleasurably incline towards each other and interact echoes the Lucretian idea of the swerve of atoms towards each other, the *clinamen*. The significance of this notion is often understood to lie in incorporating freedom into what would otherwise have been an entirely mechanistic philosophy (as in Epicurus' forerunner Democritus). In Creech's translation, owned by Wordsworth, the *clinamen* is described as seeds falling like rain:[54]

> Now *Seeds* in downward motion must *decline*,
> Tho very little from th'exactest line:
> For did they still move *strait*, they needs must fall,
> Like drops of Rain, dissolv'd and scatter'd all;
> For ever tumbling thro' the Mighty Space,
> And never joyn to make one single Mass.[55]

This notion of the *clinamen* struck imaginatively several twentieth-century thinkers. Harold Bloom adopted it for his theory of 'poetic misprision', in which the 'poet swerves away from his precursor'.[56] Gilles Deleuze reads the *clinamen* as only productive 'difference', with no positive or negative ethical valence, implying neither deviation nor freedom: 'the *clinamen* is by no means a change of direction in the movement of an atom, much less an indetermination testifying to the existence of a physical freedom. It is the original determination of the direction of movement, the synthesis of movement and its direction which relates one atom to another.'[57] Jean-Luc Nancy, on the other hand, reads it as the ethical basis of community:

Still, one cannot make a world with simple atoms. There has to be a *clinamen*. There has to be an inclination or an inclining from one toward the other, of one by the other, or from one to the other. Community is at least the *clinamen* of the individual. Yet, there is no theory, ethics, politics, or metaphysics of the individual that is capable of envisaging this *clinamen*, this declination or decline of the individual within community.[58]

That the action of the *clinamen* can be understood as both friendly 'inclination' (Nancy) and negative 'declination' (Bloom), and as neither (Deleuze), attests to its conceptual and ethical suggestiveness and ambiguity. Though Wordsworth does not use the *clinamen* concept explicitly, the question of what forces of affection and connection run through the universe seem important to his consideration of pleasure and its moral possibilities in 'Lines Written in Early Spring' and in the 'Preface' documents. His very struggle and indecision over whether there is evidence of natural pleasure, and if there is, what it means for human political life, is one strand of a long and rich history of speculation on these ideas. Furthermore, recognizing parallels between his discussions of pleasure in the 'Preface' documents and the terminology of Spinoza and Epicurus also helps to complicate the argument beyond the ideological attacks that once prevailed in criticism. His interest in metrical pleasure cannot be seen as 'simply' soporific closure or a negative disciplining of feeling, if it is recognized as standing for both physiological calming and restoration, as well as disruption and tension. It goes beyond the terms of Rousseau's *Julie* which offers an either or choice of a closed, tightly managed bourgeois economy, and the open, but tragic, energetic delights of the lovers. Pleasure in the 'Preface' seems to combine both collective harmony and openness to novelty; habit and change; determination and freedom.

CHAPTER 4

Economies of affect in The Prelude *and* Home at Grasmere

'Pleasure' in *The Prelude* is repeatedly entangled in a nexus of images of blood, breath, motion, life, spirit and gift, as evinced in the beautiful opening:[1]

> Oh there is blessing in this gentle breeze,
> That blows from the green fields and from the clouds
> And from the sky; it beats against my cheek,
> And seems half conscious of the joy it gives. (I. 1–4)

Where does the pleasure occur? On the surface of the skin, as the breeze's motion acts upon the cheek; yet this occurrence seems to return a reciprocal pleasure to the breeze, which revises our understanding of the 'blessing' that is 'in' the breeze. 'Blessing' is rooted in the Old English word 'blodsian' or 'blooded', as in daubed with blood in consecration, and over time the word crosses between bliss (Old English 'bliths') and worship, in rendering the Latin 'benedicere' as blessing (*OED*). Blessing, blissing, blooding: that the breeze 'beats' against the cheek seems to suggest that the pleasure it gives generates a heartbeat in the subject, intertwining spiritual and corporeal senses. The idea that the pleasure of nature sets a reciprocal pleasure in motion in the body, which circulates the blood and the breath, is powerfully formulated in Book II's erotic cosmology, where the poet tells us that he 'loved the sun':

> ... for this cause, that I had seen him lay
> His beauty on the morning hills, had seen
> The western mountain touch his setting orb
> In many a thoughtless hour, when from excess
> Of happiness my blood appeared to flow
> With its own pleasure, and I breathed with joy. (II. 184–93)

These lines show a startling image of circulation where all teleology and transcendence is lost in a kind of pointless, thoughtless bliss that simply echoes the unproductive sensuality ('touching') of the sun and mountain. Wordsworth insists that he loves the sun in this way *rather than* 'as I since have loved him, as pledge / And surety of our earthly life, a light / Which while we view we feel we are alive' (II. 185–7) – a strange assertion, for what is the difference between feeling alive (Rousseau's *sentiment d'existence*) and 'breathing with joy'? One reading of this is that even the discourse of 'life', of the heartbeat that circulates the blood, is at this point too teleological; the kind of intense shared pleasure of this scene is even less aim-oriented, less locatable in a human subject, than that other kind.

Turning from the *Lyrical Ballads* to Wordsworth's long narrative poems, we face a different set of questions around pleasure, partly around how to categorize them, perhaps mirroring the long poems' inherent challenge of organization of material and design. This chapter uses the concept of economy in various ways, to think about the distribution of pleasures in Wordsworth's account, and the history of representing hierarchies of different kinds of pleasure (for instance, bodily, mental and spiritual). It begins by analysing the categorization of pleasure in *The Prelude* – a poem that opens with the representation of a joy (its ambition being 'to make / A present joy the matter of my song', I. 55–6), and distinguishes between different types: 'vulgar' and 'subtler' joys, for instance. My main argument is about the ontological status of joy in the poem. This categorizing framework leads to a reading of *Home at Grasmere*, a poem which is structured around two representations of pleasure: one as calm, still gratification, and the other as endless movement and desire. To explore this further, a contrast is drawn with Bataille's account of restricted and general economies in his 1933 essay 'The Notion of Expenditure'. The chapter concludes by suggesting that *Home at Grasmere* unexpectedly offers a Wordsworthian critique of Bataille's account of bourgeois pleasure. In this way, it retrieves alternative political and ethical meanings of pleasure, in the very period associated with the rise of utilitarian and bourgeois philosophies criticized by Bataille. Consequently, it has an impact on the way we understand pleasure in the writing of figures influenced by Bataille, including Derrida, Nancy and Deleuze.

THE CLASSIFICATION OF PLEASURES IN 'THE PRELUDE'

One of the striking features of the account of pleasure in *The Prelude* is that its status and categorization is constantly under review; the poem repeatedly asks whether pleasure is an animal sensation, a kind of consciousness, a feeling of power, a feeling of community, and whether there is a 'pure' delight. Whilst on one level this hesitancy is neither surprising nor particularly problematic (it is a poem and not a treatise), it bears some closer attention because the poem *does* have a pressure towards logic, and presents those categories emphatically.[2] At times, the treatment of pleasure echoes the neuro-physiological theories of David Hartley, John Brown and Erasmus Darwin.[3] 'Fits of vulgar joy' are described in terms of vibrations, repetition and memory traces:

> that giddy bliss
> Which like a tempest works along the blood
> And is forgotten . . .
> And if the vulgar joy by its own weight
> Wearied itself out of the memory,
> The scenes which were a witness of that joy
> Remained . . . (1. 611–13, 625–8)

The description of affect as a corporeal ripple through the mind and blood, and the perceptions that become marked on the mind, strongly echoes Hartley's associationism and his influential claim in the *Observations* that 'the Pleasures and Pains of Feeling contribute, according to the Doctrine of Association, to the Formation of our Intellectual Pleasures and Pains'.[4] Feelings leave a 'trace' causing the nervous system to 'run into miniature vibrations of the same kind' when excited by the 'associated Circumstances'.[5] Hartley focuses on pain rather than pleasure 'in forming the intellectual Pleasures', because pleasures are 'faint and rare'.[6] Wordsworth seems to reverse the priority of Hartley's account, making pleasure the key associative principle, which should not surprise given the broader ontological and political importance that, as we saw in the last chapter, he attaches to pleasure. But he goes much further than Hartley in his depiction of pleasure, both in his hints at the existence of deeper and subtler pleasures than such vulgar joy, but also in his *more* bodily representation of pleasure as a whole-being event. While Hartley insists upon the body's priority in matters of mental action (in claiming that bodily sensations are the direct basis of intellectual pleasures), it seems that his interest is still in representation, in the mind's images and concepts, compared with Wordsworth's strikingly holistic, dynamic and corporeal language of pleasure, in which pleasure *is* life. Wordsworth's claim that 'my blood appeared to flow / With its own pleasure, and I breathed with joy' is only one of many links in the poem between pleasure and the life-force (11. 192–3).

This invites a medical contextualization: whilst pleasure is not pathological, and was in this sense never the direct focus of medical research, this period saw a new interest in non-pathological topics like life and health which also bore on the concept of pleasure.[7] For instance, John Brown's *Elementa Medicinae* started from the principle that health consists of a balance between the subject's own 'excitability' and the external level of 'excitation'; diseases lay in the imbalance.[8] This emphasis on balanced stimulation could have drawn from ancient theories of *ataraxia*, though Brown was rather uncertain about the role of pleasure *per se*, a weakness noted by his translator Beddoes.[9] It is unclear in his account whether pain and pleasure are sensations that arise in response to stimulation, or whether they constitute forms of stimulation, though certainly pain diminishes stimulation, and pleasure increases it.[10] There is an evident circularity here, perhaps because of a politic decision to downplay pleasure in a therapy that heavily relies on brandy and opiates. (Brunonianism was associated with hedonism from its outset, though from the reverse point of view, Brown himself was suspicious of the moralizing *anti*-hedonism of a medical culture that instituted cures of pain, discomfort and starvation; the upper-class fashion for aping poverty in the name of health.[11]) Although there was a glorious possibility of perfection – 'If the just degree of excitement could be constantly kept up, mankind would enjoy eternal health' – this balance was said to be impossible to achieve.[12] The gradual wasting of natural excitability opened the 'gate of destruction'; life, in a state of minimal stimulation, would simply shift into the state of death (a crux seen in Rousseau's *Reveries*).[13]

There are some similarities here with Wordsworth's emphasis on excitation and stimulation, and the matrix of ideas around life, health and poetry's curative effects.[14] These go beyond association psychology to imply that both poetry and our enjoyment of nature are life-enhancing, affecting every vein and muscle directly. Yet, pleasure is crucially *not* the same as excitability or nervous energy; looking closer at his use of 'pleasure' we see that it does not easily fit into modern dichotomies like physiology versus philosophy; body versus mind; corporeal versus moral.[15] This is apparent every time he tries to categorize pleasure in such way in the poem. The strongest instance is in Book I, where Wordsworth has described all his childhood 'sportive joys' in terms of vibration and motion, and then performs an apparent conceptual turn – to some readers typical of Wordsworth's transcendentalizing urge – distinguishing that kind of sportive pleasure from 'joys of subtler origin':

> Nor, sedulous as I have been to trace
> How Nature by extrinsic passion first
> Peopled my mind with beauteous forms or grand

And made me love them, may I well forget
How other pleasures have been mine, and joys
Of subtler origin – how I have felt,
Not seldom, even in that tempestuous time,
Those hallowed and pure motions of the sense
Which seem in their simplicity to own
An intellectual charm, that calm delight
Which, if I err not, surely must belong
To those first-born affinities that fit
Our new existence to existing things,
And, in our dawn of being, constitute
The bond of union betwixt life and joy. (1. 571–85)

As in the 'Preface', there is a strong yet difficult insistence on a 'subtler' pleasure ('other enjoyments, of a purer, more lasting, and more exquisite nature', 'Preface', 776–7). Since Hazlitt's memorable attack on Wordsworth's seeming lack of appetite – 'From the Lyrical Ballads, it does not appear that men eat or drink, or are given in marriage' – critics have often been troubled by this purity, finding it to indicate abstraction or disdain for life.[16] Yet, these pleasures only 'seem' to own an intellectual charm, and, as William Empson long ago noted, the word *intellectual* leads us to expect an epistemological statement but in fact what we get is an obscure ontology, 'the bond of union betwixt life and joy'.[17] Any vestigial expectation that the 'joys of subtler origin' will move us *away* from the vulgarity of sense perception is again startled when the metaphors are of intense sense perception: 'drinking in / A pure organic pleasure from the lines / Of curling mist' (1. 590–1); 'gathering ... / Through every hair-breadth of that field of light / New pleasure, like a bee among the flowers' (1. 606–8). If anything, its avowed 'purity' sounds almost to exist *in* being more hungrily sensual than the half-distracted, mixed enjoyments of 'vulgar joy'.[18]

Perhaps this distractedness is important to the interpretation of vulgar joy; we could here look to what analytic philosophy calls 'intentional' pleasures.[19] The boyish sports are directed to specific activities and objects, their pleasures have a content; whilst the 'hallowed motions' that fit a baby to the world imply a diffuse, non-directional, objectless affect ('A virtue which irradiates and exalts / All objects through all intercourse of sense', II. 259–60). This latter type is less *taking* pleasure or *getting* pleasure from something than a communicative and reciprocal event: 'From Nature largely he receives, nor so / Is satisfied, but largely gives again' (II. 267–8). But these distinctions do not completely hold up; as we shall see, childhood physical joys are also described in quite reciprocal terms. Perhaps, drawing on Gilbert Ryle, we could see the joys of subtler origin as coming from a different mode of *attention*; if sportive joys are a forgettable, physical giddy bliss, the 'motions of the sense' to which Wordsworth refers are physical perception ramped up to another level, where the enjoyment has become an end in itself, rather than a side-effect of some other purpose.[20]

In making affectivity 'first-born', Wordsworth hints that positive affect is the precondition of all other experience, perception and knowledge. The word 'pure' in this context signifies less chaste or spiritual, than radical, primary or preconditional, the experience of feeling or 'sense' in general rather than 'a sensation' in particular. In this way, as Simon Jarvis has recently argued, Wordsworth approaches a form of radical phenomenology based in an unconventional reading of Descartes and associated with the contemporary thinker Michel Henry.[21] Jarvis notes that despite his usual antipathy towards systems of philosophy, Wordsworth copied out two passages from Coleridge's transcriptions of Descartes: the description of how 'volition and fear' count 'among my ideas', and how 'my understanding' of things, truth and thought 'derive simply from my own nature', which could be seen as representing (in Jarvis' words) an 'account of affective subjectivity as such'.[22] Such evidence lends more support to the idea, contra many commentators, that Wordsworth is not reaching for an aesthetic ideology or transcendental illusion in going 'beyond' the physiological.

Yet this modern phenomenology evinces some important differences from Wordsworth's representation of that first affect. For Michel Henry, there can be no idea of community without the basis of feeling individuals: the first thing we know is that we, as an individual, feel *something*. Yet in *The Prelude* pleasure is often presented as requiring other individuals, or that feeling of 'fitting' with and against other people and other things. For instance, when the infant ontology of Book 1 recurs in the 'Blessed Babe' passage, the mother and the baby both create the influx of feeling which brings it to life, 'Like an awakening breeze':

> Along his infant veins are interfused
> The gravitation and the filial bond
> Of Nature that connect him with the world. (II. 262–4)

The lines above echo the joyful affinities of Book I, and the language of pleasurable 'fitting' that was witnessed in the 'Preface'. Metaphors of gravitation and binding recur: pleasure is regularly referred to as weighty in the poem, including in this image which ends with the unexpectedly light final image of the dream:

> oh, then the calm
> And dead still water lay upon my mind
> Even with a weight of pleasure, and the sky,
> Never before so beautiful, sank down
> Into my heart and held me like a dream. (II. 176–80)

Later, the poet's being is described as light, but again weighed down by the pleasure offered to him by natural beauty: 'Like a breeze / Or sunbeam over your domain I passed / In motion without pause; but ye have left your beauty with me' (VI. 605–7). The process of 'fitting', fitting our existence to existing things, could be seen as a version of the pleasure of being weighed down by materiality and history, bound to the earth. The inverse of the pleasure-weight theme appears in Wordsworth's description of the 'voluptuous' royal courts as *light* and unbound: 'A light and cruel world, cut off from all / The natural inlets of just sentiment' (IX. 357–8), as well as the comparison of the violent lust of the Terror's protagonists to the 'light desires' of a child, wanting his windmill to whirl faster (X. 336–45).

All of these refined yet inconclusive metaphors for pleasure show up the oddness of Wordsworth's categorization of sense perception in the 'Blessed Babe' lines, also observed by Noel Jackson who argues compellingly that 'the poet repudiates a sensationalist epistemology only to appear to subscribe to many of its protocols'.[23] Wordsworth sharply dismisses those who 'parcel out / His intellect by geometric rules' and wish to name 'the individual hour in which / His habits were first sown as a seed', *directly* before stating his own aim to 'trace / the progress of our being' and the origins of feeling (II. 208–9, 211–12, 238–9). Jackson argues that Wordsworth is offering a 'rejoinder and a more complicated return to a degraded French rationalism' in his addition of (Burkean) feeling, custom and habit to a (French) psychological model of development. In a Foucauldian vein, Jackson stresses how the passage presents the infant being 'fitted' to a *context* ('fit / Our new existence to existing things', I. 582–3), making the self 'historical from its inception'.[24] Jackson wishes to downplay that mother–child narrative of the history of emotion to prioritize the Scottish research into custom of David Hume and William Cullen. His reading is very strong, though it does not, however, consider that both historical and interpersonal bases for our affections might be opposed to, or in dialogue with, a 'pure' subjective ontology in the poem, or emphasize why the categorization of *pleasure* seems to be central to the poem's repeated proposition, withdrawal and revisiting of developmental models of sensation throughout.

The Prelude classifies pleasure in terms of age and maturity; in terms of physiological and ontological status; and in terms of individuality and communality, yet frequently these seemingly philosophical classifications prove precarious. The poem's developmental model starts *in medias res* with the boisterous raptures of the nine-year-old catalogued in Book I: egg-stealing, ice-skating, hazel-nutting and fishing. These 'boyish sports' (I. 495) are emphatically corporeal, and occasionally imply an ecstasy of physical abandon: 'we had given our bodies to the wind' (I. 479); the resonances of 'giving' here are not to be missed: the young boy's body is a part of nature and, as such, becomes almost a mere token in the exchange of natural and human forces. Pointless sensuality is again the point: 'Basked in the sun, and plunged, and basked again, / Alternate, all a summer's day' (I. 295–6). Even the apparently more domestic comforts of long evenings in cottages show a decisive physicality, recalling cosiness and physical proximity to siblings and friends. Cambridge and the summer vacations in Hawkshead provide a certain degree of difficulty for Wordsworth's account of his enjoyments. His remembered pleasures in his late teens match neither with childhood's easy intimacy with nature nor the young adult's domestic satisfactions and creative seriousness. In Cambridge, the poet asserts that he was losing 'the deep quiet and majestic thoughts / Of loneliness' in favour of 'empty noise / And superficial pastimes' (III. 210–13). But even from this vantage point, he cannot quite treacherously dismiss as false or immoral the pleasures he remembers,

> And yet
> This was a gladsome time. Could I behold –
> Who less insensible than sodden clay
> On a sea-river's bed at ebb of tide,
> Could have beheld – with undelighted heart
> So many happy youths, so wide and fair
> A congregation in its budding-time (III. 216–22)

Despite the severe criticism of Cambridge life that begins the passage, the sudden proliferation of the lines describing these youths' beauty and energy attests to the intensity of the memory. Rather unexpectedly, the explanation is that the poet's natural tendency was to sociability: 'my heart / Was social and loved idleness and joy' (III. 235–6). This pattern of criticism of shallow pleasures and self-reproving recurs in Book IV, when he describes being drawn to the feasts, dances and revelry of village life,

'This vague heartless chace / Of trivial pleasures': 'these did now / Seduce me from the firm habitual quest / Of feeding pleasures' (IV. 304–5, 277–9). He attacks them for being secondary pleasures (or, as Kant puts it, the pleasure of approbation): 'less pleasing in themselves / Than as they were a badge, glossy and fresh, / Of manliness and freedom' (IV. 275–7). This idea of false or secondary pleasures is very important to Wordsworth in the poem, and perhaps draws from Rousseau's account of *amour propre*. Having said that, the poem repeatedly reminds us of the strong purchase of our memories of pleasure. It would have been better, he writes, had he been able to study, to indulge his quiet, profound passions, but an erotic memory comes back as strongly as desire itself:

> And yet, in chastisement of these regrets,
> The memory of one particular hour
> Doth here rise up against me. . . .
> Slight shocks of young love-liking interspersed
> That mounted up like joy into the head,
> And tingled through the veins (IV. 314–27)[25]

As with the reference to the fun of Cambridge youths, Wordsworth takes a distant, spectatorial position: he does not remember *himself* drinking with the students, nor kissing a particular 'maid', but he remembers a general air of delight. For some readers, this distancing might once again indicate Wordsworth's refusal to accept the 'real' pleasure of sociability and sex; but it also attests to his interest in shared feeling. Both scenes are of communal and shared enjoyment, where the pleasure of a group 'infects' an onlooker; arguably, this hints at a broader conception of pleasure than the *private* memory of sensation. We return to the maturation of pleasures in Book v, which describes the childhood delight in imaginative fiction which at around age thirteen shifted to a different economy of reading: loving words 'For *their own sakes*' (v. 579),

> It might demand a more impassioned strain
> To tell of later pleasures linked to these,
> A tract of the same isthmus which we cross
> In progress from our native continent
> To earth and human life – I mean to speak
> Of that delightful time of growing youth
> When cravings for the marvellous relent,
> And we begin to love what we have seen;
> And sober truth, experience, sympathy,
> Take stronger hold of us; and words themselves
> Move us with conscious pleasure. (v. 558–68)

The unusual word 'isthmus' alerts us to the strangeness of comparing the birth (or, possibly, conception) of a human being to the acquisition of grown-up reading tastes. Wordsworth's developmental model has so far proceeded as follows: first, a pre-existence on our 'native continent', whose pleasures are not described; secondly, our new-born affinities, of great epistemological and ontological seriousness, where our existence is 'fitted' to existing things; thirdly, childhood joys, vulgar and sensational as they may be, but maybe more intimate and free than (fourthly) adolescent pleasures of sociability and blooming sexuality; which are nonetheless recalled with an intensity which rebukes any attempt to moralize them into unimportance. Late childhood is also given as the time of an intense craving for imaginative fiction, which is presented seemingly as a 'lower' pleasure than an adult taste for words-in-themselves – and yet is immediately recalled with an excessive, anguished nostalgia: 'I am sad / At thought of raptures now for ever flown' (v. 569–70). But this sense of loss is never long maintained within the poem: 'And yet the morning gladness is not gone / Which then was in my mind' (vi. 63–4). Repeatedly, we see a pattern whereby a developmental model is proposed and then withdrawn or re-thought.

Book viii appears initially to present pleasure's final maturation. Though London's theatres 'then were my delight' (vii. 438) and the place was 'a vivid pleasure of my youth' (vii. 151), its pleasures cannot be recuperated until Bartholomew Fair is erased by the Village Fair, introducing the 'agrarian ideal' of the poem.[26] In this book recur several of the delight motifs from Books i and ii: the motions of delight (viii. 80); the erotic cosmology of sun and mountains (viii. 117–18); the 'principles' of joy – the 'common haunts' of the green earth and 'ordinary human interests' (viii. 173, 166, 167). The figure of the Shepherd represents a high-point in the pleasure-classification scheme: the free man who can determine his own comforts and pleasures whether individual or social. This vision is transformative: 'hence the human form / To me was like an index of delight' (viii. 414–15); indicating and indexing pleasure. Then, pleasure seems to reach an apex: 'There came a time of greater dignity', when 'the pulse of being everywhere was felt' – all the 'frames of things' 'Were half confounded in each other's blaze, / One galaxy of life and joy' (viii. 624–31). Such a blaze recalls the 'Preface' description of man and objects 'acting and re-acting upon each other, so as to produce an infinite complexity of pain and pleasure' (412–14), hinting that the 'dependency sublime' (viii. 639–40) that ends the passage may refer not only or primarily to God, but to a kind of joyous interdependence of humans on each other and on natural things.

Book VI's paean to friendship, the 'joy / Above all joys' (VI. 211–12) that is Dorothy's presence, demonstrates again a form of unlocatable, non-individualized pleasure:

> And o'er the Border Beacon and the waste
> Of naked pools and common crags that lay
> Exposed on the bare fell, was scattered love
> A spirit of pleasure, and youth's golden gleam. (VI. 242–5)

This notion of scattered pleasure recurs strongly in the Revolutionary passages ('How bright a face is worn when joy of one / Is joy of tens of millions' (VI. 359–60)). Here, pleasure is catching: 'benevolence and blessedness / Spread like a fragrance everywhere' (VI. 368–9); 'delight / Was in all places spread around my steps / As constant as the grass upon the fields' (VI. 703–5). The comparison of delight to a fragrance 'spread' underlies a curious biographical anecdote: in 1797, Mary Hutchinson smelt 'a bed of stocks in full bloom', a 'pleasure' which the anosmic Wordsworth 'caught from her lips and then fancied to be his own'.[27] This spreading metaphor for pleasure appears in shorter poems, including 'Stray Pleasures', which begins: ' – *Pleasure is spread through the earth / In stray gifts to be claim'd by whoever shall find.*'[28] It describes encountering dancers, dancing merrily and freely to some music that drifts from another place; and in turn the poet 'catches' their joy.[29] 'The Barberry-Tree', mentioned in Chapter 3, is another poetic exercise about transferred delights; and likewise *The Prelude*, having 'caught' pleasure from outside, will transmit it on to its readers: 'What we have loved / Others will love, and we may teach them how' (XIII. 444–5).

Whilst the Revolutionary books are less concerned with pleasure than the 'home' books, pleasure is still relevant here as a source of emotional and aesthetic sustenance through the Terror, and in terms of the communal pleasure, the joy and optimism spread everywhere, that the poet observes and is infected by on first arriving in France. Those famous lines, 'Bliss was it in that dawn to be alive, / But to be young was very heaven!' (X. 692–3), recall infant ontological joy. The blessing of feeling one's existence becomes a kind of political homecoming: 'earth was then / To me what an inheritance new-fallen / Seems' (X. 728–30). The critique of rational (Godwinian) thought bears on the theme of pleasure. The poet tells us that under the influence of abstract thought he began to believe that reason could build everything on mental freedom: the delightful, 'glorious' idea that 'in self-knowledge and self-rule' we could shake off '[t]he accidents of nature, time, and place, / That make up the weak being of the past' (x. 818–26). Whilst this is represented as youthful arrogance, the poet still has respect for the 'noble aspiration' of the hope that man would be 'Lord of himself, in undisturbed delight' (x. 838). As we shall see in the reading of *Home at Grasmere* to follow, the idea of self-love or sovereign self-mastery suggested in the phrase 'Lord of himself' has a positive value for Wordsworth. We could read this as a merging of Epicurean and Stoic positions, and as a recollection of the *jouissance de soi* of Rousseau in his boat on Lake Bienne. There are several passages in the poem that echo that scene, most strongly in Book IV:

> When first I made
> Once more the circuit of our little lake
> If ever happiness hath lodged with man
> That day consummate happiness was mine
> Wide-spreading, steady, calm, contemplative. (IV. 127–31)

Later, in the lines describing a night-walk on the Hawkshead road, there is a suggestion both of the sentiment of existence, and of Rousseau's account of the gentle movements of the water: 'A consciousness of animal delight, / A self-possession felt in every pause / And every gentle movement of my frame' (IV. 397–9). This seems very close to Rousseau's prescription for 'neither absolute rest nor too much agitation, but a uniform and moderated movement having neither jolts nor lapses'.[30] In Book II, this Rousseauian vision of self-sufficiency appears to be involved with the fantasy that pleasure actually starts motoring the body's circulation, a hedonist homeostasis: 'when from excess / Of happiness my blood appeared to flow / With its own pleasure, and I breathed with joy' (II. 191–3). For some critics, this implies a delusion of godliness and bad aesthetic solipsism, but it reads very differently in the light of a history of Enlightenment claims that relationships and the love of others are actually dependent on forms of pleasure or self-love.[31]

The opening passage of Book XI's Restoration emphasizes those 'motions of delight' and the dynamic, interactive model of enjoyment that is so important to the poem:

> The morning shines,
> Nor heedeth man's perverseness: spring returns –
> I saw the spring return, when I was dead
> To deeper hope, yet had I joy for her
> And welcomed her benevolence, rejoiced

> In common with the children of her love,
> Plants, insects, beasts in field, and birds in bower. (XI. 22–8)

Thus, Wordsworth goes on to argue, 'complacency' (with the transitive, shared implication of the verb *complacere*, pleasing-with, as we saw in Kant's Anthropology lectures in Chapter 1), 'peace' and 'tender yearnings' had stayed with him throughout the moral crisis. What he lacked was hope: complacency is not a complete good without hope. But the passage implies that pleasure can come before hope; might even be a harbinger or condition of it. As in Rousseau's *Emile*, a certain degree of strength and joy in existence is a necessary starting point for kindness, generosity and hope.

We see another Rousseauian echo in the treatment of bad comparative pleasure. Wordsworth criticizes himself for a turn to reason: the 'narrow estimates of things' that his 'idol' of judgement rather than feeling brings about (XI. 127, 131). It is rare that the poet identifies a way that we could be 'even in pleasure pleased / Unworthily' – his word 'even' reminding us that, for Wordsworth, pleasure is *usually* an unmitigated good, except when it becomes based only on comparison and distinction (XI. 152–3). In comparative pleasure (which could be viewed as a kind of *amour propre*), the eye dominates over the 'sensuous and intellectual' creature (XI. 168). He is hungry for such pleasures 'of the outward sense', 'vivid but not profound', but this is an imperial, non-reciprocal enjoyment, desiring to see and compare without any kind of connection or reflection: 'Still craving combinations of new forms, / New pleasures, wider empire for the sight, / Proud of its own endowments' (XI. 191–4). Finally, under the influence of Mary's own enjoyments – 'She welcomed what was given, and craved no more' (XI. 206) – the poet shakes off his idolatry. This makes way for the discussion of spots of time, 'A virtue, by which pleasure is enhanced, / That penetrates, enables us to mount / When high, more high' (XI. 265–7). This is a mysterious language, overlaid with eros and echoing an ancient, meditative practice of the self.

Various philosophical registers sound in the seeming pinnacle of the poem's catalogue of pleasures, namely the twenty-one-year-old poet's ascent of Snowdon in Book VIII. A break in the mist reveals a layered scene of mountains, moon and sea, which the poet recognizes as an emblem of the imagination underlying the most stunning scenes of nature. This passage celebrates the attributes of the 'highest minds', who have a great power of imaginative connection with nature, and enjoy the 'highest bliss':

> For they are powers; and hence the highest bliss
> That can be known is theirs – the consciousness

Of whom they are, habitually infused
Through every image, and through every thought,
And all impressions; hence religion, faith,
And endless occupation for the soul,
Whether discursive or intuitive;
Hence sovereignty within and peace at will,
Emotion which best foresight need not fear,
Most worthy then of trust when most intense;
Hence chearfulness in every act of life;
Hence truth in moral judgments; and delight
That fails not, in the external universe (xiii. 107–19)[32]

This sombre, almost rather daunting, image of dependable bliss is not quite in tune with the leitmotif of unpredicted pleasure previously running through the poem. It has a definite Stoic quality, in its celebration of a calm sense of self arrived at through peace with the rational order of nature, one that will come to the fore in 'Character of the Happy Warrior' and *The Excursion*. It is notable that in all these instances, Wordsworth attributes such successful satisfaction to others, not himself, witnessed in the use of the third person plural (they, themselves, their) in almost every line from 90 to 102. In the idea of approaching an adequate understanding of the universe that will bring about a highest form of joy, there is an echo of Spinoza's ethics, though there is also a more traditional Christianity present, developed further in Wordsworth's 1850 revisions.[33] The passage therefore rings with numerous philosophical meanings – possibly providing an instance of what Thomas Kavanagh has described as the period's hybrid Epicurean-Stoicism – and the lighter language of pleasure from earlier in the poem is still sounded in that ordinary word 'chearfulness'.[34]

It must, of course, be noted that this highest bliss is *not* actually the end of the poem: it turns to the friendship of Dorothy and Coleridge, 'centring all in love, and in the end / All gratulant if rightly understood (xiii. 384–5). In *Paradise Lost*, the beauty and delight of the new creation is marred for Adam only by his human 'deficience' that without a similar species with whom to share his happiness, he will not find real contentment: 'who can enjoy alone / Or all enjoying, what contentment find?'[35] Taking Eve to bed brings about a cosmic level of rejoicing:

    . . . the earth
Gave sign of gratulation, and each hill;
Joyous the birds; fresh gales and gentle airs
Whispered it to the woods.[36]

Samuel Johnson defined congratulation as 'the act of professing joy for the happiness or success of another'.[37] Congratulation is important to Wordsworth's description of the move from taking pleasure in the objects of the world like a 'spirit / Or angel', in 'individual happiness', to a pleasure that has a 'human-heartedness' (IV. 228–9, 225).

> But now there open'd on me other thoughts,
> Of change, congratulation, and regret,
> A new-born feeling. It spread far and wide;
> The trees, the mountains shared it, and the brooks (IV. 231–4)

'Congratulation' is thus implicated in *The Prelude*'s main stated argument that the love of nature can lead to the love of man. These forms of reciprocal or interstitial pleasure were present in the opening description of the breeze on the cheek, where no clear distinction is made between the force acting and that acted upon, echoing the claim that the poet 'considers man and the objects that surround him as acting and re-acting upon each other, so as to produce an infinite complexity of pain and pleasure' ('Preface', 412–14).

TWO REGISTERS OF PLEASURE IN 'HOME AT GRASMERE'

This extraordinary and comparatively unstudied poem demonstrates the tension between two economies of pleasure that we witnessed in Rousseau's *Julie*.[38] Pleasure may be read as the conservation of forces; or it may be associated with the exceeding of norms and surpassing of systems. It shall be argued here, with reference to Bataille, that Wordsworth's interest in the former economy – the closure and completeness of bliss – has a kind of radicalism that is worthy of more interest than is usually granted to it. *Home at Grasmere* takes as its subject the poet's intense feeling of happiness and belonging, ramped up to what one is tempted to describe as a hysterical level of bliss. Since its first critical response in 1889, there has been a regular claim that there is something not quite right about the poem's almost hyperbolic joyfulness. William Minto began by describing the verse as 'of the poet's prime', and, unlike *The Prelude*, 'crossed by no disturbing currents of regret or misgiving', before a sentence later qualifying that 'There is no trace of misgiving, unless we are to find it in the very pains that he took to satisfy himself . . . that he had made no mistake in his choice of residence, and that he ought to be grateful.'[39] Through the late twentieth century, the poem was read almost exclusively in terms of these traces of misgiving. Stephen Gill commented that '[t]he poem has celebrated joy, yet the idea of joy itself clearly troubles Wordsworth'.[40] The 'pains' Wordsworth takes to emphasize joy have been read as biographical symptom: for example, in the suggestion that it evinces Wordsworth's longing for the home he lost as a child, or that it buckles under the weight of creative expectation for *The Recluse* project.[41] Sally Bushell's recent reading is premised on accepting that the text 'is about the Poet's inability to situate himself, and subsequent anxiety concerning his role and abilities'; her incisive reading of Wordsworth's revisions, she claims, confirms the existing scholarly 'consensus' about the poem's 'contradictions and false self-justifications'.[42] I wish to dissent from this consensus by showing that *Home at Grasmere* may be taken much more at its happy word: the poem offers a concerted engagement with the philosophy of pleasure. That the matter of pleasure is central to the poem's arguments is clear given *Home at Grasmere*'s overt confederacy with utopian and paradisiacal texts including *Song of Solomon*, Spenser's *Faerie Queene*, Shakespeare's romances and Milton's *Paradise Lost* and *Paradise Regained*. One of the key ideas informing Wordsworth's representation of the vale of Grasmere, drawn perhaps from the *Tempest* ('The isle is full of noises, / Sounds, and sweet airs, that give delight'),[43] is that it is a space literally full of affect: 'this whole Vale, / . . . Swarms with sensation, as with gleams of sunshine, Shadows or breezes, scents or sounds' (666–8).

Several important features of the poem's treatment of pleasure may be delineated. First, there is a dichotomy between images of pleasurable 'rest' and pleasurable 'restlessness': it will be argued that a key feature of the poem's figuration of the joy of Grasmere is the oscillation between a wish for calm satisfaction and stillness, and a wish for endless flight and the postponement of satisfaction. In terms of the poem's narrative, these images form a split between the fantasy of the poet and Emma at home, versus the restless birds of the sky. Secondly, we may consider, as we did in relation to Rousseau's *Julie*, whether this dichotomy evinces an anxiety about restless desire that it resolves by trying to conserve all energy within Grasmere, within what Bataille terms a closed economy. It thus provokes the question of whether the poem practises a kind of bourgeois economistic thinking around pleasure, inviting discussion of the idea of utility in this period. Thirdly, it will be argued that, in fact, Wordsworth ultimately equates stillness and restiveness in pleasure, because he wants to argue for what they have in common, which (somewhat surprisingly) is an insistent *unproductiveness*. Unlike the image of happiness in *The Excursion* to be discussed in the final chapter, pleasure in *Home at*

Grasmere insistently refuses to look towards any end beyond itself; and this has repercussions for the way we think about aristocratic critiques of economy like Bataille's. Finally, the way that Wordsworth figures pleasure as a stream or force beyond individuals and individual accident will be discussed, showing his interest in the transmissible, and perhaps collective, nature of affect.

Grasmere is repeatedly figured as a site of rest, calm and safety. From the beginning, with the schoolboy's precocious vision of a place where he can imagine his whole life stretching out unto death, the poem explores the desire for an unchanging 'rest': 'For rest of body 'twas a perfect place' (22). The prayer-like verse offers thanks for an end to difficulty and disturbance: 'But I am safe; yes, one at least is safe; / What once was deemed so difficult is now / Smooth, easy, without obstacle' (74–6). The landscape is entreated to 'close me in' (129), and this landscape's air of transcendental 'repose' (162) makes 'A termination and a last retreat' for the community within (166). Gesturing towards the cottage where he lives with Emma, the poet experiences a joy so complete that it tips him towards a state of perfect quietude:

> Aye, think on that, my Heart, and cease to stir;
> Pause upon that, and let the breathing frame
> No longer breathe, but all be satisfied. (99–101)

This extreme tranquillity of pleasure is a recurring vision in the poem. It recalls that ancient conception of pleasure as *ataraxia*, the absence of any disturbance or stimulation. In *The Prelude*, pleasure makes the organic frame function, it *is* breath ('from excess / Of happiness my blood appeared to flow / With its own pleasure, and I breathed with joy', II. 191–3). In *Home at Grasmere*, even the breath quietens to half-deadness. In one of the key descriptions of this experience, Wordsworth unabashedly highlights the complex, almost paradoxical, quality of a joy without *jouissance*, an undesirous delight. He hails the quality of the valley that can 'purify' and 'soothe' (391, 392):

> And steal away and for a while deceive
> And lap in pleasing rest, and bear us on
> Without desire in full complacency,
> Contemplating perfection absolute
> And entertained as in a passive sleep. (393–7)

These lines play ambivalently around their central fantasy, hinting that this kind of pleasurable rest is either implausible or deceptive or both. The word 'lap', with its sexual connotations, may allude to the delusory, druggy, deathless pleasure of Adonis entrapped in Venus' bower in the *Faerie Queene*: 'There yet, some say, in secret he does ly, / Lapped in flowres and pretious spycery, / By her hid from the world ...'[44] Tautology, characteristic of Wordsworth's writing in general and especially in *Home at Grasmere*, here is used to underline the incongruous nature of this unstimulated bliss: 'full complacency', 'perfection absolute', 'passive sleep'.[45] Wordsworth draws upon an uncommon sense of entertain as 'to hold in a state' to play up the paradoxical idea of being entertained – in the sense of stimulated and amused – in a sleep (*OED*). There are echoes of Rousseau's *Reveries*' description of 'a state in which the soul finds a solid enough base to rest itself on entirely and to gather its whole being into, without needing to recall the past or encroach upon the future ... he who finds himself in it can call himself happy'.[46] The language does not blanch at the idea that tranquil delight carries a hint of death about it, playing quite deliberately with death metaphors (a termination, an urn-like valley, stopped breath).[47]

Against this complex, ambivalent imagery of pleasurable rest, the poem poses images of restlessness. There is the guilt-stung shepherd who, after his adultery, has no 'resting-place', finding neither pleasure nor quiet but only a desire to 'fly', in keeping with the Miltonic language of Satan's restlessness that runs throughout the poem (515, 524). A more positive restlessness is presented by the circling birds, which dart from land to sky and back 'As if they scorned both resting-place and rest' (314). Such a scorning is echoed in the way the verse attempts to rest them, yet finds its own claims firmly repudiated:

> see them now at rest,
> Yet not at rest, upon the glassy lake.
> They cannot rest; they gambol like young whelps,
> Active as lambs and overcome with joy. (768–71)

The joyful movement of these birds forms the key visual motif of the poem, recurring in a number of long passages, as if to the poet they comprise both a reiterated pleasure and an ongoing riddle. In the opening lines, they are grouped together with all entrancing things that move fast on a bright March day, clouds, breezes, 'Sunbeams, Shadows, Butterflies and Birds, / Angels and winged Creatures', and it is the poet whose fantasy flight is delineated: 'To flit from field to rock, from rock to field' (31–2, 37). The first main description of the birds occurs 300 lines into the poem, where the 'jubilant' birds 'show their pleasure' in the way they 'Mount with a thoughtless impulse, and wheel there' (284, 286, 289).

Their impulsive, random moves evince pleasure-for-pleasure's sake: 'girding it about / In wanton repetition' (295–6). In contrast to the fantasy of a peaceful lack of desire, the birds are associated with temptation and narcissism:

> They tempt the sun to sport among their plumes;
> They tempt the water and the gleaming ice
> To show them a fair image. 'Tis themselves,
> Their own fair forms upon the glimmering plain,
> Painted more soft and fair as they descend,
> Almost to touch, then up again aloft. (307–12)

Though the birds initially propose a contrast with the state of being 'Without desire in full complacency' (395), Wordsworth invests his every description of them with an insistent circularity, with the consequence that they finally appear to experience something more like full complacency than desire; desire having often been understood as a consciousness of (an unsatisfiable) lack. The birds may have a kind of desirous restlessness, but like a perpetual motion machine, their pleasurable movements create reflections and images that are the source of further delight. No outside energy is required to begin the birds' entertainment; no unpleasure sets in; no sensations become jaded. This automatic delight is echoed in the very pattern of their movements, 'Hundreds of curves and circlets', which do not conflict or disrupt one another but form an endless pattern, 'that large circle evermore renewed' (298, 297). They perform in nature the fantasy that Grasmere, even in the 'daily walks / Of business', will provide 'perpetual pleasure of the sense' (210–12). This is perhaps why towards the end of the poem Wordsworth can revise his account of the birds' mad energy to represent instead a kind of 'stillness':

> And in and all about that playful band,
> Incapable although they be of rest,
> And in their fashion very rioters,
> There is a stillness, and they seem to make
> Calm revelry in that their calm abode.
> I leave them to their pleasure. (798–803)

What is the source of this 'calmness'? The subsequent lines imply that it is their role in an endlessly recurring cycle of nature, 'the life of the whole year / That is to come' (804–5). Their 'thoughtless impulse' is not the sign of a disruptive *jouissance* but rather forms part of an ongoing chain of nature (289). From the point of view of critics of Wordsworth's aesthetic ideology, this claim for 'calm revelry' may seem simply paradoxical or bad faith. Or worse: is it an attempt to recuperate all joyful energy, all disruptive desire, to Grasmere's closed economy?

BOUNDED OR 'BOURGEOIS' PLEASURE?

Twentieth-century theory has considered a calm, bounded form of pleasure to exemplify 'bourgeois' rationality, notably Georges Bataille in his 1933 essay 'The Notion of Expenditure'.[48] In *Home at Grasmere*'s avowal of what Bataille describes as utility's goal, 'pleasure – but only in a moderate form, since violent pleasure is seen as *pathological*, and particularly in the kind of pleasure-conservationism introduced above, it might appear to propose a highly utilitarian vision of human life which, according to Bataille, utterly limits that life.[49] The poem reiterates various limitations to the energy and movement that it first propounds, most strikingly in 'bounding' the imaginative movement of the narrator to the geographical space of the vale, but also in that odd revision of the birds' enormous playful energy to one of a form of 'stillness'. Bataille argues that modern, rational 'utility' proposes an efficient balance of the production and consumption of goods and the reproduction and conservation of life, excluding 'non-productive expenditure' within social life, like the 'great and free' feudal-era practices of 'luxury, mourning, war, cults, the construction of sumptuary monuments, games, spectacles, arts, perverse sexual activity (i.e. deflected from genital finality)'.[50] Whilst pleasure is purportedly the goal of modern utility, in actual fact it becomes a mere 'concession' or 'diversion', outside the main focus which is 'productive social activity' as an end; this denial of waste and excess offers a false description of human life; experience will only begin when non-teleological energies are liberated.[51] For Bataille, modern intellectual systems of utility are aporetic: 'it is constantly necessary to return, in the most unjustifiable way, to principles that one would like to situate beyond utility and pleasure: *honor* and *duty* are hypocritically employed in schemes of pecuniary interest'.[52] Indeed, this analysis might find evidence in the way that *Home at Grasmere* seems finally to renounce 'enjoyment' in favour of 'duty' (878–9).

But whilst *Home at Grasmere* in certain respects (perhaps unsurprisingly from a historical point of view) reinforces aspects of the bourgeois / utilitarian restricted economy, there are other moments where it seems to reflect quite knowingly on that very dilemma, and look for ways of unlimiting human life from closed economic forms. Most importantly in this context is the poem's striking refusal to suggest a productive role for pleasure. An extraordinary feature of *Home at Grasmere* is what Kenneth Johnston calls its 'rubric of circularity'.[53] Rather than forcing pleasure into an ends-oriented economic system, Wordsworth is deeply interested in the non-teleological aspects of a very ordinary pleasure. This is emphatically non-reproductive (cue, perhaps, the subject matter of a non-sexual sibling romance) and non-productive in the economic sense (thus Grasmere's 'bounty' and Wordsworth's idleness). Whilst such moderate pleasure might not represent the 'limit experiences' proposed by Bataille, Wordsworth's excessive, 'absurdist' treatment of bourgeois pleasure might be seen along the lines of those who, as Bataille admiringly puts it, 'push the consequences of current rationalist conceptions as far as they will go'.[54]

This is witnessed in moments where Wordsworth is quite explicit about the question of the teleology of pleasure. In admiring the movement of 'shadows, butterflies and birds', he feels their joy transferred or conducted to him, but towards an 'end' which is mooted briefly before immediately being refuted in favour of perpetual motion across the space of Grasmere:

> I seemed to feel such liberty was mine,
> Such power and joy; but only for this end:
> To flit from field to rock, from rock to field,
> From shore to island, and from isle to shore,
> From open ground to covert, from a bed
> Of meadow-flowers into a tuft of wood,
> From high to low, from low to high, yet still
> Within the bound of this huge concave; here
> Must be my home, this Valley be my World. (35–43)

This repetitive, destination-less movement has been read as 'in essence the same as stasis', 'confinement', a 'psychic predicament', but taking the affirmative argument more literally, we see Wordsworth as playing quite ironically with the idea that his transferred pleasure in the natural world should have any end.[55] Instead of an end to liberty, power and joy, we are presented with an expense of energy purely for the joy it gives. This movement is emphatically bounded, however, in a way that might sound restrictive or repressive, but is perhaps neither, if we follow what Johnston described as the poem's 'centripetal' logic: 'The freedom the boy feels is in fact a process of continual rebounding, because the definition of freedom in Grasmere is freedom to move within set bounds.'[56] Johnston explains this structure in terms of a Romantic question of self and community; yet, the emphasis on binding and pleasure is so strikingly affirmative that it is hard to avoid the feeling that the poet is arguing a more theoretical point.

At stake seems to be a principle of pleasure based on repetition and not egress. A kind of pleasurable energy that would allow the boy to flee the limits of Grasmere might dissipate on its route; it could reach a destination or a purpose, thus making pleasure subordinate to something else; or it could suggest a relationship with lack, because it would represent a transition from a lesser state to a greater, or a greater to a lesser. By binding this energy firmly in Grasmere, Wordsworth is highlighting the self-sufficiency of this automatic delight. This echoes Rousseau's depiction of Clarens: no money must leave the estate; its controlling presence, Wolmar, must be an atheist so that no spiritual lack is admitted into the system. Whilst Wordsworth's poem does not go this far, there is an interesting indecision about whether the poet's happiness *is* ultimately religious:

> Oh, if such silence be not thanks to God
> For what hath been bestowed, then where, where then
> Shall gratitude find rest? Mine eyes did ne'er
> Rest on a lovely object, nor my mind
> Take pleasure in the midst of [happy] thoughts,
> But either She whom now I have, who now
> Divides with me this loved abode, was there
> Or not far off. (102–9)

That crucial word 'rest' is here deployed in a powerfully circular way. Rather than answering the question of whether pleasurable silence *is* a religious thanksgiving, the thought associatively keeps moving with the word 'rest', dislodging it into another context, that of the shared experience of pleasure. We are unsure whether the apparently rhetorical question about worship remains rhetorical, or whether it is undermined by the turn towards human fellowship which provides an alternative, 'proper' answer, or whether the shared experience is meant to confirm and develop the thanksgiving possibility. And, in fact, the 'rest' of this question is continually postponed throughout the sentence by way of the series of conjunctions, 'ne'er, nor, either, or'. The idea of pleasure as being not end-directed but rather a shareable and renewable 'resource' is confirmed by the general impression of feeling in Grasmere. Sensations and emotions in the vale are represented as having a tendency to transfer from one being to another, and to be experienced collectively ('Joy spreads, and sorrow spreads', 664). We often hear that the energy and pleasure of the natural scene is transferred or conducted from the creatures or objects (recurrently the flying birds) to the observer: 'Who could look / And not feel motions there?' (24–5). This emotional movement is at play in the arrival of Emma and the poet in the valley, where the trees, brooks and sunbeams appear to interrogate and then well-wish the human travellers, ending in an intermingled joyful affect: 'They were moved, / All things were moved; they round us as we went, / We in the midst of them' (234–6). As in *The Prelude*, this scene echoes Milton's description of the earth's rejoicing or 'congratulation' when Adam and Eve consummate their love.[57]

The poem also appears to advance a view that there is a 'stream' of pleasure that persists beyond individual subjectivity. This appears in relation to the attempt to understand the place of crime and death in Grasmere: the disturbing idea that a shepherd may have shot the pair of swans with which the poet and Emma identified themselves. This critical thought about a Grasmere inhabitant is itself first represented as a kind of crime, a lack of faith in the perfection of the vale, before the poetic voice reassures himself by way of a strange analogy:

> What if I floated down a pleasant stream
> And now am landed and the motion gone –
> Shall I reprove myself? Ah no, the stream
> Is flowing and will never cease to flow,
> And I shall float upon that stream again. (381–5)

These gnomic lines, almost like something from an ancient philosophical dialogue, suggest the need for a 'faith' *in* pleasure, echoing both 'Lines Written in Early Spring' and *The Prelude*'s admiring account of those who possess 'delight / That fails not' (XIII. 118–19). Pleasure, to which the 'stream' is directly linked by the use of that keyword 'motion', is here elevated into a cosmic force, an impression confirmed by the increasingly religious tone: 'By such forgetfulness the soul becomes – / Words cannot say how beautiful. Then hail!' (386–7). The description of the process as 'forgetfulness' is ambiguous, associating the stream of pleasure with Lethe. It is not quite clear what would be forgotten (the negativity? the self-reproving?), but the overall sense of the lines is that pleasurable ease is a natural state of being, and one in which we must trust.

Some further comparisons may be suggested between Wordsworth's poem and forms of radical naturalism. The distinction between motion and rest that we have been tracing in *Home at Grasmere* is crucial to Spinoza's philosophy of nature; and there are powerfully pantheistic moments in Wordsworth's poem (for instance, the birds move 'As if one spirit was in all and swayed / Their indefatigable flight', 300–1). When Arnold picks up on Wordsworth's stream of being metaphor (citing *The Excursion*'s 'might stream of tendency') he also compares it with the Spinozistic *conatus*. 'That *stream of tendency by which all things seek to fulfil the law of their being*.'[58] Whilst for Spinoza joy is always a good, there is a distinction between the joy that acts on you (a passion), and a joy that arises when a body fully possesses its own power of acting: 'when the mind conceives itself and its power of acting, it rejoices (by P53). But the mind necessarily considers itself when it conceives a true, or adequate, idea (by IIP43). But the mind conceives some adequate ideas (by IIP40S2). Therefore, it also rejoices insofar as it conceives adequate ideas, that is (by P1), insofar as it acts.'[59] As Deleuze paraphrases Spinoza:

The word *blessedness* should be reserved for these active joys: they appear to conquer and extend themselves within duration, like the passive joys, but in fact they are eternal and are no longer explained by duration; they no longer imply transitions and passages, but express themselves and one another in an eternal mode, together with the adequate ideas from which they issue.[60]

This idea of an *adequate* pleasure is useful to think alongside Wordsworth's hyperbolic joy, and it provides a gloss on its circularity, timelessness and self-sufficiency. This image of a maximized pleasure shows up a blind spot in Bataille's aristocratic critique of pleasure and utility. Spinoza's attempts to imagine a kind of joy without desire or loss could hardly be called bourgeois by Bataille (it would be anachronistic for one), and perhaps neither should Wordsworth's. Bataille does not have space for ordinary pleasure in his philosophy; for him, it can only be understood in terms of self-preservation and the bad economy of 'life'. This comes from his reading of Hegel's fable of master and slave: that the master must stay alive though he has staked his life in order to win recognition means that he is really *enslaved* to life, its conservation and its reproduction.[61] Bataille may be a thinker of *jouissance* and eroticism but in his work they always imply death and the dissolution or unbinding of the subject. One might argue that this lets teleology in by the back door; that Wordsworth's *endless* movement of pleasure within a closed system is less teleological than Bataille's blazing flights of eros, which in escaping the 'system' have a certain direction.[62] In any case, Wordsworth's poem demonstrates the inescapable difficulty of determining the meaning of pleasure, and its relation to death and stillness. In this sense, it anticipates the provocation of Freud's theory of the pleasure principle and the death drive: two principles that, as much as he tries to separate them, collapse into one another.[63]

Such speculations also help reframe *Home at Grasmere*'s themes of subjectivity and mastery. It has an odd, sometimes paradoxical, language of lordship: shadows and Angels 'that are Lords / Without restraint of all which they behold'; an 'unappropriated bliss' that has found 'an owner' and a 'Lord'; a happiness that does *not* enable him to 'take possession of the sky' (32–3, 85–7, 278). For David Simpson, the language of ownership may be metaphorical or psychological but inevitably invokes the 'sphere of public language . . . earthly authority and possession of the land'.[64] He adds, '[s]ince Wordsworth did *not* own the vale, such a projection must remain at the level of the imaginary. Indeed it had best remain so, since it is in clear conflict with the cohesive and egalitarian society that the poem postulates for the locality.'[65] Certainly, there is an evident tension; though one that is *overtly* incongruous, hinting at something more knowing than a literalist reading might claim. Wordsworth rebuffs the common economic and political meanings of lordship and possession in several ways. First: in what sense can 'unappropriated bliss' actually *be* owned? Only in a transformed sense of 'enjoyment' – a kind of owning that does not exclude any other owners. The multiplicity of owners and lords is important to the poem; for instance, the elements, insects and angels that are all 'Lords'. Their sheer heterogeneity and multiplicity implies that lordship is not power of the one over all others; *not* the power of Adam to name everything which he sees.[66] Perhaps this underlies Wordsworth's astonishingly hubristic claim that 'among the bowers / Of blissful Eden this was neither given / Nor could be given' (123–5). The 'lordly birds' are the strongest emblems of sovereignty, a power that derives from their self-generating delight and circularity, whose calls recur through the poem, 'Admonishing the man who walks below' (151), and later, a 'reiterated whoop / In manner of a bird that takes delight / In answering to itself' (410–12). Delight thus refines the meaning of mastery. One might read these plays on lordship as trying to delineate a pleasurable power in powerlessness: 'I seemed to feel . . . Such power and joy; but only for this end: / To flit' (35–7). An insight into these lines may be gained from Spinoza's idea of blessedness as a form of sovereign self-activity, and from Bataille's idea that sovereignty, as opposed to mastery, stands for a power that serves no purpose other than itself, and does not need to enslave in order to be realized.[67]

Yet, why can Wordsworth *not* be sovereign as a bird? The poem seems undecided, moving between the claim that in Grasmere he has achieved this intensity of pointless delight and power; and the claim that he has not yet reached it, or cannot. Some of the poem's delicacy and interest resides in the fact that the consummation and joy of which it speaks depends on conviction and trust – 'if sound be my belief' (93), 'this Vale so beautiful / *Begins* to love us!' (268–9), 'confident, enriched at every glance, / The more I see the more is my delight' (716–17). Many readers have looked askance at this occasional wavering, as if to say that Wordsworth is afraid of life's real suffering and negativity (despite Wordsworth's frank engagement with the 'Realities of life' argument, 54–63 – and 'real life' is a theme of 'The Happy Warrior', discussed in Chapter 5). Instead, perhaps we could read it as testament to the complex relation of pleasure to trust and hope, and the increase which each bring to each other. The prosody speaks this, with its strong iambic pentameter sped up with occasional little dactylic inrushes – 'Long is it since we met to part no more' (171); 'Thrice hath the winter Moon been filled with light' (257) – as if to suggest the tremulousness of expectation that resolves into steady calm. And the threat of pain and 'reality' is not evaded: the poet repeatedly argues that Grasmere is not a place free of suffering and nor did he expect it to be, and his two stories of cottagers, later incorporated into *The Excursion*, are meant (perhaps not quite successfully) to acknowledge this. To the Malthusian argument that Nature demands 'Her tribute of inevitable pain' (841), the poet responds with a pragmatic kind of language as if to suggest that it is not a choice of either all misery or all bliss:

> Yet temper this with one *sufficient* hope
> (What need of *more?*): that we shall neither droop
> Nor pine for want of pleasure in the life . . .
> . . . And if this
> Were not, we have *enough* within ourselves,
> *Enough* to fill the present day with joy
> And *overspread* the future years with hope (844–62, my italics)

This language of adequacy and abundance is very important to the poem: 'more' appears some twenty-seven times in MS B. This may seem to some readers to indicate that dreaded bourgeois moderation and economism – worry not, there is plenty of joy saved in the larder – but there may be something modestly philosophical in this language of adequacy. Pleasure, it argues, is not dialectical: not affirmation or negation; absence or presence. Nevertheless, any wavering or pragmatism is suddenly hardened into an unexpected derision of pleasure in favour of duty, just as Bataille predicted:

> But 'tis not to enjoy, for this alone
> That we exist: no, something must be done.

I must not walk in unreproved delight
These narrow bounds and think of nothing more,
No duty that looks further and no care. (874–9)

These lines reverse the sentiment of Wordsworth's 1807 sonnet, 'Nuns Fret Not at their Convent's Narrow Room', which describes how, for one who has 'felt the weight of too much liberty', to be 'bound' might be both pastime and solace.[68] After all the non-teleological language of *Home at Grasmere*, we hear that the poet must find an *end*. It is described in terms of the first *non*-shared affect – 'Possessions have I, wholly, solely mine, / Something within, which yet is shared by none' – a riddling locution, only more perplexing when the poet goes on to declare his desire to 'impart' and 'spread' this unshared thing (897–8).[69] But perhaps this is the nature of a gift; to impart something that no one yet shares. This thing is of course his poetry, which grows into full view in the beautiful cadences of the Verse Prospectus that close the manuscript.

The logic of these final pages in relation to the earlier fantasies is difficult, and Wordsworth's editors suggest that the passage from the self-reproving up to the Verse Prospectus was added in 1806 on Coleridge's return to England, representing 'an abrupt transition to the proper philosophical mode' linked to poems such as 'Ode to Duty', 'Character of the Happy Warrior' and 'Peele Castle'.[70] As we shall consider in the next chapter, Coleridge's anti-hedonism and anti-Epicureanism is registered in tension points in Wordsworth's writing, as is the question of poetic labour in general.[71] Yet, if one does not want to close this question with a biographical answer, we might consider how the reproving of enjoyment is played out. The intervening lines summarize *The Prelude*'s tale of the simultaneous development and coexistence of joys throughout age. First, the poet admits his ongoing (childish) desires for action – 'I wish, / I burn, I struggle' (932–3) – before renouncing them ('farewell to the Warrior's deeds', 953) on the instruction of Nature. Yet, warrior deeds are replaced quickly with a milder ambition: giving utterance to emotions. The Verse Prospectus that follows hardly jettisons 'delight' in favour of a more productive and teleological account of the world; rather, the poet will sing 'Of joy in widest commonalty spread', of 'Paradises and groves / Elysian', and of the fitting of man and world, a key pleasure-metaphor we shall explore in more detail in the 'Preface' documents (968, 996–7).

One reading has been to suggest that Wordsworth's 'crisis' derives from the fact that he can only be a recipient of the bountiful goods of Grasmere – a crisis that can only be resolved by gift exchange, as he prepares to give back his sole possession to the world.[72] This gift language accords closely with the argument presented in this chapter, for how pleasure redefines terms of mastery and ownership. But for Modiano, the poet 'crumbles under the burden of his own gift-giving ambitions ... [and] is again assaulted by fears of death'.[73] For that reading, the circularity of the poem 'becomes a trap, a "hall of mirrors" with no way out'.[74] Rather, the reading here has suggested that this circularity, and even the deliberate play on the desire for deathliness and quietude, is not a delusion but rather an integral part of the poem's attempt to think through the philosophy and sociology of pleasure, and the stress it places upon a non-teleological, non-productive vision of bliss. The intellectual context for this vision is hinted at in an earlier passage, after the poet's description of the transmissible affect that 'swarms' through the vale.

> Nor deem
> These feelings – though subservient more than ours
> To every day's demand for daily bread,
> And borrowing more their spirit and their shape
> From self-respecting interests – deem them not
> Unworthy therefore and unhallowed. No,
> They lift the animal being, do themselves
> By nature's kind and ever present aid
> Refine the selfishness from which they spring (667–75)

This passage shows how aware Wordsworth was of a tradition of thought on pleasure as self-interest, as well as the centrality of ordinary pleasure for his social and philosophical attitudes. It suggests a redefinition of 'self-love' and 'self-interest'. Such ordinary feelings are 'fit associates' of the 'Joy of the highest and the purest minds'; the poet makes it clear that it is *unclear* how one would separate out sensual and transcendental pleasure. 'They blend with it congenially', offering 'health', and are a kind of 'animating thought' which makes labour seem a 'glad function natural to Man' (682–90). There is an essential circularity to this kind of pleasure; self-interest circles around on itself to become something more multitudinous and reciprocal. Pierre Force's study of the doctrine of self-interest shows us how the charge of tautology was often made against claims such as Pascal's that 'we always will what we will'. Augustine wrote that 'being led on by one's will is not much, if one is not also led on by pleasure. What is it to be led on by pleasure? It is finding one's will in God.'[75] These claims have strong parallels in *Home at Grasmere*, though always underscored with epistemological and political doubt, or perhaps simply openness.

CONCLUSION: THE CIRCULARITY OF PLEASURE

This and the previous chapter have shown that a powerful characteristic of Wordsworth's first-decade writing is to generate theories of pleasure in his readers. They have also suggested that philosophical and scientific frameworks seem repeatedly to come short of this 'grand elementary principle' ('Preface', 399–400) of his poetry: a 'principle' both in the sense of proposition and ethical creed. This pattern is strongly evident in *The Prelude*, which repeatedly promises a philosophical classification of delights that is constantly open to revision. We have seen that Wordsworth's use of 'pleasure' often evinces a rhetorical generality and circularity, but that these features are themselves important, because he is interested in the collective (general) dimension of pleasure, as well as in its lack of teleology, and productivity. Critics have seen his use of tautology in a deconstructive vein, showing the inherently supplementary, negative and regressive character of language; instead, this chapter has tried to present it as a deliberate engagement with traditions of thought on pleasure. Although this chapter has focused on work up to 1806, these questions about pleasure as circular 'entrapment' or deeper 'freedom' recur in later writing, for instance in the apparently light piece 'Gold and Silver Fishes, in a Vase' (composed 1829, published 1835). Here, the poet compares the freely moving lark and bee with the goldfishes, who 'in lasting durance pent, / Your silent lives employ / For something more than dull content, / Though haply less than joy' (ll. 5–8). This casual-serious precision about the definition of contentment changes to a more open question about whether in fact there *is* 'joy' and 'meaning' in the 'motions' of the fish, whether they 'with conscious skill / For mutual pleasure glide' (ll. 10–14, 29–30).[76]

The image of an untroubled and non-stimulating bliss reaches back to some of the earliest theories of pleasure in the Greek and Indic traditions.[77] Rousseau and Wordsworth both attempt to formulate a kind of pleasure not founded on lack (or desire, or want), and not involving power, but one that is complete in itself; they represent it in a similar scene of floating on water.[78] For Rousseau, the image comes out of a sense that social life as it stands threatens all genuine pleasure with the constant imagination of alternatives, and the relentless way that competitiveness between individuals undermines any possibility of enjoying what one has. Wordsworth also draws from Rousseau's understanding of how sociality transforms experience, and our tendencies for domination and subjugation, but his play on economic themes suggests that he is also responding to late eighteenth-century political economy, finding ways to talk about pleasure that are not entirely bound up with models of individualism and economic productivity. One can see this even more clearly by way of a later image of calm delight in Adorno's 1951 *Minima Moralia*:

Enjoyment itself would be affected [if mankind were freed from want], just as its present framework is inseparable from operating, planning, having one's way, subjugating. *Rien faire comme une bête*, lying on water and looking peacefully at the sky, 'being, nothing else, without any further definition and fulfilment', might take the place of process, act, satisfaction, and so truly keep the promise of dialectical logic that it would culminate in its origin. None of the abstract concepts comes closer to fulfilled utopia than that of eternal peace.[79]

For Adorno, this image is motivated by an attempt to think of an 'emancipated society' not as the maximization of 'human possibilities and the richness of life' but one precisely freed from production, the 'blind fury of activity', even creativity: those desiderata which may be seen as historical aspects of the 'bourgeois outlook'.[80] Adorno's notoriously 'ascetic' views of the experience of art in *Aesthetic Theory*, including his stress on dissonance and difficulty, have recently been reconsidered by Ross Wilson, who finds a dialectical conception of the relation of asceticism and voluptuousness running through various of his works: aesthetic, philosophical and social-theoretical. As Wilson notes, this of course has a negative-utopian element: '[i]n its attachment to material things, materialism both conforms to currently prevailing conditions and raises its gaze beyond them to a world in which material desires would finally be fulfilled'.[81] Adorno's emphasis on the double or dialectical nature of pleasure finds a new lineage in the eighteenth-century philosophy and poetry described in this book.

The question of Wordsworth's notion of a 'pure' pleasure remains: is it something pre-reflective, pre-sexual, pre-relational, almost pre-experiential? Is it akin to the Kantian *sensus communis* that we considered in the first chapter, a kind of feeling of attunement and universality that must be in place before we can think at all? And, once again, how do we get from here to the 'real' world? Before seeing how Wordsworth tries to do this in a new language of 'happiness' in *The Excursion*, the most anthropological and social-reform oriented of his works, we might briefly consider Sebastiano Timpanaro's idea of pessimistic hedonism, elaborated in relation to the Italian poet Leopardi. Like Adorno, Timpanaro is interested in the limit-point of Marx's utopianism and particularly in how we can envisage the role of 'nature' in relation to the happiness promised by freedom from oppression.[82] Drawing on Rousseau, though also unintentionally echoing Wordsworth's lament in 'Early Spring', Timpanaro points out how 'nature is "good" in contrast to a repressive and ascetic education or a progress which perpetually creates new false needs in us', yet is also a cruel stepmother who thrusts sickness, old age and death in the way of our happiness: a cruelty for which the means of production cannot be held entirely responsible.[83] Timpanaro's attention to the false consolation of a spiritualized pessimism, the 'mystical desire for annihilation', also echoes Wordsworth's suspicion of the idealization of 'a universe of death / The falsest of all worlds' (XIII. 141–2). Hedonistic pessimism recognizes man's need for happiness in this world, which Timpanaro wants to give the 'full, strong sense' it had in the eighteenth century, as 'a need which, though it could never be fully satisfied, was nonetheless impossible to suppress'.[84] In *The Prelude*, Wordsworth writes measuredly, perhaps guardedly, of the geography of political action, which takes place:

> Not in Utopia – subterraneous fields,
> Or some secreted island, heaven knows where
> But in the very world which is the world
> Of all of us, the place in which, in the end,
> We find our happiness, or not at all. (x. 723–7)

That quietly searing final clause, 'or not at all', leaves the idea, and possibility, of happiness an open question. As Keston Sutherland has recently shown, in a closer-than-close reading of the manuscript revisions of those final lines in relation to the theme of 'doubt', one of the ways in which Wordsworth's use of 'our happiness' here differs from common eighteenth-century usage is that 'it irresistibly connotes the possibility that our happiness is *somewhere* in the way that places, people and real, physical objects are'.[85] This is an intellectual temptation that well describes *The Excursion*'s project and its attempt to locate happiness not in the abstract commonality of *The Prelude* that stands behind the inter-subjective self, but in and through a dramatized actual community, of encounters, conversations and life-narratives. This is worked through in the framework of the term 'happiness', a term that, as we shall see, puts pleasure to work in a political and social narrative.

CHAPTER 5

The politics of happiness in The Excursion

THE HAPPINESS OF THE HAPPY WARRIOR

> Who is the happy Warrior? Who is he
> Whom every Man in arms should wish to be?
> – It is the generous Spirit, who, when brought
> Among the tasks of real life, hath wrought
> Upon the plan that pleased his childish thought:
> Whose high endeavours are an inward light
> That make the path before him always bright:
> Who, with a natural instinct to discern
> What knowledge can perform, is diligent to learn;
> Abides by this resolve, and stops not there,
> But makes his moral being his prime care;
> Who, doom'd to go in company with Pain,
> And Fear, and Bloodshed, miserable train!
> Turns his necessity to glorious gain;
> In face of these doth exercise a power
> Which is our human-nature's highest dower;
> Controls them and subdues, transmutes, bereaves
> Of their bad influence, and their good receives;
> By objects, which might force the soul to abate
> Her feeling, rendered more compassionate;
> Is placable because occasions rise
> So often that demand such sacrifice;
> More skilful in self-knowledge, even more pure,
> As tempted more; more able to endure,
> As more expos'd to suffering and distress;
> Thence, also, more alive to tenderness.[1]

At first glance, it is hard to believe that 'Character of the Happy Warrior' was composed only a little after the thirteen-book *Prelude* and *Home at Grasmere*, in winter 1805–6, and published with 'Stray Pleasures' in 1807's *Poems, in Two Volumes*. Nothing could be further from the utopian images of non-productive bliss and inter-affective subjectivity traced in the preceding chapter than this relentless image of military happiness. The poem describes a person and a life (of tasks, plans, resolve and sacrifice) completely at odds with the persona (full of doubts, unfinished tasks and quiet joyful passivity) of *The Prelude*. Rather than the 'grand elementary principle of pleasure' said to define human action and being in the 'Preface' (399–400), the Happy Warrior's 'law is reason ... the best of friends'; in place of the unowned, infinitely shared delights of *The Prelude*, it is said of the Warrior that he 'in himself possess his own desire' (27–8, 38). The Warrior's movements, unlike the unending circularity of the birds and poet in *Home at Grasmere*, are perfectly directional: he 'keeps faithful with a singleness of aim' (40), will never be betrayed by 'thought of tender happiness' (73) and,

> Who, not content that former worth stand fast,
> Looks forward, persevering to the last,
> From well to better, daily self-surpast (74–6)

There is no talk here of perfect complacency or congratulation, but only restless redefinition. Finally, instead of the breathing which forms a powerful image of non-teleological delight in sensual existence in *The Prelude* and *Home at Grasmere*, the Happy Warrior 'draws / His breath in confidence of Heaven's applause' (82–3).

Critical attention to 'The Happy Warrior' has been scant, and has primarily focused on its connection to a clutch of poems in which Wordsworth memorialized his brother John after his drowning off the *Earl of Abergavenny* in 1805.[2] Wordsworth's Note in *Poems, in Two Volumes* states that it was inspired by the death of Lord Nelson the same year.[3] Richard Matlak has shown that George Beaumont encouraged Wordsworth to frame the poem in this way, ostensibly to gain more public attention for the (implicit) elegy to John; Matlak reads the poem as a site of tension over Nelson's and John's differing public reputations.[4] Despite a critical drubbing for its 'monotonous' couplets and 'generalized vocabulary', carrying 'no tradition or voice that is alive', the poem has survived in two contexts under the literary-critical radar: military culture and, perhaps more oddly, virtue ethics.[5] The term 'Happy Warrior' appears to have been coined by Wordsworth (*OED*), but has later uses in the contexts of war and politics; a library catalogue search reveals it to be a highly popular title for biographies of statesmen and generals from the late nineteenth century onwards. Perhaps this popularity stems from the purported circulation of the poem amongst troops in the Crimea; one can also imagine glum Victorian schoolboys reciting those heroic couplets.[6] William Hazlitt mentioned the 'Happy Warrior' briefly in his 1821 essay on heroism:

> A soldier is a perfect hero but that he is a mere machine. He is drilled into disinterestedness, and beaten into courage. He is a very patriotic and romantic automaton. He has lost all regard for himself and concern for others. His life, his limbs, his soul and body, are obedient only to the word of command . . . from the madman to Mr Wordsworth's 'Happy Warrior' there is but one step.[7]

According to Hazlitt, the modern soldier has the appearance of heroism in his disinterestedness and willingness to sacrifice life, but in an age of Epicurean philosophy, what has been lost is the 'blind attachment to individuals or to principles', even old-fashioned prejudice and good hating, which make martyrdom heroic.[8] Hazlitt's essay implicitly argues that the progressive attack on religion encouraged by 'a sceptical, dispassionate, Epicurean work, like Bayle's *Dictionary* or Hume's *Essays*, has created two deplorable anti-types: those sensitive, sensual, life-protecting, interested individuals (for example the weeping female consumer of novels he describes), and those who perform disinterestedness mechanically as duty.[9] There are only two options: bodily self-interest and disinterested mechanism – unless you are the ideologue and good hater Hazlitt – and Wordsworth's poem, squaring a blandly perfect performance of one's tasks without any specific idea at stake, represents the weak, modern incarnation of those wild-eyed fanatics that Hazlitt cannot help but admire.

The fact that Hazlitt contextualizes the poem within Epicureanism and ideas about self-interest is one incentive to investigate the 'happiness' of the Warrior. In so doing, the poem begins to look like a reflection on the history of conceptions of positive affect. Both J.L. Austin and Martha Nussbaum after him used 'Character of the Happy Warrior' to emphasize the gap between Aristotelian *eudaimonia* and a simple utilitarian picture of pleasure. Austin wrote sarcastically, 'I do not think Wordsworth meant . . . "This is the warrior who feels pleased."'[10] In various essays critiquing Bentham's pleasure-based account of happiness, Nussbaum uses the poem to highlight the alternative 'English tradition concerning happiness that Wordsworth's poem embodied':[11]

> As Austin saw, the important thing about the happy Warrior is that he has traits that make him capable of performing all of life's many activities in an exemplary way, and that he acts in accordance with those traits. He is moderate, kind, courageous, loving, a good friend, concerned for the community, honest, not

excessively attached to honor or worldly ambition, a lover of reason, an equal lover of home and family.[12]

Nussbaum's emphasis on the Warrior's successful 'performance' at life could more sceptically be regarded as a version of what Adorno called the 'blind fury of activity' and the maximization of 'human possibilities' in bourgeois, economically 'productive' models of happiness.[13] Nussbaum's reading is, of course, anchored in Greek philosophy. Aristotle's notion of *eudaimonia*, usually translated as happiness or flourishing, is a rather obscure concept expressing striving and activity, in accordance with a sense of the purpose of one's life as a whole. Aristotle called it 'the active exercise of his soul's faculties in conformity with excellence or virtue'; and pointed out that 'to be happy takes a complete lifetime'.[14] One of the chief ways to frame the difference between *eudaimonia* and utilitarian conceptions of happiness-as-pleasure is by teleology. For Aristotle, *eudaimonia* concerns not only the narrative of a man's whole life, but the teleology of man as a member of a species: how he achieves the fullest flourishing that is his natural and social destiny. In the words of one critic, happiness is theoretical: 'the actions of life as a whole are only done well, not through subjection to, or knowledge of, a strict *techne*, but through the ongoing creation and reassessment of one's happiness or *eudaimonia*. Happiness and *theoria* are mutually defined.'[15] Yet, Jonathan Lear has suggested that there is an intrinsic disturbance in the teleology of *eudaimonia*. He calls happiness in the *Nicomachean Ethics* 'an enigmatic signifier', which seduces us (in the psychoanalytic sense), captivating us with unconscious messages like those a parent transmits to a child. Unhappily, he observes, the *Ethics* suggest that most people are not and will never be happy, that even the elite, leading an ethically virtuous life, achieve only a second-rate happiness, and that an inactive contemplative life is the most happy, but only achievable for brief periods if at all:

Thus by injecting happiness as the organizing goal of human teleology Aristotle manages to disrupt the teleological structure itself. For he has made it virtually impossible for humans to fulfil their nature. Although the teleological worldview is used to give content to what happiness consists in, once the picture is filled out it puts pressure on the teleological worldview itself.[16]

Lear argues that in fact the 'enigmatic signifier' of happiness serves to 'promote discontent and valorize death'.[17] Is this one way to understand what seems most odd to modern eyes in Wordsworth's poem: the cheerful violence of the man who, in the 'heat of conflict', is 'happy as a Lover' (53, 51)?

The poem insists that a well-lived, happy life is by definition laced with suffering. '*Tender* happiness' risks distracting the Warrior, but this warlike happiness feeds off the violence around it: 'doom'd to go in company with Pain, / And Fear, and Bloodshed, miserable train! / Turns his necessity to glorious gain' (12–14). And yet at times the poem echoes *The Prelude*'s language of transmuting pain and unsympathetic objects into sympathetic joy, as if the Warrior was one of those 'higher minds' described at the poem's climax. He also exhibits aesthetic and hedonistic sensibilities, furnished with memories for times of struggle:

> a Soul whose master-bias leans
> To homefelt pleasures and to gentle scenes;
> Sweet images! which, wheresoe'er he be,
> Are at his heart. (59–62)

Hazlitt's logic suggests that there is no paradox in this poem's blend of violent and hedonist traits; modern religious scepticism has made it inevitable by vitiating the possibility of real ideals. Whilst Hazlitt's comments make the poem emblematic of modernity, one may also situate it within an older tradition: the *beatus ille* theme ('Happy is he who . . .') which has both Greek (*makarismos*) and Hebrew (*ashrei*) antecedents, and is familiar from Psalms ('Blessed is he who . . .'). The most influential literary *beatus ille* text is probably Horace's Second Epode singing the joys of rural obscurity, which, in Dryden's translation, begins:

> How happy in his low degree,
> How rich in humble poverty, is he,
> Who leads a quiet country life!
> Discharged of business, void of strife,
> And from the griping scrivener free.[18]

Although there is an obvious dissonance between this 'country life' and the battle where Wordsworth's poem begins, there are many common features, particularly the theme of self-possession and the simple domestic life to which the Warrior returns. Formally, Wordsworth's interrogative structure and the use of balanced heroic couplets also suggest a connection, though the didactic, almost catechistic progression of the work is slightly unsettled by Wordsworth's use of fricative relative pronouns (Who, Whom, Whose), setting off a slightly ghostly, whispering echo throughout in the alliteration with the keywords 'warrior' and 'wish'. The central motifs of the *beatus ille* tradition – and its philosophical questioning of pleasure and happiness – are also woven through Wordsworth's long poem *The Excursion*, the subject of the remainder of this chapter.[19]

'THE EXCURSION'

Like the 'Happy Warrior', *The Excursion* is concerned with how to define a happy life, and, like that work, it places the philosophical treatment of affect within a public and national context, also faintly traced with death. John Barrell reminds us of the layers of meaning in the word 'excursion', from ex-cursus, a running out, escape from confinement; drawn from military campaigns and fortification, it dramatizes struggle, though it also suggests a journey with the explicit intention of returning.[20] *The Excursion* was completed just as Napoleon's defeat was announced in April 1814, and to some extent it attempts to voice historical optimism. In the raising of its central character 'The Solitary' from despondency to gladness, it purports to cheer and invigorate a disenchanted, depoliticized generation still stinging from the moral failure of the French Revolution two decades previously. To *some* extent, generations of readers have responded very differently and drawn from it a wide range of political interpretations, and, as I aim to show, the theme of happiness within the poem is not the least part of this problem. Many memorable early reactions showed the poem's troubling nature, from Hazlitt's comments on its 'overwhelming, oppressive power', Francis Jeffrey's 'This will never do!' and Mary Shelley's neat 'much disappointed. He is a slave.'[21] As Philip Connell has elucidated, after the initial dislike and hesitation, the poem was viewed as primarily concerned with religious crisis, and then from the 1870s began to be read in secular and social terms, ultimately as prophetic of the impact of industrialization. Read as evincing Wordsworth's mature political position, *The Excursion* has variously been taken as 'a demonstration of the author's political apostasy, a vindication of his enduring radical sympathies, and even as the literary manifesto of an English "environmental tradition"'.[22] Connell finds some truth in all these versions of the Lake Poets' careers and *The Excursion* itself: still committed to 'radical' agrarian virtue, newly trying to accommodate with liberal Toryism, supporting commerce and strongly interested in Malthusian proposals for popular education, the later identifiable with both radical and 'liberal-conservative' positions.[23]

Focusing on the poem's treatment of pleasure and happiness lends support to this modern view of the mixed political inclinations of Wordsworth's thought in the second decade of the nineteenth century. At the same time, it encourages us to think about *The Excursion* as existing both within its time and its politics (the modern, historicist take), and as insightful with respect to a longer philosophical framework (the Victorian, spiritual take), because the theme of pleasure was then, as it is now, alive in social thought. Coleridge's demand, in his letter of 1798, that Wordsworth's *Recluse* should serve an anti-Epicurean purpose in response to the despondency following the French Revolution, helps justify a view of *The Excursion* as deeply involved with the intellectual history of pleasure, as well as its early nineteenth-century politicization. The poem may be seen as reformulating the utopian possibilities of the 'bliss' of 'that dawn' described in the Revolution books of *The Prelude* (x. 692–3), the brimming hope shared by ordinary people that led Saint-Just to declare to the National Convention that 'Le bonheur est une idée neuve en Europe.'[24] Žižek glosses this as establishing 'happiness as a political factor', and as 'a radical renunciation of the decadent pleasures of the *ancien régime*'.[25] Happiness, in this reading, is the egalitarian and ascetic alternative to the sickly aristocratic factors of enjoyment and pleasure, ciphers of luxury and social and economic inequality. I would contend that 'happiness' *is* a political factor in *The Excursion*, though what I see as Wordsworth's own 'happiness turn' does not exactly mirror Žižek's model of radical renunciation. One could say that *The Excursion* takes the still, circular and passive pleasures in *The Prelude* and *Home at Grasmere* and tries to lend them some direction: instead of stopping stock-still in Grasmere's perfect peace, the Wanderer takes the road.

One model for a revolutionary, *moving* and crucially labour-based image of happiness in the poem is that furnished by *Paradise Lost*. Milton's epic was invoked in the 'Verse Prospectus' and Charles Lamb first recognized how it underlay *The Excursion*'s project.[26] Stuart Peterfreund observed that *The Excursion* precisely reverses the movement of the final lines of *Paradise Lost*.[27] As Milton's poem takes its human protagonists from Eden to a 'parched' plain and 'torrid heat',[28] so Wordsworth's counter-current is from a hot plain ('Across a bare wide Common I was toiling / With languid feet', I. 21–2) to a beautiful valley in which one might think, as the Pastor claims, 'That Paradise, the lost abode of man, / Was raised again' (IX. 714–15). Peterfreund focuses on the parallels between the Wanderer and the archangel Michael, and between the Pastor and Raphael. But a further set of parallels can be found between both poems' investment in the question of post-revolutionary optimism. Milton's poem meditates on the ambiguous nature of human pleasure; representing both the perfection of pre-lapsarian existence and the Serpent's promise alongside Eve's sensual weakness. Happiness has two faces: that bestowed by God, and that which man and woman can forge for themselves in a fallen world. Desire, exemplified by Satan, represents lack and discontent; Satan's inability to enjoy finally spurs him on to the temptation of Eve, 'Envying our happiness and of his own / Despairing.'[29] In Milton's Eden, where Adam and Eve find themselves placed 'In all this happiness', there are no seasons but spring, and just a little horticulture, which only enhances pleasure: 'no more toil / Of sweet gard'ning labour than sufficed / To recommend cool Zephyr, and made ease / More easy.'[30] After the Fall, Adam rebukes Eve's suicidal urge as a sign merely of 'life and pleasure overloved', and promises instead the more limited possibility of a laborious happiness.[31] She will suffer pains of childbirth but they will be 'recompensed with joy'; as for man, 'with labour I must earn / My bread; what harm? Idleness had been worse; / My labour will sustain me.'[32] Further, they will learn to shelter themselves with God's instruction so to have a life passed 'commodiously', 'with many comforts', until the final rest of death.[33] The very last lines of *Paradise Lost* see Adam and Eve setting out to choose 'Their place of rest': 'with wand'ring steps and slow, / Through Eden took their solitary way.'[34]

Wordsworth's *Excursion* takes up the same images, of wandering and solitariness in seeking a place of rest, and the shaping of compromised contentment in a fallen world. He and Milton represent work, human relationship and home-making as the means of an ordinary happiness on this earth, as opposed to an unearthly, paradisiacal bliss. Labour is a consistent emphasis in *The Excursion*'s stories of the villagers and their lifelong 'work' of happiness. They are prefaced with a living example of a poor couple dwelling high in the mountains whose labours 'beguile' time: 'intermingled work of house and field . . . sufficient to maintain / Even at the worst, a smooth stream of content' (v. 710–14). This smooth stream recalls the argument of *Home at Grasmere* for a stream of pleasure that persists beyond the vagaries of daily accident. Yet here, rather than being a natural blessing, the stream is maintained through labour; a model of happiness that emerges partly from the Protestant tradition.[35] As Darrin McMahon has argued, Luther attacked 'the privileged place of suffering in the Christian tradition', affirming that 'All sadness is from Satan.' Whilst Protestantism 'saddled human beings with a renewed awareness of their dependence and sin', it also 'set men and women free to search for happiness on the hallowed ground of God's creation'.[36] *The Excursion*'s model of happiness as an artful work or *skill* of managing pleasures and needs is also linked to agrarian virtue. In *The Prelude*, the self-sufficiency and daily labour of the shepherd was a powerful image of both heroism and an 'index of delight' (VIII. 415); his serenity and self-possession is a key aspect of the *beatus ille* trope, drawing from Lucretius, Horace and

Virgil.[37] In *The Excursion*, we hear of the young shepherd who 'Can portion out his pleasures, and adapt, / His round of pastoral duties' (IV. 800–1). His 'experience' and 'knowledge' aid him to know his precise needs and how to answer them (IV. 807–11), constituting him as one who 'breathes / For noble purposes of mind', whose 'heart / Beats to the heroic song of ancient days' (IV. 826–8). This is a subtly different kind of 'heroism' – a virtuous *souci de soi*, or care of the self – from that which was witnessed in 'Character of the Happy Warrior'.

The difference between Wordsworth and Coleridge's philosophical reference points on the themes of happiness and pleasure further illuminates *The Excursion*. In his *Philosophical Lectures*, Coleridge stressed how blessedness, which the 'ancients' called *ataraxia* or *eudaimonia*, stems from 'having been born in such an hour and climate under such and such a circumstances'.[38] This focus on circumstance rather than work is even more strongly brought out in Coleridge's *Opus Maximum* (c. 1819–23) where happiness must be distinguished from willed action and achievements, preserving a quasi-Kantian account of morals. There, happiness is 'the aggregate of fortunate chances; but our birth, wealth, person, natural talents, opportunities of cultivating them, health, country . . . are all prizes in the lottery of life'.[39] As Thomas McFarland has shown, Coleridge's writing was riven by a consistent, nearly obsessional anti-Epicureanism that also informed his interactions with Wordsworth over the meaning of *The Recluse* and, particularly, the status of pleasure within it.[40] Coleridge wrote to Wordsworth around 1799 to urge on the composition of *The Recluse*, imagining it as an anti-Epicurean corrective:

My dear friend, I do entreat you go on with 'The Recluse'; and I wish you would write a poem, in blank verse, addressed to those, who, in consequence of the complete failure of the French Revolution have thrown up all hopes of the amelioration of mankind, and are sinking into an almost epicurean selfishness, disguising the same under the soft titles of domestic attachment and contempt for visionary *philosophes*. It would do great good.[41]

Coleridge's letter (like Hazlitt's heroism essay) represents Epicureanism as a default intellectual position for those fleeing political engagement; a soft and lazy alternative to visionary political thinking.[42] Verbal echoes of Coleridge's letter reappear all over Wordsworth's poetry, and he drew directly from it in the rhetorical climax of the energetic first draft of the 'poem to Coleridge':

> If, 'mid indifference and apathy
> And wicked exultation, when good men

> On every side fall off we know not how
> To selfishness, disguised in gentle names
> Of peace and quiet and domestic love –
> Yet mingled, not unwillingly, with sneers
> On visionary minds – if, in this time
> Of dereliction and dismay, I yet
> Despair not of our nature, but retain
> A more than Roman confidence, a faith
> That fails not, in all sorrow my support,
> The blessing of my life, the gift is yours
> Ye mountains, thine, O Nature. Thou hast fed
> My lofty speculations, and in thee
> For this uneasy heart of ours I find
> A never-failing principle of joy
> And purest passion. (1799, II. 480–96; retained in the
>   1805 and 1850 versions)

Though there are some word-for-word borrowings, the poet's refusal of an equation between Epicureanism and selfishness subtly alters Coleridge's letter. Perhaps this is why his principle is 'more than Roman', i.e. exceeding Stoicism, despite the long-recognized significance of Stoicism to *The Excursion*.[43] These *Prelude* lines provide a gloss on *The Excursion*'s main narrative of the Solitary's despondency and correction: 'good men' becoming selfishly withdrawn and intellectually cynical, to be answered by Nature's pleasure principle. The Wanderer's Christian-Stoic admonition against the Solitary again almost ventriloquizes Coleridge:

> For who could sink and settle to that point
> Of selfishness; so senseless who could be
> In framing estimates of loss and gain,
> As long and perseveringly to mourn
> For any Object of his love, removed
> From this unstable world, if he could fix
> A satisfying view upon that state
> Of pure, imperishable blessedness (IV. 59)

But what sounds like an exhortation to look beyond human experience to Heaven is complicated by the Wanderer's warning that despising 'Earth' and renouncing happiness is the 'easy' path (IV. 130–1). Coleridge says something like this in 'Dejection: An Ode', where suffering and joylessness has become 'the habit of [his] soul', but 'sensual' is still a term beyond the intellectual pale.[44] *The Excursion* on the other hand counterposes and weaves together Stoic, Christian *and* Epicurean themes of pleasure and happiness.

The Excursion grants a certain authority to a Stoic definition of happiness residing in conformity with nature; yet, the poem raises questions over man's relationship to natural cheer, and the way in which contingency and material conditions underlie the potential for happiness. Other characters defend a position of Epicurean withdrawal through a complex analogy with asceticism, which offers a subtle critique of contemporary attitudes.

'Steady' is one of the key markers for Stoicism in Wordsworth's writing, used to effect in the aspiration of the 'Preface' to the *Lyrical Ballads* to look 'steadily'. The need to approach suffering with equanimity is raised in the prologue to *The Excursion*, in the Verse Prospectus, where the witnessing of 'ill sights', 'solitary anguish' and a 'storm of sorrow' will not, the poet prays, make him 'downcast or forlorn' (74–81). The development of this capacity is also said to be the beneficial purpose of the epitaphs of Books 6 and 7, 'words of heartfelt truth, / Tending to patience when Affliction strikes' (VII. 1074–5). The Wanderer is steadfast against passion: 'In his steady course, / No piteous revolutions had he felt, / No wild varieties of joy and grief' (I. 387–9). His undoubted authority in the poem seems to derive partly from the military and masculine associations of the Stoic hero (archetypally, Marcus Aurelius). The 'dissolution' described by Shaftesbury, and the happiness of the one who can confront it, appears in the powerful vignette of the Ruined Cottage. Time has passed, and it is covered with weeds, grass, 'silvered' in rain; it is 'an image of tranquillity', which makes our 'sorrow and despair' at time's ruination appear merely 'an idle dream' which cannot keep hold over the 'enlightened spirit'. The fluid, melting imagery and syntax of fourteen lines receives a brisk and emotionally dissonant summation: 'I turned away, / And walked along my road in happiness (I. 972–84).[45] As David Simpson has it: 'It is not in itself shocking that a man of faith should find a way of coming to terms with the miseries in the world; but Wordsworth elects to work up this acceptance into what is almost a language of pleasure.'[46] But on a Stoic account, it is important that the term is 'happiness' and not pleasure: *hedone* is (with sorrow, desire and fear) one of the passions and affections that aim at external objects, obstructing virtuous self-sufficiency. Sympathy, friendship and love are meaningful as large-scale universal principles, but not in specific instances, where they risk disturbing calm. The sufferings of others are of limited importance, because they are irrelevant to one's own virtue and thus one's happiness.[47]

The Wanderer's 'happiness' may be read in terms of this absolute acceptance of the law of nature, and the refusal to be bound by the experiences of others. The aesthetic experience of nature gives the Wanderer a moment of insight, the *phronesis* described by Diogenes Laertius: knowledge of what is good and evil and what is neither good nor evil, through which the Wanderer recalls that passions are an 'idle dream'. Free of the binding impact of particular relationships, the Wanderer experiences a Marcus Aurelius-like universal sympathy:[48]

> by Nature tuned
> And constant disposition of his thoughts
> To sympathy with Man, he was alive
> To all that was enjoyed where'er he went,
> And all that was endured; for, in himself
> Happy, and quiet in his cheerfulness,
> He had no painful pressure from without
> That made him turn aside from wretchedness
> With coward fears. He could *afford* to suffer
> With those whom he saw suffer. (1. 391–400)

These final lines slightly revise the description of the Wanderer's Stoic self-sufficiency, setting the achievement of this 'Happy' calm within specific enabling conditions: a procedure of the poem as a whole, which sets big philosophies alongside social and historical circumstance. Wordsworth takes special pains to delineate the Wanderer's background. There are certain overlaps with *The Prelude* poet, in the natural education in 'heavy' pleasures ('they lay / Upon his mind like substances, whose presence / Perplexed the bodily sense', 1. 137–9) and a grateful existence. But the Wanderer's solitude is far more intense than that of *The Prelude* boy. He grew up in a poor, pious and excessively strict family and learnt to take enjoyment in nature, but always 'in solitude and solitary thought', 'unvexed, unwarped / By partial bondage' (1. 383–7). Not everyone can steer clear of 'partial bondage', as the contrast with Margaret makes clear. Margaret is first introduced as possessing a 'steady mind': 'framed' as one who '[m]ight live on earth a life of happiness' (1. 544–50). That she was constitutionally or temperamentally set up to be happy but was thwarted by material and political conditions is part of what we could call the poem's realism. 'Two blighting seasons' and 'the plague of war' strike down a 'happy Land' (1. 568–71). The Wanderer can '*afford* to suffer' but artisans with 'wives and children' (1. 592) and a need for daily bread cannot merely float above the *adiaphora*, indifferent things of this world.

The question of nature places further pressure on a Stoic conception of happiness. Ever-virtuous, the Wanderer calls off his tale of Margaret's suffering, adverting to its inappropriateness at the hot noonday when 'all things' are either at 'rest' or are 'cheerful' (I. 625–6). 'Why,' he asks, should we turn away from 'natural wisdom' and 'natural comfort', and 'thus disturb / The calm of nature with our restless thoughts?' (I. 629–34). These lines seem to express a distinction between the happy, unreflecting immediacy of natural existence, and the unhappy, mediated reflexivity of rational man. Later, the Solitary demands to know if the epitaphs can show any achievement of happiness better than the limit-case of a cow's contentment: 'to graze the herb in thoughtless peace, / By foresight, or remembrance, undisturbed!' (v. 325–6). The dismissal of bovine happiness stretches back at least to Aristotle: 'The utter servility of the masses comes out in their preference for a bovine existence [the life of enjoyment]' – and forward to Nietzsche.[49] Reflective, melancholy men, anchored in time and memory, wrote Nietzsche, 'cannot help envying them [cattle] their happiness', in lines that also evoke Keats' 'Ode to a Nightingale'.[50] Nietzsche argued that happiness is 'the ability to forget or, expressed in more scholarly fashion, the capacity to feel *unhistorically* during its duration'.[51] The man who cannot forget will not only be unable to experience happiness, but 'he will never do anything to make others happy'; thus, culture's act of 'forgetting' is necessary to morality.[52] The Solitary is unable to forget his painful past, and this has moral resonances: he must be taught to do so (as the Wanderer can forget the ruined cottage) in order to get somewhere and to do some good.

Yet as we have seen in 'Lines Written in Early Spring', animal immediacy – the generality of positive affect amongst animals and plants – cannot always provide a simple opposition to human unhappiness. Whilst *The Excursion* raises a set of ideas, or fantasies, about happiness as a creaturely, natural and even inhuman state of existence, the verse also subtly undermines such a split between pure unmediated natural cheer and rational unhappy consciousness. The Wanderer initially claimed that instead of experiencing sad thoughts, one should be like the cheerful things, like the 'multitude of flies' whose sound fills the air; but the strange effect of the imagery is to link the flies (which feed noisily if happily on dead matter) with the sad notions, that 'feeding on disquiet, thus disturb / The calm of nature with our restless thoughts' (I. 633–4). The Poet's own natural being is disturbed by the Wanderer's tale of Margaret: 'a heart-felt chillness in my veins' (I. 649) displaces the warm summer day, and his hunger for the story means he suddenly finds ordinary conversation 'tasteless'. On the Poet's insistence that he continue, the Wanderer revises his idea that sad thoughts are merely destructive, arguing that in 'mournful thoughts' there is a 'future good' and a 'power to virtue friendly' (I. 662–5). Sadness cannot just be erased in conformity with cheerful nature; it must be told; narratives must keep moving forwards, or the poem will come to a standstill.

This is a distinctive feature of a long narrative poem that is supposedly about 'retirement' and the associated philosophies of pleasure. In Book III, the Poet deliberately provokes the Solitary by attacking a 'Philosophy', personified as 'timid', 'reserved', 'inert', 'weak' and 'tame' (III. 344–52), who

> Did place, in flowery Gardens curtained round
> With world-excluding groves, the Brotherhood
> Of soft Epicureans, taught – if they
> The ends of being would secure, and win
> The crown of wisdom – to yield up their souls
> To a voluptuous unconcern, preferring
> Tranquillity to all things. (III. 350–9)

This very long verse sentence contains an abundance of breaks and interruptions: parentheses which themselves contain a list, and the separation of the main verbs 'placed' and 'taught' from their objects, 'Brotherhood' and 'to yield'. This prosody suggests staginess and sophistry; the Solitary's response, by contrast, is melodic in its impassioned eloquence. He offers a subtle, yet spirited, vindication of the Epicurean project of gaining peace: 'mortal life's chief good / And only reasonable felicity' (III. 372–3). Our 'longing' for 'tranquillity' and 'repose' is, as Epicureans argued, a 'universal instinct' (III. 404–5). Somewhat surprisingly, the Solitary draws a comparison with the hermits and anchorites of early Christianity, arguing that their ascetic withdrawal must not be misconstrued by moderns as a mere flight from worse pains in the real world, such as persecution, guilt, pride and betrayal, but rather as a clear choice of one who:

> ... compassed round by pleasure, sighed
> For independent happiness; craving peace,
> The central feeling of all happiness,
> Not as a refuge from distress or pain,
> A breathing-time, vacation, or a truce,
> But for its absolute self (III. 387–91)[53]

Here, this positive peace in its own right recalls the images of rest and self-sufficiency explored in *Home at Grasmere* and *The Prelude*, and again invites comparisons with Rousseau's scene of a-temporal bliss, 'precious *far niente*', at Lake Bienne: 'a sufficient, complete and perfect happiness which leaves no emptiness to be filled in the soul'.[54] In both this ideal and in his isolated and paranoid earlier state, the Solitary might start to look like a cipher for Rousseau. Through its ambiguous treatment of the Solitary's 'correction', the poem may seem at times to plead for Rousseau's counterfactual return to the public-political sphere, and at other moments, to offer a quiet defence of the utopian principles and the forms of selfhood traced in his late work.

The poem's dialogue between different views of happiness and pleasure also enlists the ideas we saw in 'The Happy Warrior', and problematizes the heroic definition of life given by the shorter poem. Through the Solitary's criticism of the misguided violence of youth, *The Excursion* falls more in line with *Home at Grasmere*'s idea that the Realities of Life may not be defined by toughness and suffering (*Home at Grasmere*, 54–63). In justifying his current beliefs in peace and retirement, the Solitary describes how as 'a forward Youth', he was 'ever prone / To overweening faith', 'inflamed, / By courage, to demand from real life / The test of act and suffering', with 'dreadful' result (III. 421–5). The terms echo the Happy Warrior's 'tasks of real life' and 'suffering', and the belief that he is 'more able to endure, / As more exposed to suffering and distress' (ll. 4, 24–5). In rejecting this image of striving and self-exceeding, the Solitary seems to speak against the Happy Warrior's idea that we can recuperate suffering to good. It is important that he characterizes this as a kind of 'faith': faith in *The Excursion* usually means the Wanderer's general religion of Providence and Nature. Here, 'overweening faith', a kind of oxymoron, implies a misguided belief in negation which is as false as a misguided belief in harmony. It finds its parallel in *The Prelude*'s attack on the belief in 'a universe of death / The falsest of all worlds' (1805, XIII. 141–2).

Later in *The Excursion*, heroic happiness is again put into dialogue with forms of sensual pleasure, though here these forms find their defender in the Poet. The Wanderer has been expounding a vision of happiness as progressive knowledge: 'Happy is He who lives to understand! / Not human nature only, but explores / All Natures' (IV. 351, 385–7). The Poet finally manages to interrupt the seemingly unstoppable Wanderer, and suggests that perhaps 'the dignity of Life is not impaired' by ordinary and everyday gratifications, the satisfaction of 'the humbler cravings of the heart' and the 'pure sensations' of solitude and rural life (IV. 354–68). The Wanderer agrees, but elevates the rhetoric beyond domesticity with metaphors of eagles, sky, soul and heaven. His practical advice is to conform with natural rhythms in Stoic style: 'withdraw yourself from ways / That run not parallel to Nature's course. / Rise with the lark!', which will bring about sound repose (IV. 489–91). Again, the Poet interrupts, and puts quite a different emphasis on joy, described as a powerful experience of embodiment that takes us out of limited 'sensibility'. In our very mingled physicality we paradoxically become 'spirit': 'Oh! what a joy it were, in vigorous health, / To have a Body . . . And to the elements surrender it / As if it were spirit!' (IV. 508–13). This is exuberant, even ecstatic, in the original sense of the word. Wordsworth revised this passage after 1836, so that in the 1845 edition, the Poet's speech ends in a rather King Lear-like invitation to the elements to 'Rage' and 'mingle [. . .] [w]ith this commotion'.[55] The Poet seems even himself surprised at the eruption of this passionate and radical account of pleasure: 'Be as a Presence or a Motion – one / Among the many there' (IV. 520–1). The Wanderer, somewhat predictably, responds by converting this joyful philosophy of presence to a time-bound, more individualized, system for curing later 'cares and sorrows' with memories of such 'desires', 'delight' and 'spots' (IV. 541–7). Yet it is striking that this simple, sensual image of pleasure retains such prominence in the poem. Pleasure is never disparaged by any of the characters, except in passing in the Poet's hope in Book VI that candidates for the Church will be 'Detached from pleasure, to the love of gain / Superior' (VI. 46–7). Even in this conventional, Establishment rhetoric, the Poet does not claim that the ministers will be 'disinterested': they will experience delight, only, in their duty (VI. 49).

The representation of 'self-love' or interestedness in the poem is another point where *The Excursion*'s surprising sympathy with pleasure may be witnessed. The Wanderer angrily attacks 'Philosophers' who suggest the universe is only a reflection of 'proud Self-love', but not, as one might expect, according to conventional morality, because the soul is capable of disinterest, but rather because the soul is composed of 'twice ten thousand interests' (IV. 984–6).[56] Unlike Coleridge, and after him Hazlitt, who are keen to prove that disinterest is a real psychological and moral possibility, *The Excursion*'s critique of that image of 'proud Self-love' is much more Shaftesburian in claiming that egoistic philosophy is not 'realistic', and rather has underestimated the very multiplicity of our interests and natural affections. Yet, as we saw in relation to Shaftesbury, the idea of a natural pleasurable responsiveness can also appear coercive. This problem, too, is traced in *The Excursion*, where by the very fact of its dialogic, dramatic form, philosophical positions are always turned over by means of a character's response.

The Solitary recognizes the attractiveness of the idea of our soul's multiple interests and joys, but states the impossibility of simply being able to 'Resolve' to be happy; he cannot 'fly' when his very wings are 'shorn' (IV. 1078–81). The Wanderer insists otherwise: the Solitary's own words reflect back upon the assembled group a happiness that he must be forced to recognize. He is told that his sad 'discourse' has, against his own intentions, 'caught at every turn / The colours of the sun' (IV. 1115–19). That verb 'caught' is ostensibly innocent, but it hints at entrapment, where the healthy discipline of pleasure recommended shades into a more violent disciplining *with* pleasure. The strictness of the Wanderer's authority in this respect is confirmed a few lines later with the additional suggestion that not only has the Solitary's poetry betrayed him into the collective vision of happiness, so too does he perform unwitting prayer: 'Here you stand, / Adore, and worship, when you know it not' (IV. 1141–2). His 'thought' and 'intention' are weak in light of the body's sensitivity to pleasure: 'Yes, you have felt, and may not cease to feel' (IV. 1145). In light of this, the only meaning of 'gloom' can be a childish resistance to a maternal power of good: 'Acknowledge that to Nature's humbler power / Your cherished sullenness is forced to bend' (IV. 1184–5). One must 'bend' to happiness, and once this is recognized there is also no choice but to act and think in moral goodness. The Wanderer describes a glorious feedback loop of pleasure and goodness, whereby man 'needs must feel / The joy of that pure principle of love / So deeply, that ... he cannot choose / But seek for objects of a kindred love in fellow-natures and a kindred joy' (IV. 1206–11). The discipline of pleasure will lead to the habit of goodness, 'the glorious habit by which Sense is made / Subservient still to moral purposes' (IV. 1243–4). This reminisces upon the desire of 'A Fragment on Morals' (1798) for a system of morals of such pleasurable 'power' that it would form our habits.[57] But here, the loop of discipline, pleasure and goodness becomes a massive engine of conversion, first of sights and sensations – all sensations will work to 'raise' our 'soul': 'Whate'er we see, / Whate'er we feel, by agency direct / Or indirect shall tend to feed and nurse / Our faculties' (IV. 1266–9); second, the conversion of others to happiness in a 'spreading' which anticipates the explicit colonialism of Book VIII: 'with the will, confer / The ability to spread the blessings wide / Of true philanthropy' (IV. 1238–40).

The question of the law and discipline of happiness invites comparison with Kant's practical philosophy. For Kant, happiness is a necessary end common to all humans and part of their essence; neither a gift nor a right, but a tormenting need, consequent upon our frailty: 'a problem imposed upon him by his finite nature itself, because he is needy'.[58] Our need for happiness clamours for our attention, and though we cannot be rid of it, we must learn sometimes to ignore its voice: 'pure practical reason does not require that one should *renounce* claims to happiness but only that as soon as duty is in question one should *take no account* of them'.[59] Happiness can never be a universal concept: first, because it relates to subjective feelings of pleasure and displeasure, and so is 'a very *contingent* practical principle, which can and must be different in different subjects, and hence can never yield a law', and secondly, because epistemological limitations mean that we can never know what we really want: 'In short, he is not capable of any principle by which to determine with complete certainty what would make him truly happy, because for this omniscience would be required.'[60] Thirdly, there is a problem of contingency: 'both the circumstances of the times and the highly conflicting but always changing illusion in which someone places his happiness (though no one can prescribe to him in what he should place it)' make it 'unfit' to be a legislative principle.[61] Such an idea, finally, is foolishly tautological: 'one never commands of someone what he unavoidably wants already'.[62] Thus, a maxim of happiness in government can lead only to 'conflict, and the complete annihilation of the maxim itself and its purpose', as well as tyranny: 'The sovereign wants to make the people happy in accordance with his concepts and becomes a despot; the people are not willing to give up their universal human claim to happiness and become rebels.'[63]

These references to 'the people' invite us to reconsider happiness in the larger 'sociological', empirical or anthropological perspective of *The Excursion*, in its central books (v, vi and vii) probably written in 1813–14, several years after the initial development of the opening around the 'Ruined Cottage' text, and moving away from the predominantly ethical debates of the Wanderer, Poet and Solitary.[64] Wordsworth's *Essays on Epitaphs* were composed around the same time, leading many critics to focus on the poem's language of death and the grave, and the connection of writing and death.[65] Yet, happiness is also at stake in these essays: the second *Essay on Epitaphs* insists upon charting 'blessings' and 'achievements'. Aristotle's claim that plot works according to the logic of happiness and unhappiness is relevant to the status of these stories: 'because tragedy is mimesis not of persons but of action and life; and happiness and unhappiness consist in action'.[66] The epitaphic form taken by the Pastor's response argues that you can call no man happy until he is dead; that death provides a unique vantage point from which to judge the successful flourishing, or the failure to flourish, of individuals. Wordsworth wonders how many know of the 'trials to which Men in a lowly condition are subject, or of the steady and triumphant manner in which those trials are often sustained, but they themselves'.[67] These words, 'trials' and 'steady', suggest once again that Protestant idea of happiness as labouring in a fallen world, and Stoic equanimity in the face of suffering.[68]

The epitaphs in the long poem are precipitated by the Solitary's scepticism about what we can tell from the mere appearance of a 'large and populous Vale' ('Summary of Contents').[69] Books VI and VII consider the varying degrees of satisfaction, and in some cases happiness, achieved in the face of adverse circumstance on the part of individual, deceased villagers. By showing the Solitary examples or standards, he is intended to find a framework into which to insert his own experiences, and so to leave his depression. Yet, the epitaphs make uncomfortable reading: the suffering and loneliness many of them convey seem hardly to answer the Solitary's demand to see someone preserved, in the way the Wanderer has extolled, 'From painful and discreditable shocks' or 'unsanctioned fear' (v. 358–60), or even the Poet's request to see some who are 'warmed or cheered' by the light of duty, or had 'a blest old age!' (v. 380, 385). The houses seem 'To give assurance of content within; / Embosomed happiness, and placid love' (v. 409–10). But these appearances can be deceptive: the Solitary himself, following his misfortunes in the late days of the French Revolution, had a 'zeal / Which showed like happiness' (II. 298–9). As he adds, sceptically, with reference to the valley, life 'Is fashioned like an ill-constructed tale', starting with 'fair adventures' and ending with 'Old things repeated with diminished grace' (v. 427, 429).

The discussion of the villagers often takes the form of an analysis of the condition of England, comparing different segments of society and types of life, again pointing up the political ambivalence of the poem's 'happiness' theme. The Wanderer tells the impoverished, hard-working couple that they were paradoxically blessed:

> O happy! yielding to the law
> Of these privations, richer in the main!
> While thankless thousands are opprest and clogged
> By ease and leisure – by the very wealth
> And pride of opportunity made poor;
> While tens of thousands falter in their path,
> And sink, through utter want of cheering light (v. 832–8)

This paradoxical happiness to be derived from being poor, as with the echoes of physico-theology considered in Chapter 3, has a ring of William Paley's and Bishop Watson's conservative pamphleteering. Paley wrote that society's apparent fortunates were 'exceedingly oppressed' by their idle, unengaged lives.[70] Bishop Watson, in the course of his attack on the French Revolution, argued that inequality was a 'spur to industry and frugality', bringing 'virtues' to the poor.[71] Wordsworth wrote, but did not publish, a stinging response to the latter in his 'Letter to the Bishop of Llandaff', though he did not touch on the question of happiness and pleasure.[72] Yet, despite the overlap between the Wanderer and Paley, there is a key difference: Paley claims that God allocates equal joys to all creatures, whilst the Wanderer points out that the town-dwelling masses 'sink' without the energy and fortitude provided by the simple enjoyment of existence ('cheering light'). In the early nineteenth century (as Connell argued with respect to the political ambiguity of the education reforms), references to joy and happiness seem to enable both justifications of the status quo and an attack on the division of labour and industrialization. Wordsworth seems to push towards the second of these positions. The agrarian ideal shows up the vast inequalities opening up in towns and cities, inequalities of wealth and work that make both poor and rich unhappy, resonating with modern centre-left economic theories of happiness like Richard Layard's, as well as with Adorno's negative-utopian image of happiness. David Simpson drew from Adorno in describing Wordsworth's labour ideal as 'a fusion of poverty and possessiveness, and work and leisure. One should have enough to live on, but only *just* enough.'[73] He suggests that for Wordsworth 'authentic pleasure' is 'not antithetical to pain and hardship, but continuous with them . . . constituted by strenuous effort rather than by passive leisure, and thus belongs within a community governed by undivided labour in a pre-commercial phase'.[74] In *The Excursion* the golden age promised by the *beatus ille* seems almost to have been restored by this farming community and its utopian affective possibilities.

   But one of the fascinating things about *The Excursion* is that it cannot stop generating examples and arguments. So, whilst the story of the hardworking, pre-commercial couple seems to demonstrate the possibility of achieved pleasure, the rest of the catalogue given by the Pastor presents plenty of 'trials' – to recall the arguments of the second *Essay on Epitaphs* – though without much evidence of that 'triumphant manner' with which they sustain them. The villagers hardly achieve a glorious reconciliation with life; 'satisfaction with one's whole existence', as Kant described it.[75] A summary of the first dozen reminds us how problematic these tales are. The first three encapsulate gradual reconciliation to failed love, perseverance in attaining riches and a life of rakishness only calmed in death. We hear of the lifelong fellowship of two sparring friends; and the epitaph of a woman who, in spite of the supposedly happiness-prone environs of the valley and its community, maintains a forceful *ressentiment* up to her deathbed. She cannot submit or reconcile her character and her intelligence, 'like the imperial Thistle', to 'the harsher servitude' that is her lot as a female and a poor one (VI. 704, 719). Her whole tale resists redemption according to the schema, but, by the time of the 1845 edition, the Pastor manages to extract a Christian-Stoic message: 'She spake, yet, I believe, not unsustained / By faith in glory ... She, who had rebelled, / Was into meekness softened and subdued.'[76] The seventh epitaph is for Ellen, the first named subject, described as 'hapless' (lacking a happy destiny?); abandoned by the man who has impregnated her, she finds an unexpected joy in her child. When her baby dies after she takes on work as a wet-nurse, she grieves, but 'tutors' herself to find 'pleasure in endurance' (VI. 1047–8). Wilfred is an adulterer who is punished for his taking of 'troubled joy' by an ensuing guilt which strips all positive affect from his world: 'No pleasure in the beauty of the day' (VI. 1142–3). We hear of a widowed father, the sight of whose family of six 'budding' daughters, 'a happy family', shows that despite his continued sadness his 'whole House seems filled with gaiety', and his dead wife can be deemed 'Thrice happy' at the merry life that her family achieved without her (VI. 1169, 1166, 1228, 1229).[77] The seeming paradox here is that the father remains miserable and all the surplus happiness is ascribed to the mother – who remains dead. Book VII tells of a bright young parson who sadly outlives his entire, beloved family, the respectively deaf and blind dalesmen and how they endured their 'sad privation', an optimistic logger (one of only two 'epitaphs' for living characters) and the tale of a dead, much-loved toddler.

The Pastor's faith is meant to fill in some of these unsatisfying gaps in happiness – in the reassurance that the mother's spirit lives on, or through the consolation that Ellen rejoined her baby in the next world – but the reader may feel a residual discomfort that the tranquil resolution described still does not compensate for the prior suffering encountered. The unsuccessfulness of the epitaphs as a reply to the demands in Book V of the Poet and Solitary to show people 'withdrawn from Passion's crooked ways' or 'thoroughly fortified' by faith (V. 350–1) has often been noted. Hazlitt wondered, 'why introduce particular illustrations at all, which add nothing to the force of the general truth'.[78] Of recent critics, Kevis Goodman has asked why the Pastor recounts, as supposed consolation, 'life after life of abandoned promise and deviation, lives if not of quiet desperation then certainly of disappointed aspiration'.[79] By way of

D'Israeli's *Dissertation on Anecdotes* and Freud's *Beyond the Pleasure Principle*, Goodman argues that the epitaphs' healing effect is *meant* to lie in the strangely blasé passing from one story to the next. 'They attempt to perform mastery' over the past by stimulating the listener through the cycle of storytelling itself: and this forms part of Wordsworth's deliberate refusal 'to gratify the desire for the immediacy of the past, or intimacy with the dead'.[80] Yet, Goodman's compelling account of the poem's 'resounding, ironic inadequation' once again reveals the difficulty of absorbing this 9,000-line poem as a whole, partly because she does not try to account for why the poem moves directly from historiographical incertitude to the two didactic themes that have caused modern readers much consternation: contemporary education schemes and the argument for colonization.[81]

The poem segues into broader geo-political concerns by means of the final three epitaphs given by the Pastor: for a soldier, a patriotic peasant and addressing the tomb of a long-dead knight. With the encomium for the soldier Oswald, politics and war enter the peaceful valley and jack up the rhetoric from the domestic-sentimental to the public-patriotic register. 'Happiness' remains the leitmotif. Oswald's happiness and that of the ten young men he takes with him to war are directly linked to their patriotism and militarism; urgently excited for departure, 'Measuring the soil beneath their happy feet' (VII. 798), the war feels to them like 'A festival of unencumbered ease' (VII. 801). In a grander symbolic gesture, the humble Peasant-youth is presented as the embodiment of the enduring spirit of an essentially happy country, despite the negative effects of her own technological and economic advances:

> In spite of vice, and misery, and disease,
> Spread with the spreading of her wealthy arts,
> England, the ancient and the free, appeared
> In him to stand before my swimming eyes,
> Unconquerably virtuous and secure. (VII. 874–8)

This claim for the persistence of the spirit of an older, purer England – currently blighted by industry and consumerism – is reinforced by the final epitaph, turning to feudal England at the grave of Sir Alfred Erthing. The Wanderer's reflection on the loss of chivalric values in his own lifetime moves him to comment on the environmental and social crisis of the current day. Roads have multiplied, hamlets have swollen into towns, the seas are crowded with trading ships; and huge factories and mills have become modern temples of 'perpetual sacrifice' to the idol of

accumulation (VIII. 186). The Wanderer's main focus is on the loss of
comfort and pleasure caused by industrialization. His rhetorical set-piece
is a description of a young factory boy, whose loss of pleasure is characterized as the loss of auto-affection, a kind of bodily self-pleasure in
perception or apperception:

> The limbs increase; but liberty of mind
> Is gone for ever; and this organic Frame,
> Which from heaven's bounty we receive, instinct
> With light, and gladsome motions, soon becomes
> Dull, to the joy of her own motions dead;
> And even the Touch, so exquisitely poured
> Through the whole body, with a languid Will
> Performs its functions; rarely competent
> To impress a vivid feeling on the mind
> Of what there is delightful in the breeze,
> The gentle visitations of the sun,
> Or lapse of liquid element – by hand,
> Or foot, or lip, in summer's warmth – perceived. (VIII. 323–35)

The interplay of enjambment and caesura in this passage aurally and
visually reinforces the conceptual flow and stoppage of pleasure. That
'exquisite touch' may be an echo of the lyrical-satirical treatment of poetic
sensation in Pope's *Essay on Man*: 'The spider's touch, how exquisitely
fine! / Feels at each thread, and lives along the line.'[82] Wordsworth's
passage reiterates the emotional and physical atrophy attributed to contemporary 'forces' in the 'Preface' to the *Lyrical Ballads*, which 'blunt the
discriminating powers of the mind and, unfitting it for all voluntary
exertion, ... reduce it to a state of almost savage torpor' (1850,
ll. 161–4). The Wanderer's language of breezes, gladness, gifts and joy
mark this as a *Prelude*-like, lyrical moment within *The Excursion*, but its
reference to 'liberty of mind' brings up different questions – around
liberalism, utilitarianism and nationalism – with which the remainder of
the poem is preoccupied.

The last books oscillate between the idea that England is indeed a
'happy Island', particularly in contrast with a Europe described as
oppressed, dark and wretched (IX. 412–17), and may transfer its blessings
to the wider world; and that industrialization has degraded its delights, as
in the set-piece above. The over-determined image of England as a 'happy
land' has a long history, taking in, for example, John of Gaunt's 'Scept'red
Isle' speech in *Richard II*: 'This happy breed of men, this little world ...
This blessed plot, this earth, this realm, this England.'[83] More's *Utopia*

and Francis Bacon's *New Atlantis* are dotted with happy islands, whilst the mythological archetypes were the Greek Islands of the Blessed – the land of eternal bliss near the setting sun – and biblical accounts of Israel.[84] From the late fourteenth century, England's providential destiny was connected with Israel, and Linda Colley has argued that a national myth of Israel-like blessedness became widespread in the eighteenth century.[85] Britons, she argued, believed that 'almost by definition, they were blessed, and these blessings had a material as well as a spiritual form ... under God, they were peculiarly free and peculiarly prosperous'.[86]

Wordsworth's use of 'happy island' imagery in *The Excursion* appears to build on an everyday discourse of England's blessedness, but it undermines contemporary rhetoric in suggesting that modern commercial habits – 'her wealthy arts' – are precisely what obscure a deeper, more ancient potential for happiness envisaged as a universal freedom and dignity. The ambivalence around this image is evident when the Pastor compares the pre-'Jehova' age of barbarism and idolatry to the present:

> So wide the difference, a willing mind
> Might almost think, at this affecting hour,
> That Paradise, the lost abode of man,
> Was raised again: and to a happy Few,
> In its original beauty, here restored. (IX. 712–16)

The qualifiers ('willing', 'might', 'almost') heighten the uncertainty produced by the caesurae that break each line into an expansive thought and a restraining after-thought. The word 'Few' is charged in the poem, from the Verse Prospectus' quotation of Milton: 'fit audience let me find though few!',[87] to the Solitary's negative demand: 'Not for a happy Land do I enquire, / Island or Grove, that hides a blessed few' (V. 345–6), and the Pastor's question: whether the wretched are 'of one species with the sheltered few' (V. 949). These questions of selection and election become increasingly urgent in the poem. The Solitary offers a third, sceptical perspective on the idea of England's happiness or degradation, arguing that degradation and unfreedom are ancient. He cites the pleasure-less and 'profitless' English beggars of the commons, and the 'thriving churl' who ekes out a blank, limited existence in the countryside:

> his Country's name
> Her equal rights, her churches and her schools –
> What have they done for him? And, let me ask,
> For tens of thousands uninformed as he?
> In brief, what liberty of *mind* is here? (VIII. 431–5)

That phrase 'liberty of mind' again opens up a new vista on the problematic of pleasure and happiness, one that also speaks to the genesis of liberalism from utilitarianism. An intermediary answer to the Solitary's political scepticism comes via the appearance of a glowing young girl and two cheerful boys: the Pastor's graceful daughter, son and his friend. They are meant to evidence what the Wanderer calls 'an *active* principle' of the universe (IX. 3); a principle of affirmation, which seems to return to the language of unowned delight and the feeling of existence traced in my last chapter:[88]

> Whate'er exists hath properties that spread
> Beyond itself, communicating good,
> A simple blessing, or with evil mixed;
> Spirit that knows no insulated spot,
> No chasm, no solitude; from link to link
> It circulates, the Soul of all the worlds.
> This is the freedom of the universe;
> . . . we live by hope
> And by desire; we see by the glad light
> And breathe the sweet air of futurity;
> And so we live, or else we have no life. (IX. 10–16, 23–6)

These lines represent many of the rather ambitious, abstract philosophical-political ideas about pleasure and nature that we discovered in Wordsworth's earlier work as well as in Rousseau. This mixing and spreading, as in the 'Preface' ('acting and re-acting upon each other, so as to produce an infinite complexity of pain and pleasure', 413–14), hints at something like a radical naturalism. It redefines 'freedom', perhaps with calculated paradox, as interconnection and binding, as well as understanding 'life' as optimism. Echoing Rousseauian themes delineated in Chapter 2, the Wanderer stresses that physical comfort and pleasure are a prerequisite for hope: 'bodies crushed by unremitting toil' cannot believe in the kindness of Nature (IX. 97). Man used as a means, 'without acknowledgment / Of common right or interest in the end', will lack motivation to do good, as well as being alienated from his true sensual-moral freedom (IX. 118–19). 'True equality', according to the Wanderer, is the availability to all of the sensual experience that is a free gift of nature. Echoing the thought of 'Lines Written in Early Spring', the Wanderer notes that observing the generality of pleasure in nature will also bring sad thoughts to the mind:

> The charities that soothe, and heal, and bless,
> Are scattered at the feet of Man – like flowers.
> . . . He, whose soul,

Ponders this true equality, may walk
The fields of earth with gratitude and hope;
Yet, in that meditation, will he find,
Motive to sadder grief, . . .
And for the injustice grieving, that hath made,
So wide a difference betwixt Man and Man. (IX. 238–53)

This definition of 'true equality' as pleasure is reiterated when the
Wanderer notes that whatever may happen to the two boys, one poor,
one rich, 'sure it is that both / Have been permitted to enjoy the dawn'
(IX. 280–1); in this they have 'been fairly dealt with', receiving 'justice' in
terms of both 'body and mind' (IX. 286–8). But the lines still hold a gap
open between what they call 'true equality' and something like real or
economic 'injustice' – and *The Excursion* goes much further than 'Early
Spring' in voicing a solution.

The means of healing the 'difference' between men is a proposal for
a utilitarian system of schooling. The 'Madras' or monitorial system for
schooling was a concept of cheap, universal education whereby students were educated (using exercises and tests), and disciplined by
senior students, rising to a single superintendent. Wordsworth was
preoccupied with Andrew Bell's educational theories during the intense
phase of *The Excursion*'s composition.[89] In a note to the poem, Wordsworth is lavish in praise of Bell's system: 'it is impossible to overrate
the benefit which might accrue to humanity from the universal application of this simple engine under an enlightened and conscientious
government'.[90] Though critics have seen Wordsworth's interest in
utilitarian education as a contradiction of his seemingly more radical
or idealist moments, Connell makes the point that it was a locus of
conservative and radical interest.[91] One can further understand its
importance to Wordsworth by keeping fully in view the concept of
the 'equality' of pleasure as common ground between his radicalism
and his seemingly liberal-Tory identifications. Utilitarian schooling
will offer children civilizing tools for freedom and pleasure, and prevents them from having 'to drudge through weary life' (IX. 306).
According to Bentham, the 'inspection principle' of the Panopticon
was designed to release *more* time for children's play, rather than being
hostile to it:

During the hours of business, habit, no longer broken in upon by accident would
strip the master's presence of its terrors, without depriving it of its use. And the
time allotted for study being faithfully and rigidly appropriated to that service,
the less of it would serve.[92]

So Wanderer describes the boys' schooling:

> A few short hours of each returning day
> The thriving prisoners of their village-school:
> And thence let loose, to seek their pleasant homes
> Or range the grassy lawn in vacancy;
> To breathe and be happy, run and shout,
> Idle – but no delay, no harm, no loss. (IX. 258–63)

Such schooling will thus advance the 'true equality' of pleasure, bringing together children once divided by poverty; their idle happiness, like the economics of *Home at Grasmere*, will incur no 'loss'.

From the point of view of modern anti-colonialism, however, the education schemes *are* politically unprogressive. The just apportioning of means to happiness becomes the basis not only of joyful 'reproduction' at home but also a reproduction of the 'happy Island' abroad. The education eulogized by the Wanderer is a crucial plank in the solution to 'redundant' population: the feared crisis of resources through human reproduction that Malthus outlined in 1798. James Mill reluctantly admitted that not only would Britain be unable to supply the means of men's subsistence, it would not furnish the means of their happiness – 'those other things, by the enjoyment of which the life of man is preferable to that of the brutes' – unless the population was somehow restricted.[93] Given the practical and moral difficulties of disincentivizing sex, colonization appeared the only solution. According to the Wanderer, the universal piety that will result from basic universal education and 'joy' are the motive powers of the imperial project:

> avaunt the fear
> Of numbers crowded on their native soil,
> To the prevention of all healthful growth
> Through mutual injury! Rather in the law
> Of increase and the mandate from above
> Rejoice! – and Ye have special cause for joy. (IX. 365–70)

The 'special cause' lies in the sea's ardour for Britain's 'swarms', as her cast-off population is 'Bound to establish new communities / On every shore' (IX. 381–2). The 'brightness' of 'the happy Island' glows as 'Oppression' covers Europe, pointing up the need to 'Show to the wretched Nations for what end / The Powers of civil Polity were given' (IX. 417–18). Addressing 'British Lawgivers', with an urgent series of 'nows', the Wanderer insists that 'Your Country must complete / Her glorious destiny' (IX. 410–11). The world will thereafter be fertilized with civilization, as the spreading of Britain enables the transmission of happiness to less fortunate countries. Enraptured with these political-philosophical solutions, the now-expanded group of listeners are surprised by the sight of a beautiful ram across the water, alluding to the imperial destiny traced in Virgil's *Aeneid.*

There are several questions posed by this dramatic climax to the poem (which is, however, not its ending). First, why should universal education 'avaunt' the Malthusian fears? And secondly, what has rejoicing and joy to do with the imperial project? The surface-level claim is that the educated populace will succeed abroad; that the sea will naturally welcome the industrious, as the Virgilian metaphor of the bee-hive indicates.[94] But on a deeper level, it could be interpreted as a corollary of the metaphorical association between happiness and 'spreading' explored in this chapter. Élie Halévy argued that the antinomy of utilitarianism was between Smith's natural harmony of interests (the invisible hand), and Bentham's artificial identification of interests (the Panopticon). Likewise, *The Excursion* believes on the one hand that happiness spreads naturally ('Even 'till the smallest habitable rock, . . . bloom / With civil arts, that send their fragrance forth', IX. 389–93); on the other, it hints that such apparently humane and liberating aspirations may have a coercive mandate. The question of colonialism was already a tension point in utilitarian philosophy. Jeremy Bentham was a lifelong anti-colonialist, for both ethical and economic reasons, who in 1793 wrote to Talleyrand an open letter challengingly entitled *Emancipate your Colonies!* But Halévy pointed out that 'in so far as [utilitarian] philosophy advocates the artificial and despotic identification of interests, might they not be tempted to consider the colonial empire as a vast field for experiments in philanthropy and reform?'.[95]

The identification of a conflict between the poem's humanist aspirations for happiness and its imperialist message might be said to be anachronistic; yet, one can see tensions registered in the closing verse. A dissenting voice comes from the Lady who has joined the group, who mutters, during the trance of collective happiness ('Gathered together, all, in still delight'), that the Wanderer is an 'eloquent Old Man' who construes harmony from a trick of the light: 'His mind gives back the fairest forms of things, / Caught in their fairest, happiest attitude!' (IX. 459, 462, 466–7). In the spell of his rhetoric, she can 'see / Even as he sees', but, she sighs, such a 'serene and bright' picture cannot last in a world where beauty and peace are so evidently transient (IX. 468–9, 471). Her whispered interruption alters the emotional landscape of the closing verses. There is a turn to a more local and limited kind of pleasure:

making a fire, eating, gathering flowers: 'trivial occupations well devised, /
And unsought pleasures springing up by chance' (IX. 521–2). The Solitary
then provides the second major interruption to the closing scene,
attempting to draw attention to the abandoned ashes of the fire:

> 'The Fire, that burned so brightly to our wish,
> Where is it now? Deserted on the beach
> It seems extinct; nor shall the fanning breeze
> Revive its ashes. What care we for this,
> Whose ends are gained? Behold an emblem here
> Of one day's pleasure, and all mortal joys!
> And, in this unpremeditated slight
> Of that which is no longer needed, see
> The common course of human gratitude!' (IX. 550–78)

Drawing attention to the word 'emblem', Alison Hickey comments that
'the remark is fundamentally disturbing, rather than just ungraciously
morose. It mocks the very notion of signification.'[96] However, the
emblem is specifically an emblem of pleasure and joy. The Solitary's
denunciation of *The Excursion*'s themes of happiness, his claims for the
non-reciprocity of pleasure, 'disturbed not the repose / Of the still
evening', and no character directly answers him (IX. 559–60). It is not
the most powerful of attacks: there is bathos in sympathy with a bonfire
(in the 1845 edition described as 'Dying, or dead!'), and one might
interpret the speech as indicating the almost comic resistance of the
Solitary to the pleasures all around him. The collectivity of the experience
of this 'refulgent spectacle' is stressed; everyone is eager 'To impart a joy,
imperfect while unshared' (IX. 611, 587). The Pastor offers a rapturous
service, expressing a wish that the lonely peasant will one day be 'happy in
himself' (IX. 672). In the last lines of the poem, by leaving for his 'one
Cottage in the lonely dell', the Solitary refuses to join the collective 'happy
few' around the Vicar (IX. 772, 715). The Solitary does, however, 'promise'
to 'share' in the experience of pleasure:

>   But, ere he turned
> Aside, a welcome promise had been given
> That he would share the pleasures and pursuits
> Of yet another summer's day . . .
>   'Another sun',
> Said he, 'shall shine upon us, ere we part, –
> Another sun and peradventure more;
> If time, with free consent, be yours to give, –
> And season favours.' (IX. 773–82)

Perhaps this willingness is meant to indicate the first sign of the Solitary's acceptance of the priest's terms; his outburst at the bonfire would be the final spasm of his depression. Yet, Wordsworth deliberately leaves open the question of the 'Degree of healing to a wounded spirit' that has actually been brought about through the Wanderer's and the Poet's debates on happiness (IX. 785). Some readers take the ending's openness to show a hesitation or indecision; others find it representative of Wordsworth's achievement.[97] At the poem's close, 'celestial splendours' are replaced with a 'grey' sky and 'inferior lights . . . too faint almost for sight' (IX. 758, 760–1), substituting for religious sublimity the markers of ordinary domestic life that finally take centre stage. One way of reading the ending is to understand it as highlighting a simple, provisional pleasure as the first step on the way to a happiness that cannot yet, without violence, be conceived: that which the narrator's 'future Labours may not leave untold' (IX. 795).

CONCLUSION

As twentieth-century philosophers turned to *eudaimonia* because they perceived it as making more room for contingency, vulnerability and context than the modern ethical traditions, Kantianism and utilitarianism, we might see a parallel with Wordsworth's move towards narratives of happiness in his 1814 poem. *The Excursion* tries to 'realize' the utopian idea of shared pleasure central to *Home at Grasmere* and *The Prelude*, by embodying it in varied, contingent life-stories (epitaphs), giving it a historical framework of circumstance, suffering and flourishing. Nussbaum commented in *The Fragility of Goodness* that '[t]he Aristotelian view of the human being as a being both capable and vulnerable, in need of a rich plurality of life-activities (a conception that he takes over, in many ways, from the tragic poets), has striking resonance for contemporary thinking about welfare and development'.[98] But, I would suggest, *The Excursion* also performs an immanent critique of such modern conceptions of happiness as end-directed, productive and involved with narrative, informed by Aristotle's teleological conception of *eudaimonia*. Happiness, theorized as productive work or labour, drives the poem towards a normative and teleological model, and it forms part of the inspiration for, and authority of, the colonial project in Book IX. On the level of character, the coercive nature of happiness in the poem is presented in the Solitary's desperate reply to the Wanderer's prescriptions, and the seeming failure of his 'cure'; perhaps also why the poem ends with the Solitary's minimal commitment only to 'share the pleasures and pursuits / Of yet another summer's day' (IX. 775–6). One can thus see *The Excursion* as representing a defence of 'ordinary', passive, unproductive pleasure, untied to larger narratives and ends. Despite this final uncertainty, and the pain and disagreement that leave their traces throughout the whole poem, we must nonetheless recognize the challenge that the poet undertakes in trying to understand the human question of happiness on a larger, anthropological scale. Ultimately, the poem may be seen as parallel to Kant's analysis of the problem of trying to legislate for, or to normativize, happiness; though, despite his concerns about the undemocratic or illiberal possibilities of philosophies of happiness, he admitted that they are of great human significance.[99] 'Certainly, our well-being and woe count for a *very great deal* in the appraisal of our practical reason and, as far as our nature as sensible beings is concerned, *all* that counts is our *happiness.*'[100] Wordsworth's poetic project in *The Excursion* can be acknowledged as successful in teaching us, as the Pastor says of the epitaphs, 'To prize the breath we share with human kind; And look upon the dust of man with awe' (v. 658–9). As much as Wordsworth's poetry theorizes the way that pleasure is communal and connecting, so too does his verse apprehend the very shared ground of the human longing for happiness.

Conclusion

The writers featured in this book – Shaftesbury, Rousseau, Kant, Wollstonecraft and Wordsworth – may not initially have appeared to be obvious figures upon whom to centre a study of Enlightenment pleasure, especially sage Kant with his punctiliously regular walks round Königsberg and solemn Wordsworth with his poems on tombstones and thorn-trees. Yet (biographical counter-examples aside: Kant is said to have loved raucous dinner parties and Wordsworth is said to have had an immoderate fondness for Cheshire cheese and 'a convulsive inclination to laughter about the mouth'), both wrote of a 'principle of pleasure' which they viewed as central to their thought; both understood pleasure as epistemological and ethical in character. These writers' earnestness about pleasure has sometimes led (except in the case of confessional Rousseau) to patronizing charges of prudishness or asceticism. But I have attempted to defend and delineate their serious kind of thought about simple, sensuous or existential pleasure.

For Shaftesbury and Kant, a concept of shared pleasure emerges from a framework of aesthetic ideas. Shaftesbury attempts to redefine his contemporaries' notions of self-interest and show that they depend upon a performative contradiction; instead, individual and communal ends cannot simply be opposed. The *sensus communis* refers to the pleasure that arises from a sense of belonging to the human species and to a commonality caused by a natural feeling of pleasure in order. Kant defines the pleasure of community cautiously and as bearing a complex relation to cognition. In reading the Third Critique alongside the *Anthropology*, one finds various ways that the pleasure of the beautiful may be characterized; as still, calm and closed, or in terms of movement, liveliness or openness, all of which interpretive possibilities subtly shape the links that have been made between Kant's aesthetics and political theory. For both Kant and Shaftesbury, anthropology is something of a disruptive discourse: the comparative perspective problematizes an *a priori* understanding of pleasure.

Kant may have learnt this disruptive anthropology from Rousseau. Rousseau's philosophy frequently demonstrates a negative view of sociability, and of the violence and competition that may define collective experience more often than peace and pleasure. In Rousseau, nevertheless, there is an ideal of subjectivity as grounded in pleasure, witnessed in his key ideas of *amour de soi* and the sentiment of existence. Despite the apparent privacy and individuality of such subjective feeling, pleasure in Rousseau is frequently 'allocentric', a feeling defined with reference to others. Of all the thinkers presented here, Rousseau seems to show most powerfully the ethical ambivalence of pleasure; in particular, how the blissful feeling of being alive might be linked to a feeling of mastery. Wollstonecraft's response to Rousseau is of great interest in this context, for she is deeply conscious of the ambivalence of pleasure. She decries the political violence against women that it entails, while maintaining a deep attachment to the utopian, radical idea of intersubjective delight; on this reading, the negative view of pleasure in the *Vindication* is a condition of possibility for the hedonism of *Maria*.

Wordsworth's poetry and prose is absorbed in the history of thought about pleasure and the epistemological and political issues shown in Part I. From the *Lyrical Ballads*, exemplified in 'Lines Written in Early Spring', through the whole *Recluse* project, Wordsworth registers the contemporary political contradictions of a general or collective pleasure, whilst holding fast to the utopian and redemptive ideal of pleasure in the Enlightenment. The obsessive return to pleasure throughout the 'Preface' documents help to refine our view of Wordsworth's relation to utilitarianism, and they are texts which may be seen to continue both ancient and Kantian debates about the nature of pleasure and its relation to community. Wordsworth's *Prelude* presents pleasure in various, sometimes competing, categories and frameworks, though the reciprocity of pleasure remains a central aspiration of the poem. *Home at Grasmere* represents the point in Wordsworth's oeuvre at which the image of passive, circular, non-teleological delight reaches its fullest power. The mildness of this image could lead twentieth-century anti-utilitarian thinkers of 'excess' to view this pleasure as a bourgeois restriction of human life, but looked at differently, it offers a political radicalism of its own, as well as gently suggesting some of the limitations of twentieth-century accounts of pleasure. Nonetheless, a tension begins to emerge in *Home at Grasmere* between a static bliss and an idea of happiness as action and work, one which deepens in poems like 'Character of the Happy Warrior' and *The Excursion*. The central metaphor of the 'spreading' of joy becomes, in *The Excursion*, implicated in normative and even coercive social systems, as Kant predicted in his concerns about 'happiness' in his practical philosophy.

These readings have demonstrated the wide range of historical and theoretical meanings that the term possesses. Pleasure's status as primarily biological and sensual or representational and imaginative remains an open question in these texts. Indeed, the traditional hierarchy of pleasure as spiritual, intellectual and sensual, which goes back to Plato and is associated with St Paul, has emerged only occasionally in this book. Pleasure stands for our ordinary physical existence, and sometimes for our animal nature; yet, it is also represented as historical in its instantiations, shaped by our learnt habits, and attesting to human cultural and preferential diversity as well as to a simple universal experience. Pleasure can be seen as a freedom from the travails of self-preservation to reflect on the world and create a pleasure from it (as Marx and Adorno sometimes seem to imply); it might form part of a humanism defined as 'the possibility men have to oppose the biological constraints of the species'.[2] Then again, Wordsworth's poetic idea that our pleasure is enjoyably reciprocal with breezes and periwinkles suggests a different kind of ecological utopianism. Both these frameworks for thinking about human pleasure and its relation to nature are laced with nostalgia and loss: an Edenic inscription in Kant's idea about the loss of a pleasure that was once in cognition, Rousseau's supplementary logic of pleasure, and Wordsworth's paradisiacal language. As Walter Benjamin once suggested, the 'dialectic of happiness' involves this mixture of hope and loss, involving the first (unattainable) bliss and the elegiac dream of its recurrence.[3]

William Wordsworth is the defining literary figure for a philosophically oriented study of pleasure. Responding to and reshaping a whole range of Enlightenment discourses on happiness, self-interest and bliss, he insistently referred to pleasure from the start to the end of his writing career. This book has argued that one can trace a distinctive strain of thought about pleasure in the eighteenth century that culminates in Wordsworth's compelling, challenging treatment. The distinctiveness of this thought is that pleasure, rather than being represented as something essentially private or individual, is frequently defined in broader, social terms. In the twentieth and twenty-first centuries, there is a tendency to represent pleasure as individualist, even selfish, and therefore of little ethical or political importance. In the eighteenth and early nineteenth centuries, this image of pleasure was less fixed. Issues around pleasure included the socially just distribution of pleasure; how pleasure might form bonds of community; the idea that pleasure might lend a feeling of power associated with personal domination; pleasure's status in the natural versus the social orders. In the texts discussed in this book, we may find resources to rethink a simple dismissal of the ideology of collective pleasure, as well as to rethink the assumption that subjectivity should be characterized as essentially tragic, located in loss. These writings suggest that joy, affirmation and existential delight have their own ethical possibilities and are not merely bland, politically passive modes of being; they illuminate the meanings of pleasure for modernity.

Notes

INTRODUCTION

1 'Quare etiam atque etiam, ut dico, est communi' voluptas', Titus Carus Lucretius, *De Rerum Natura*, 4.1207, ed. and trans. W.H.D. Rouse and M.F. Smith (Loeb Classical Library; Cambridge, MA: Harvard University Press, 1975). The translation is from Jean-Luc Nancy, *A Finite Thinking*, trans. and ed. Simon Sparks (Stanford University Press, 2003), p. 199.

2 On the cultural history of pleasure, luxury and consumption see Roy Porter and Marie Mulvey Roberts, eds., *Pleasure in the Eighteenth Century* (Basingstoke: Macmillan, 1996); C.J. Berry, *The Idea of Luxury: A Conceptual and Historical Investigation* (Cambridge University Press, 1994); Neil McKendrick, John Brewer and J.H. Plumb, *The Birth of a Consumer Society: The Commercialization of Eighteenth-Century England* (London: Europa, 1992); and Maxine Berg, *Luxury and Pleasure in Eighteenth-Century Britain* (Oxford University Press, 2005).

3 As far as I am aware, there is no existing history of the idea of pleasure. The definitive survey of ancient pleasure philosophy is J.C.B. Gosling and C.C.W. Taylor, *The Greeks on Pleasure* (Oxford: Clarendon, 1982); from within the analytic tradition, Leonard Katz's entry 'Pleasure' in the *Stanford Encyclopedia of Philosophy* is the most comprehensive. See also Darrin McMahon's fine study, *Happiness: A History* (New York: Atlantic Monthly Press, 2005).

4 Katz, 'Pleasure'.

5 Ibid.

6 John Locke, *An Essay concerning Human Understanding* (Oxford World's Classics; Oxford University Press, 2008), II.vii.1, p. 70.

7 Ibid., II.vii.2, p. 70.

8 Ibid., II.vii.2, p. 70.

9 Ibid., II. vii.3, p. 71.

10 Ibid., II. xx.1, p. 136.

11 On the Epicurean dimensions of Locke's thought, see Nevin Leddy and Avi Lifschitz, eds., *Epicurus in the Enlightenment* (Oxford: Voltaire Foundation, 2009), and Catherine Wilson, 'Epicureanism in Early Modern Philosophy', in James Warren, ed., *The Cambridge Companion to Epicureanism* (Cambridge University Press, 2009), pp. 266–86.

12 Samuel Johnson, 'Pleasure', in *A Dictionary of the English Language*, 5th edn, 2 vols. (London: Strahan, 1785), II.

13 'Pleasure', s.v. *The Encyclopedia of Diderot & d'Alembert*, Collaborative Translation Project, trans. Robert H. Ketchum (Ann Arbor: Scholarly Publishing Office of the University of Michigan Library, 2007), http://hdl.handle.net/2027/spo.did2222.0000.826. Trans. of 'Plaisir' in Denis Diderot and Jean Le Rond D'Alembert, *Encyclopédie, ou Dictionnaire raisonné des sciences, des arts et des métiers, par une société de gens de lettres*, 35 vols. (Paris [Geneva]: Briasson et al., 1751–80), XII, 689. See G.H. Nadel, 'Pouilly's Plagiarism', *Journal of the Warburg and Courtauld Institutes*, 30 (1967), 438–44 (p. 439).

14 See Adam Potkay, *The Story of Joy: From the Bible to Late Romanticism* (Cambridge University Press, 2007), for a strong interpretation of this term through a host of philosophical and literary texts.

15 Benedict de Spinoza, *Ethics*, trans. Edwin Curley (London: Penguin, 1996), p. 77. See the discussion in Gilles Deleuze, *Spinoza: Practical Philosophy*, trans. Robert Hurley (San Francisco: City Lights, 1988), p. 50, and Antonio Damasio, *Looking for Spinoza: Joy, Sorrow and the Feeling Brain* (Orlando: Harcourt, Inc., 2003).

16 Jonathan Israel, *Radical Enlightenment: Philosophy and the Making of Modernity 1650–1750* (Oxford University Press, 2001), and John Robertson, *The Case for the Enlightenment: Scotland and Naples, 1680–1760* (Cambridge University Press, 2005); for a literary engagement with Spinozism, see Marjorie Levinson, 'A Motion and a Spirit: Romancing Spinoza', *Studies in Romanticism*, 46 (2007), 367–408.

17 Translation by William F. Wertz, www.schillerinstitute.org/transl/trans_schil_2poems.html#the ode to joy. See Potkay's discussion in *The Story of Joy*.

18 Karl Marx and Frederick Engels, 'Critique of Modern German Philosophy according to its Representatives Feuerbach, B. Bauer and Stirner', *Collected Works*, 50 vols. (London: Lawrence and Wishart, 1975–90), V, *1845–7*, p. 46.

19 Friedrich Nietzsche, *On the Genealogy of Morals: A Polemic*, trans. Douglas Smith (Oxford University Press, 1996), p. 13. See also the discussion of Kantian disinterestedness, pp. 83–4.

20 Albert Hirschman, *The Passions and the Interests: Political Arguments for Capitalism before its Triumph* (Princeton University Press, 1977), pp. 36–42.

21 Istvan Hont, 'The Early Enlightenment Debate on Commerce and Luxury', in Mark Goldie and Robert Wokler, eds., *The Cambridge History of Eighteenth-Century Political Thought* (Cambridge University Press, 2006), pp. 379–415; Thomas Dixon, *The Invention of Altruism: Making Moral Meanings in Victorian Britain* (Oxford University Press, 2008); Pierre Force, *Self-Interest before Adam Smith: A Genealogy of Economic Science* (Cambridge University Press, 2003).

22 Christian Maurer, 'Self-Love in Early Eighteenth-Century British Moral Philosophy: Shaftesbury, Mandeville, Hutcheson, Butler and Campbell', Institut de philosophie, Université de Neuchatel, Neuchatel (2009).

23 See also the discussion of interest in nineteenth-century French thought in Tzvetan Todorov, *Imperfect Garden: The Legacy of Humanism* (Princeton University Press, 2002), pp. 207–25. Simon Jarvis has argued that 'The separation of pleasures into sensual pleasures, on the one hand, and disinterested (or, alternatively, "ideological") pleasures on the other, is governed by the progressive perfection of the distinction between production and consumption in modern economic reason', *Wordsworth's Philosophic Song* (Cambridge University Press, 2007), p. 126.

24 See especially Leddy and Lifschitz, eds., *Epicurus in the Enlightenment*, and Warren, ed., *The Cambridge Companion to Epicureanism*.

25 Warren, *The Cambridge Companion to Epicureanism*, p. 5.

26 Brad Inwood and L.P. Gerson, trans. and ed., *The Epicurus Reader: Selected Writings and Testimonia* (Indianapolis: Hackett, 1994), p. 30.

27 Gosling and Taylor, *The Greeks on Pleasure*, p. 353.

28 Gosling counters that 'living a life free of disturbance is not just a matter of staying alive and not being disturbed, as with a person under heavy sedation, but living the sort of life specific to the being in question', ibid., p. 361.

29 There is a useful discussion of self-interest in Pascal and Augustine, in Force, *Self-Interest*, pp. 50–2.

30 Cited, along with examples of Vico and Voltaire's response to Locke as Epicurean, in Matthew Niblett, 'Man, Morals and Matter: Epicurus and Materialist Thought in England from John Toland to Joseph Priestley', in Leddy and Lifschitz, eds., *Epicurus in the Enlightenment*, pp. 137–59. For a modern usage, see E.A. Driscoll, 'The Influence of Gassendi on Locke's Hedonism', *International Philosophical Quarterly*, 12 (1972), 87–110.

31 In economics, see Richard Layard, *Happiness: Lessons from a New Science* (London: Allen Lane, 2005); in positive psychology see, for instance, the work of Dan Gilbert and James Pawelski. For a critical discussion of this turn, see Sara Ahmed, 'The Happiness Turn', and my essay 'Walking back to Happiness', *New Formations*, 63 (2007–8), 7–14 and 138–44.

32 See the fine study by John E. Crowley, *The Invention of Comfort: Sensibilities and Design in Early Modern Britain and Early America* (Baltimore: Johns Hopkins University Press, 2000).

33 Matthew Arnold, 'Preface' to *Poems of Wordsworth* (London: Macmillan, 1879), v–xxvi (xxi) (reprinted as 'Wordsworth' in *Essays in Criticism: Second Series* (London: Macmillan, 1888), pp. 122–62).

34 Ibid., xviii, xix. See also 'Spinoza and the Bible' and 'The Bishop and the Philosopher', in Matthew Arnold, *Lectures and Essays in Criticism*, ed. R.H. Super (Ann Arbor: University of Michigan Press, 1962).

35 John Keble, *Keble's Lectures on Poetry, 1832–1841*, trans. Edward Kershaw Francis, in Gavin Budge, ed., *Aesthetics and Religion in Nineteenth-Century Britain*, 1 (Bristol: Thoemmes Press, 2003). See, for example, James K. Chandler, *Wordsworth's Second Nature: A Study of the Poetry and Politics*

(University of Chicago Press, 1984), xv–xvii, and David Simpson, *Wordsworth's Historical Imagination: The Poetry of Displacement* (New York: Methuen, 1987), p. 9.

36 Allan Wade, ed., *The Letters of W.B. Yeats* (London: Hart-Davis, 1954), p. 590.
37 'The Culture Industry: Enlightenment as Mass Deception', in Theodor Adorno and Max Horkheimer, *Dialectic of Enlightenment*, trans. John Cumming (London: Verso, 1979), pp. 120–67 (p. 144).
38 Lionel Trilling, 'The Fate of Pleasure', in *Beyond Culture: Essays on Literature and Learning* (Oxford University Press, 1980), pp. 57–88 (p. 51).
39 Roland Barthes, *The Pleasure of the Text*, trans. Richard Miller (New York: Hill & Wang, 1975), pp. 39, vii.
40 Rick Rylance approaches this claim in *Roland Barthes* (New York: Harvester, 1994), pp. 84–5. Michael Moriarty showed instead how Barthes wished to avoid 'a new stereotype' about contented pleasure in *Roland Barthes* (Cambridge: Polity, 1991), p. 151.
41 Barthes, *Pleasure of the Text*, pp. 57–8.
42 Ibid., p. 22.
43 Idleness and passivity are treated in different ways in Anne-Lise François, *Open Secrets: The Literature of Uncounted Experience* (Stanford University Press, 2008), and Richard Adelman, *Idleness, Contemplation and the Aesthetic, 1750–1830* (Cambridge University Press, 2011).
44 See Deleuze's response to Barthes in Gilles Deleuze, 'Dualism, Monism and Multiplicities (Desire–Pleasure–*Jouissance*): Seminar of 26 March 1973', trans. Daniel Smith, *Contretemps*, 2 (2001), 92–108; and on the debate between Deleuze and Foucault concerning the term of pleasure, see Gilles Deleuze, 'Désir et plaisir', *Magazine Littéraire*, 325 (October 1994), 59–65.
45 Fredric Jameson, 'Pleasure: A Political Issue', in *Formations of Pleasure* (London: Routledge and Kegan Paul, 1983), pp. 1–13 (p. 5).
46 Ibid., p. 10.
47 Ibid., p. 6.
48 Terry Eagleton, *The Ideology of the Aesthetic* (Oxford: Basil Blackwell, 1990), p. 9.
49 For instance, see Paul de Man's reading of renunciation in Rousseau and Wordsworth, in 'The Rhetoric of Temporality', in *Blindness and Insight: Essays in the Rhetoric of Contemporary Criticism*, 2nd edn (Minneapolis: University of Minnesota Press, 1983), pp. 187–228 (p. 205); Geoffrey Hartman's focus on apocalypse in *Wordsworth's Poetry 1787–1814* (New Haven: Yale University Press, 1964); and Frances Ferguson's reading of Wordsworth as ascetic in *Wordsworth: Language as Counter-Spirit* (New Haven: Yale University Press, 1979). Jacques Derrida attended to pleasure in *The Post Card: From Socrates to Freud and Beyond*, trans. Alan Bass (University of Chicago Press, 1987), pp. 40, 77, and in *Of Grammatology*, trans. Gayatri Chakravorty Spivak, 2nd edn (Baltimore and London: Johns Hopkins University Press, 1998).

50 Those who noticed the omission include Don Bialostosky in *Making Tales: The Poetics of Wordsworth's Narrative Experiments* (University of Chicago Press, 1984), pp. 28 and 88 n. 13, and David Simpson, who commented briefly that '[t]he place of pleasure in Wordsworth's analysis of the condition of England cannot be overemphasized', *Historical Imagination*, pp. 63–4.

51 Susan Manning celebrated Burns' honest pleasure and saw Wordsworth's account as puritan, disciplinary and solipsistic: Susan Manning, 'Burns and Wordsworth: Art and "The Pleasure which There Is in Life Itself"', in Porter and Roberts, eds., *Pleasure in the Eighteenth Century*, pp. 183–206 (pp. 190–1).

52 Jarvis' *Wordsworth's Philosophic Song* brilliantly exposes the problematic intellectual assumptions of such a methodology.

53 Michael Hardt and Antoni Negri, *Multitude: War and Democracy in the Age of Empire* (London: Penguin, 2006); Barbara Ehrenreich, *Dancing in the Streets: A History of Collective Joy* (London: Granta Books, 2007).

54 See especially the work of Susan Meld Shell. Romantic scholars drawing on this new anthropology include Simon Swift, *Romanticism, Literature and Philosophy: Expressive Rationality in Rousseau, Kant, Wollstonecraft and Contemporary Theory* (London: Continuum, 2006), and David L. Clark, in 'We "Other Prussians": Bodies and Pleasures in De Quincey and Late Kant', *European Romantic Review*, 14 (2003), 261–87.

55 See *Textual Practice*, 22: 1 (2008), passim, especially Emma Mason and Isobel Armstrong, 'Introduction', 1–19, and Peter de Bolla, 'Afterword', 145–50. Teresa Brennan argues in *The Transmission of Affect* (Ithaca: Cornell University Press, 2004) that only recently have we located feeling 'in' the individual, p. 2; Rei Terada discusses the way that emotion undermines the notion of subjectivity, *Feeling in Theory: Emotion after the 'Death of the Subject'* (Cambridge, MA: Harvard University Press, 2001), p. 3; Frances Ferguson, in *Pornography, the Theory: What Utilitarianism Did to Action* (Chicago University Press, 2004), looks at how individuals rely on 'social structures to produce motives and affections in themselves', p. 32; Nancy Yousef looks at the emotional and literary consequences of the fact of human dependency in *Isolated Cases: The Anxieties of Autonomy in Enlightenment Philosophy and Romantic Literature* (Ithaca: Cornell University Press, 2004), p. 3.

56 Adorno and Horkheimer, *Dialectic of Enlightenment*.

57 Alongside Jarvis, see Peter de Bolla, *Art Matters* (Cambridge, MA: Harvard University Press, 2001); John J. Joughin and Simon Malpas, eds., *The New Aestheticism* (Manchester University Press, 2003); and the 'Introduction' to James Chandler and Maureen N. McLane, eds., *The Cambridge Companion to Romantic Poetry* (Cambridge University Press, 2008), p. 5.

58 See particularly Thomas H. Schmid and Michelle Faubert, eds., *Romanticism and Pleasure* (New York: Palgrave Macmillan, 2010). Taking their lead from recent studies of Romantic consumption and taste as well as the 1990s work of Roy Porter, Susan Manning and others, Schmid and Faubert assert that the 'dichotomy – or, more properly, the fluid relationship – between sensual and aesthetic / cultural aspects of pleasure remains critically productive'

(p. 9). Unlike my study, theirs steers away from the philosophical tradition on pleasure exemplified by Kant, with a broadly historicist approach that sets Romantic pleasure in terms of 'cultural discourses' of the late eighteenth century, including psychiatry, psychology, disease, addiction and colonialism. Many of the book's contributions are premised on a sceptical opposition between a material pleasure and an ideological, abstract or transcendent version of it, as well as a philosophical pessimism concerning the inevitable interdependence of pleasure and pain; my work is more optimistic about the political dimensions of pleasure.

59 Letter to Carl Leonhard Reinhold, December 1787, Immanuel Kant, *Philosophical Correspondence*, trans. and ed. Arnulf Zweig (Cambridge University Press, 1999), p. 272.

60 For a discussion of such continuity, see Marshall Brown, 'Romanticism and Enlightenment', in Stuart Curran, ed., *The Cambridge Companion to British Romanticism* (Cambridge University Press, 1993), pp. 25–47 (p. 44).

61 See Robert Mauzi, *L'idée du bonheur dans la littérature et la pensée francaises au XVIIIe siècle* (Paris: Éditions Albin Michel, 1979; repr. 1994), p. 18, for a summary of Shaftesbury's impact on French thought, as well as John Andrew Bernstein, *Shaftesbury, Rousseau, and Kant* (New Jersey: Associated University Presses, 1980), p. 60, on Montesquieu as the link between Shaftesbury and Rousseau. On Shaftesbury's influence on German ideas and aesthetics see Ernst Cassirer, *The Platonic Renaissance in England*, trans. James Pettegrove (Edinburgh: Thomas Nelson, 1953), pp. 198–202.

62 Wordsworth refers to Shaftesbury in his *Essay, Supplementary to the Preface* (1815) as 'an author at present unjustly depreciated', W.J.B. Owen and Jane Worthington Smyser, eds., *The Prose Works of William Wordsworth*, 3 vols. (Oxford: Clarendon Press, 1974), III, p. 72. On Wordsworth's reading of specific texts by Shaftesbury, see Duncan Wu, *Wordsworth's Reading 1800–1815* (Cambridge University Press, 1996), p. 62. On Shaftesbury's influence on Wordsworth, see Newton P. Stallknecht, *Strange Seas of Thought: Studies in William Wordsworth's Philosophy of Man and Nature* (New York: Edwin Mellen, 2000), pp. 140–51, and Stuart Allen, *Wordsworth and the Passions of Critical Poetics* (Basingstoke: Palgrave Macmillan, 2010). According to Wu, Wordsworth had read Rousseau's *Social Contract* and *Discourse on Inequality* by 1793, and *Emile* by 1796, which is mentioned in the Preface to the *Borderers*, Duncan Wu, *Wordsworth's Reading 1770–1799* (Cambridge University Press, 1993), p. 119. Wordsworth does not appear to have owned a copy of Wollstonecraft's *Vindication*, but it was in the Stowey Book Society, in Wrangham's library, and extracted in newspapers; see Wu, *Wordsworth's Reading 1770–1799*, p. 139. There is some evidence that Wollstonecraft's *Letters from Sweden* influenced *The Ruined Cottage* and *Adventures on Salisbury Plain*; Coleridge apparently read it in 1796, and Wordsworth had a copy of the second edition; Wu, *Wordsworth's Reading 1770–1799*, p. 152.

63 Wu, *Wordsworth's Reading 1770–1799*, pp. 80–1; see also Paul Hamilton, *Coleridge and German Philosophy* (London: Continuum, 2007).

64 *Spectator*, No. 411, Saturday, 21 June 1712, in Robert J. Allen, ed., *Addison and Steele: Selections from the Tatler and the Spectator* (Orlando: Holt, Rinehart and Winston, 1970), p. 399.

65 Ibid., p. 399. Addison's ideology is discussed in Terry Eagleton, *The Function of Criticism: From the Spectator to Post-Modernism* (London: Verso, 1984).

66 Letter to Fordyce, 18 June 1742, cited in Robin Dix, *The Literary Career of Mark Akenside: Including an Edition of his Non-Medical Prose* (Cranbury, NJ: Rosemont, 2006), pp. 74–5.

67 Wordsworth, 'Preface' to the *Lyrical Ballads*, in Owen and Smyser, eds., *Prose Works*, II, p. 139. See, for instance, Robin Valenza, *Literature, Language, and the Rise of the Intellectual Disciplines in Britain, 1680–1820* (Cambridge University Press, 2009).

1 AESTHETICS OF PLEASURE: SHAFTESBURY, KANT AND THE *SENSUS COMMUNIS*

1 Benjamin Rand, ed., *The Life, Unpublished Letters and Philosophical Regimen of Anthony, Earl of Shaftesbury* (London: Swan Sonnenschein, 1900), p. 146. This is the only available English edition of the *Askemata*, and it is highly edited with modernized spelling; a more recent scholarly edition is *Exercises*, trans. Laurent Jaffro (Paris: Aubier, 1993). See the discussion of the *Askemata* in Robert Voitle, *The Third Earl of Shaftesbury: 1671–1713* (Baton Rouge: Louisiana State University Press, 1984), pp. 135–63.

2 Rand, ed., *Philosophical Regimen*, p. 143.

3 Ibid., pp. 144–5.

4 Ibid., p. 151.

5 Adam Smith, *Lectures on Rhetoric and Belles Lettres*, ed. J.C. Bryce (Indianapolis: Liberty Fund, 1993), pp. 56–7.

6 See Maurer, 'Self-Love'; Force, *Self-Interest*; Daniel Carey, *Locke, Shaftesbury and Hutcheson – Contesting Diversity in the Enlightenment and Beyond* (Cambridge University Press, 2006); S.L. Darwall, *The British Moralists and the Internal Ought, 1640–1740* (Cambridge University Press, 1995). An example of the earlier reading is Ernst Cassirer, *The Philosophy of the Enlightenment*, trans. F.C.A. Koelln and J.P. Pettegrove (Princeton University Press, 1951).

7 These individual texts were all published as one volume in 1711, and references here are all to Shaftesbury (Anthony Ashley Cooper, Third Earl of Shaftesbury, *Characteristics of Men, Manners, Opinions, Times*, ed. Lawrence Klein (Cambridge University Press, 1999), and will be given in parentheses in the text.

8 'A Search into the Nature of Society' was added to the second edition of the *Fable* (1723), Bernard Mandeville, *The Fable of the Bees and Other Writings*, ed. E.F. Hundert (Indianapolis: Hackett, 1997), p. 135.

9 Ibid., p. 323.

10 Ibid., p. 333.

11 Ibid., p. 337.

12 Ibid., p. 334.
13 Ibid., p. 369.
14 In the English texts and translations discussed here, both *sensus communis* and common sense are used: sometimes they are clearly differentiated, but, as in the case of Shaftesbury and Kant, different terms and derivations may be used in tandem. I generally use *sensus communis* but will highlight differences in usage where necessary; in the case of Arendt, I deploy the phrase of her translators, 'common sense', for consistency with her quotations.
15 William Empson, *The Structure of Complex Words*, 3rd edn (London: Penguin, 1995), p. 265.
16 Raymond Williams, *Keywords: A Vocabulary of Culture and Society* (London: Croom Helm, 1976), s.v. 'Common'.
17 Daniel Heller-Roazen, *The Inner Touch: The Archaeology of a Sensation* (New York: Zone Books, 2007), p. 21.
18 This is the translation given by Heller-Roazen, which he references as *De Anima*, 3.2.427a27. Another translation (though the line appears to be 3.1.425a) reads, 'We have then a common sense which apprehends common sensibles, not incidentally; and it is not a special sense', Aristotle, *On the Soul*, trans. W.S. Hett (Loeb Classical Library; Cambridge, MA: Harvard University Press, 1985), p. 145.
19 Heller-Roazen, *The Inner Touch*, pp. 37–8.
20 Hans-Georg Gadamer, *Truth and Method*, trans. and revised Joel Weinsheimer and Donald G. Marshall, 2nd edn (London: Sheed & Ward, 1989), p. 21.
21 See Brian Cowan, 'Reasonable Ecstasies: Shaftesbury and the Languages of Libertinism', *Journal of British Studies*, 37:2 (1998), 111–38, on Shaftesbury's treatment of sexuality.
22 Howard Caygill, *The Art of Judgement* (Oxford: Basil Blackwell, 1989), p. 50.
23 Ibid., p. 61.
24 Ibid., pp. 53, 61.
25 Lorraine Daston and Katharine Park, *Wonders and the Order of Nature, 1150–1750* (New York: Zone Books, 1998), p. 201.
26 Ibid., p. 205.
27 Rand, ed., *Philosophical Regimen*, p. 49.
28 Ibid., p. 161.
29 Ibid., p. 163.
30 Ibid., p. 55.
31 Carey, *Locke, Shaftesbury and Hutcheson*.
32 Mandeville, *The Fable of the Bees*, p. 324.
33 Voitle's major monograph on Shaftesbury gives *Sensus Communis* only a couple of pages, suggesting that it was merely a lower-level staging of his serious work. Voitle, *The Third Earl of Shaftesbury*, p. 333.
34 Sophia Rosenfeld, in *Common Sense: A Political History* (Harvard University Press, 2011), has recently argued that the Whiggish early eighteenth-century invention of common sense had a different, accidental kind of plurality built in (though she makes no reference to its link with theories of pleasure): 'it

simultaneously created just the opposite of what it promised: a mechanism for producing and even intensifying ideological strife within the context of this increasingly instable political order', p. 54.

35 Giambattista Vico, *On the Study Methods of Our Time*, trans. Elio Gianturco (Indianapolis: Bobbs-Merrill Company, 1965), pp. 19, 34.

36 Ibid., p. 21.

37 Ibid., p. 34.

38 Gadamer, *Truth and Method*, pp. 21, 22.

39 Ibid., pp. 21–2.

40 Ibid., p. 25.

41 Ibid., p. 25.

42 Ibid., p. 27.

43 Ibid., p. 34.

44 Ibid., p. 34.

45 Ibid., p. 41.

46 Ibid., pp. 271–7.

47 Kant, *Correspondence*, p. 272.

48 Immanuel Kant, *Critique of Judgment*, trans. Werner S. Pluhar (Indianapolis: Hackett Publishing Company, 1987), §29, p. 125. All further references (section and page number) to this edition will be given after quotations in the text.

49 Henry E. Allison, *Kant's Theory of Taste: A Reading of the 'Critique of Aesthetic Judgment'* (Cambridge University Press, 2001), p. 145.

50 See Ross Wilson, *Subjective Universality in Kant's Aesthetics* (Oxford: Peter Lang, 2008), for a full exposition of this theme.

51 The notion of what grounds another process or system in Kant is complex; see *A Kant Dictionary* (Oxford: Blackwell, 1995), s.v. 'Ground'. Paul Guyer considers Kant to have intended the common sense of §21–2 to bear a very strong function in the *Critique*, though he finds three major problems in Kant's argument for the *sensus communis*, concluding that it must remain 'an open question' whether Kant's strange doubts about the constitutive or regulative function of common sense are meant to 'remind us of its indeterminate applicability', or actually to bring his first justification of common sense into doubt, and thus 'prepare the way for a second attempt at a deduction of aesthetic judgment', *Kant and the Claims of Taste*, 2nd edn (Cambridge, MA: Harvard University Press, 1997), p. 272. Henry Allison sees common sense as not the *quid juri* of beauty, but rather a 'digression' on cognition, in line with the main argument of his book, that the question of the normativity of taste must be separated from its 'moral or systematic' significance; thus the demand for agreement in common sense is independent of morality: see Allison, *Kant's Theory of Taste*, pp. 53, 146.

52 John H. Zammito, *The Genesis of Kant's Critique of Judgment* (University of Chicago Press, 1992), pp. 272–3.

53 Thomas De Quincey, 'The Last Days of Immanuel Kant', David Masson, ed., *Collected Writings of Thomas De Quincey*, 14 vols. (London: A. & C. Black, 1897), IV, pp. 339–40.

54 See Clark, 'We "Other Prussians"'.

55 This draws from Gilles Deleuze, *Kant's Critical Philosophy: The Doctrine of the Faculties*, trans. Hugh Tomlinson and Barbara Habberjam (London: Athlone Press, 1984), p. 3.

56 Nancy, *Finite Thinking*, p. 201.

57 Deleuze, *Kant's Critical Philosophy*, p. 4.

58 On the place of 'life' in the *Critique of Judgment*, see: Wilson, *Subjective Universality*; Peter Fenves, *Late Kant: Towards Another Law of the Earth* (London: Routledge, 2003), p. 21; Howard Caygill, 'Life and Aesthetic Pleasure', in Andrea Rehberg and Rachel Jones, eds., *The Matter of Critique: Readings in Kant's Philosophy* (Manchester: Clinamen Press, 2000), pp. 79–92.

59 Fenves, *Late Kant*, p. 9.

60 Ibid., p. 9.

61 Ibid., p. 19.

62 On the presence of reflective judgement in the *Critique of Pure Reason*, see Béatrice Longuenesse, *Kant and the Capacity to Judge: Sensibility and Discursivity in the Transcendental Analytic of the 'Critique of Pure Reason'*, trans. Charles T. Wolfe (Princeton University Press, 1998). On the question of whether pleasure is posterior to judging, see Stanley Corngold, 'What is Radical in Kant's "Critique of Aesthetic Judgment"?', in *Complex Pleasure: Forms of Feeling in German Literature* (Stanford University Press, 1998), pp. 48–58, which will be discussed in Chapter 3.

63 Kant's idea of 'attention' is echoed in Gilbert Ryle, 'Pleasure', in *Collected Papers*, 2 vols. (London: Hutchinson, 1971), II, 325–35, repr. from *Proceedings of the Aristotelian Society* (1954), suppl. vol. XXVIII, pp. 135–46.

64 Jay Bernstein, *The Fate of Art: Aesthetic Alienation from Kant to Derrida and Adorno* (Cambridge: Polity, 1992), p. 58.

65 Ibid., p. 53.

66 Ibid., p. 64.

67 Ibid., p. 61.

68 On this pleasure as a form of future-directed intentionality, see Rachel Zuckert, *Kant on Beauty and Biology: An Interpretation of the Critique of Judgment* (Cambridge University Press, 2007), pp. 141–3.

69 Béatrice Longuenesse has likewise stressed that Kantian pleasure is 'strikingly active. Both kinds of pleasure are characterized by a specific effort, or striving: either an effort to produce (or reproduce) the object whose representation is accompanied by the feeling of pleasure; or the effort to remain in the state in which the mind affects itself, through its own activity, with a feeling of pleasure', *Kant on the Human Standpoint* (Cambridge University Press, 2005), p. 270 n. 7.

70 On the conception of pleasure as dynamic and corporeal see Caygill, 'Life and Aesthetic Pleasure', pp. 79–92.

71 Fenves, *Late Kant*, p. 23.

72 Allen W. Wood, *Kant's Ethical Thought* (Cambridge University Press, 1999), pp. 274–5.

73 Ibid., p. 251.
74 Ibid., p. 302.
75 Ibid., p. 302.
76 Ibid., p. 303.
77 Ibid., p. 318.
78 Swift, *Romanticism, Literature and Philosophy*, pp. 56–7.
79 Kant presented lectures on anthropology from 1772 to 1796, which he published in 1798 as a textbook entitled *Anthropologie in pragmatischer Hinsicht abgefaßt von Imamnuel Kant*, of which various English translations are available; the one used here is *Anthropology from a Pragmatic Point of View*, trans. and ed. Robert B. Louden (Cambridge University Press, 2006). All further references (page numbers) to this translation will be given after quotations in the text. Alongside this textbook, there are reflections and drafts for the lectures, as well as students' lecture notes, which were first published in a critical edition, *Kants gesammelte Schriften*, in 1997, contributing to a surge of new interest in Kantian anthropological thought.
80 Susan Meld Shell, 'Kant's "True Economy of Human Nature": Rousseau, Count Verri and the Problem of Happiness', in Brian Jacobs and Patrick Kain, eds., *Essays in Kant's Anthropology* (Cambridge University Press, 2003), pp. 194–229 (p. 221).
81 Ibid., pp. 197, 216.
82 Ibid., p. 215.
83 Immanuel Kant, *Anthropology from a Pragmatic Point of View*, trans. and ed. Mary J. Gregor (The Hague: Martinus Nijhoff, 1974), p. 203.
84 De Quincey, 'The Last Days of Immanuel Kant', p. 335.
85 This is Heller-Roazen's gloss / translation of Aristotle's discussion of friendship in the *Nicomachean Ethics, Inner Touch*, p. 298. He draws on Giorgio Agamben, 'L'amizia', which is available in English as 'On Friendship', trans. Joseph Falsone, in *Contretemps*, 5 December 2004, http://sydney.edu.au/contretemps/5december2004/agamben.pdf.
86 *Kant Dictionary*, s.v. 'Common Sense'.
87 David Ingrams, *Reason, History and Politics: The Communitarian Grounds of Legitimation in the Modern Age* (New York: SUNY, 1995), p. 280.
88 Hannah Arendt, *The Origins of Totalitarianism* (London: André Deutsch, 1986), pp. 476–7.
89 Hannah Arendt, *The Human Condition* (University of Chicago Press, 1958; repr. 1970), p. 283.
90 Hannah Arendt, *The Life of the Mind: One/Thinking* (New York and London: Harcourt Brace Jovanovich, 1971), p. 50. The phrase evokes Marx's discussion of species-being in the *Economic and Philosophical Manuscripts*.
91 Arendt, *Life of the Mind*, pp. 80, 79.
92 Ibid., p. 59.
93 See the discussion in Howard Caygill, 'The Shared World – Philosophy, Violence, Freedom', in Darren Sheppard, Simon Sparks and Colin Thomas, eds., *On Jean-Luc Nancy: The Sense of Philosophy* (London and New York:

Routledge, 1997), pp. 19–31, and in Linda M.G. Zerilli, '"We Feel Our Freedom": Imagination and Judgment in the Thought of Hannah Arendt', *Political Theory*, 33 (2005), 158–88.

94 Hannah Arendt, 'The Crisis in Culture', in *Between Past and Future: Eight Exercises in Political Thought* (London: Penguin, 1977), pp. 197–226 (p. 222).

95 See Ronald Beiner, 'Interpretive Essay', in Hannah Arendt, *Lectures on Kant's Political Philosophy*, ed. Ronald Beiner (Brighton: Harvester Press, 1982), pp. 89–156, and Patrick Riley, 'Hannah Arendt on Kant, Truth and Politics', *Political Studies*, 35:3 (1987), 379–92.

96 Arendt, 'Crisis in Culture', p. 223.

97 Ibid., p. 225.

98 Arendt, *Lectures*, p. 70.

99 Arendt, 'Crisis in Culture', pp. 220–1.

100 Zerilli, '"We Feel Our Freedom"', p. 171.

101 Ibid., p. 183, italics hers.

102 Beiner, 'Interpretive Essay', p. 118.

103 Arendt, *Lectures*, p. 30.

104 Julia Kristeva, *Hannah Arendt*, trans. Ross Guberman (New York: Columbia University Press, 2001), p. 178.

105 Ibid., p. 300.

106 Rei Terada, 'The Life Process and Forgettable Living: Arendt and Agamben', *New Formations*, 71 (2011), 95–109.

107 Simon Swift, 'Hannah Arendt's Tactlessness: Reading Eichmann in Jerusalem', *New Formations*, 71 (2011), 79–94 (94).

108 Ronald Beiner, 'Rereading Hannah Arendt's Kant Lectures', in Ronald Beiner and Jennifer Nedelsky, eds., *Judgment, Imagination and Politics* (Lanham: Rowman and Littlefield, 2001), pp. 91–101, repr. in Garrath Williams, ed., *Hannah Arendt: Critical Assessments of Leading Political Philosophers*, 4 vols. (London: Routledge, 2006), IV, pp. 254–64 (pp. 260, 259).

109 Beiner, 'Rereading Hannah Arendt's Kant Lectures', p. 259.

110 Jean-François Lyotard, 'Sensus Communis', trans. Marion Hobson and Geoff Bennington, *Paragraph*, 11:1 (1988), 1–25 (14).

111 Ibid., p. 13.

112 Ibid., p. 11.

113 Ibid., p. 21.

114 Ibid., p. 22.

115 Ibid., p. 12.

116 Ibid., p. 22.

117 This trend could be said to begin with Thomas Weiskel, *The Romantic Sublime: Studies in the Structure and Psychology of Transcendence* (Baltimore: Johns Hopkins University Press, 1976), and was followed by numerous monographs and articles on the sublime in both French and Anglophone literary criticism and philosophy.

118 Paul de Man, 'Phenomenality and Materiality in Kant', in Andrzej Warminski, ed., *Aesthetic Ideology* (Minneapolis: University of Minnesota Press, 1995), pp. 70–90 (p. 73), my italics.

119 Frances Ferguson, *Solitude and the Sublime: Romanticism and the Ethics of Individuation* (New York: Routledge, 1992), p. 45.

120 Ibid., p. 45.

121 Kath Renark Jones, 'Exposing Community: Towards a Dynamic of *Commercium*', in Andrea Rehberg and Rachel Jones, eds., *The Matter of Critique: Readings in Kant's Philosophy* (Manchester: Clinamen, 2000), pp. 129–46 (p. 130).

122 Ibid., p. 132.

123 Ibid., pp. 135–6.

124 Vivaswan Soni, 'Communal Narcosis and Sublime Withdrawal: The Problem of Continuity in Kant's Critique of Judgment', *Cultural Critique* 64 (2006), 1–39 (25).

125 Ibid., 30.

126 Ibid., 29.

127 For a history of the epistemic value of pain, see George Levine, *Dying to Know: Scientific Epistemology and Narrative in Victorian England* (Chicago University Press, 2002).

128 Soni, 'Communal Narcosis and Sublime Withdrawal', 29.

129 Caygill, 'The Shared World', p. 23.

130 Georges Bataille, *Eroticism*, trans. Mary Dalwood (London: Penguin, 2001), p. 22.

131 Ibid., p. 17.

132 Maurice Blanchot, *The Unavowable Community*, trans. Pierre Joris (New York: Station Hill Press, 1988), p. 17.

133 Ibid., pp. 17, 18.

134 Jean-Luc Nancy, 'The Inoperative Community', in *The Inoperative Community*, ed. and trans. Peter Connor et al. (Minneapolis: University of Minnesota Press, 1991), pp. 1–42 (p. 14).

135 Ibid., pp. 25–6.

136 Ibid., p. 3.

137 Ibid., p. 19.

138 Ibid., p. 20.

139 J.-L. Nancy, *Le plaisir au dessin: carte blanche à Jean-Luc Nancy* (Paris: Hazan; Lyon: Museée des Beaux-Arts de Lyon, 2007), p. 20. Further references are given in parentheses; rough translations are my own.

140 Nancy, 'Inoperative Community', p. 34.

141 The frontispiece to Hobbes' *Leviathan* provides a powerful image of sublime, fearful community. In the early twenty-first century, political campaigns both in Britain and the US have defined community negatively by threat and terror.

142 Hardt and Negri, *Multitude*, p. 224.

143 Jon Mee, *Romanticism, Enthusiasm, and Regulation: Poetics and the Policing of Culture in the Romantic Period* (Oxford University Press, 2003).
144 Allen, *Wordsworth*, p. 13.

2 POWERS OF PLEASURE: ROUSSEAU AND WOLLSTONECRAFT

1 Raymond Trousson, quoted in Leopold Damrosch, *Jean-Jacques Rousseau: Restless Genius* (Boston, MA: Houghton Mifflin, 2005), p. 48.
2 Jean-Jacques Rousseau, *The Confessions and Correspondence including the Letter to Malesherbes*, in *The Collected Writings of Rousseau*, 12 vols. (Hanover: University Press of New England, 1995), v, p. 48.
3 Illnesses included depression, stomach problems, an enlarged prostate, gout, dropsy, insomnia, liver problems, neurological problems after being hit by a dog, pneumonia, short-sightedness, tinnitus, toothache and venereal disease: see Damrosch, *Rousseau*, p. 556.
4 It has recently been translated for the first time in *Autobiographical, Scientific, Religious, Moral, and Literary Writings*, in *Collected Writings of Rousseau*, ed. Kelly and Masters, XII, pp. 57–61.
5 Irving Babbitt, *Rousseau and Romanticism* (Boston, MA: Houghton, 1919), p. 307.
6 Ernst Cassirer, *The Question of Jean-Jacques Rousseau*, trans. and ed. Peter Gay (New York: Columbia University Press, 1954).
7 Ibid., p. 109.
8 Ibid., p. 81.
9 George Armstrong Kelly, 'General Overview', in Patrick Riley, ed., *The Cambridge Companion to Rousseau* (Cambridge University Press, 2001), pp. 8–56 (p. 15).
10 De Man, 'Rhetoric of Temporality', p. 203.
11 Ibid., p. 204.
12 Ibid., p. 207.
13 Derrida, *Of Grammatology*, p. 280.
14 Ibid., p. 166.
15 Jean-Jacques Rousseau, *The Reveries of the Solitary Walker, Botanical Writings, and Letter to Franquières*, in *Collected Writings of Rousseau*, VIII (2000), p. 36. Further references to this edition are given in parentheses after quotations in the text.
16 Derrida, *Of Grammatology*, p. 280.
17 Ibid., p. 155.
18 Ibid., p. 143.
19 Ibid., p. 163.
20 Ibid., pp. 142–3.
21 Michel Foucault, *The History of Sexuality: An Introduction*, I, trans. Robert Hurley (New York: Random House, 1978), p. 45.
22 Ibid., p. 45.

23 Ibid., pp. 85, 91.
24 'Introduction', to Jean-Jacques Rousseau, *Julie, or the New Heloise*, in *The Collected Writings of Rousseau*, ed. Kelly and Masters, VII, p. xiv. All further references to this edition will be given in parentheses in the text.
25 Nancy, *Le plaisir*, p. 20.
26 William Ray has written of a shift from the romance's 'erotic suspense' to the political allegory's 'cognitive mode of pleasure', in 'Reading Women: Cultural Authority, Gender and the Novel: The Case of Rousseau', *Eighteenth-Century Studies*, 27 (1994), 421–47 (430).
27 For an extensive discussion of Rousseau's domestic economy, see Bertil Fridén, *Rousseau's Economic Philosophy: Beyond the Market of Innocents* (Dordrecht and London: Kluwer Academic, 1998).
28 Jean-Jacques Rousseau, *Emile, or, On Education*, trans. Allan Bloom (New York: Basic Books, 1979), 80. All further references to this edition will be given in parentheses in the text.
29 See, for instance, N.J.H. Dent, *Rousseau: An Introduction to his Psychological, Social and Political Theory* (Oxford: Basil Blackwell, 1988), and the important recent study, Frederick Neuhouser, *Rousseau's Theodicy of Self-Love: Evil, Rationality and the Drive for Recognition* (Oxford University Press, 2008).
30 N.J.H. Dent, *A Rousseau Dictionary* (Oxford: Blackwell, 1992), s.v. 'Amour de soi'.
31 Jean-Jacques Rousseau, *Rousseau, Judge of Jean-Jacques: Dialogues*, in *Collected Writings of Rousseau*, ed. Kelly and Masters, I. All further references to this edition will be given in parentheses in the text.
32 Rousseau drafted a refutation of *De L'esprit*, which is thought to have been material for his *Sensitive Morality; or, the Wise Man's Materialism*. See 'Notes on Helvétius' *On the Mind*', in Rousseau, *Autobiographical Writings*, in *Collected Writings of Rousseau*, ed. Kelly and Masters, XII, pp. 204–12.
33 Kelly, 'A General Overview', p. 23.
34 This transitivity arguably presents another version of what Susan Moller Okin called the 'functionalism' of Western philosophy's attitudes towards women, in *Women in Western Political Thought* (Princeton University Press, 1979). Instead of asking 'what is woman?', she argues that male philosophers have asked 'what is woman for?'; we might say that Rousseau's answer is 'to give pleasure'.
35 See Lynda Lange, 'Rousseau and Modern Feminism', in Lynda Lange, ed., *Feminist Interpretations of Jean-Jacques Rousseau* (University Park, PA: Pennsylvania State University Press, 2002), pp. 24–41.
36 Barbara Taylor, *Mary Wollstonecraft and the Feminist Imagination* (Cambridge University Press, 2003), p. 80.
37 Ibid., p. 79.
38 Susan Meld Shell, 'Emile: Nature and the Education of Sophie', in Patrick Riley, ed., *The Cambridge Companion to Rousseau* (Cambridge University Press), pp. 272–301 (p. 291).
39 Ibid., p. 291.

40 Taylor, *Feminist Imagination*, pp. 77, 90–1.
41 Meld Shell, 'Nature and the Education of Sophie', p. 294.
42 Mary Wollstonecraft, *A Vindication of the Rights of Men, with, A Vindication of the Rights of Woman*, ed. Sylvana Tomaselli (Cambridge University Press, 1995). All page references to this edition will be given in parentheses in the text.
43 On the pleasures of sugar as advancing Western capitalism, see Sidney W. Mintz, *Sweetness and Power: The Place of Sugar in Modern History* (New York and Harmondsworth: Viking Penguin, 1985).
44 Cora Kaplan, *Sea Changes: Essays in Culture and Feminism* (London: Verso, 1986), p. 39.
45 Thomas Pfau, *Romantic Moods: Paranoia, Trauma and Melancholy, 1790–1840* (Baltimore: Johns Hopkins University Press, 2005), p. 97.
46 See, for example, Ewa Badowska, 'The Anorexic Body of Liberal Feminism: Mary Wollstonecraft's *A Vindication of the Rights of Woman*', *Tulsa Studies in Women's Literature*, 17:2 (1998), 283–303, reproduced in Harriet Devine Jump, ed., *Mary Wollstonecraft and the Critics, 1788–2001*, 2 vols. (Routledge: London, 2003), II, pp. 320–40. For Badowska, who argues that Wollstonecraft's text follows an 'anorexic logic' where words and food are confused, Wollstonecraft's fear of dirtiness evinces a desire to 'contain the incorporative and excretory processes that threaten the integrity of the female person' (p. 330).
47 Spinoza, *Ethics* (III, P2), p. 71.
48 Adriana Craciun, 'Violence against Difference: Mary Wollstonecraft and Mary Robinson', in Greg Clingham, ed., *Making History: Textuality and the Forms of Eighteenth-Century Culture* (= *Bucknell Review* 42:1 (1997)), III–41 (126).
49 Alexander Pope, 'Epistle to a Lady: Of the Characters of Women', in F.W. Bateson, *The Twickenham Edition of the Poems of Alexander Pope*, 10 vols. (London: Methuen, 1951), III-ii, pp. 46–74 (p. 67).
50 See especially the work of Simon Swift, Barbara Taylor and Susan Meld Shell.
51 The thirty-two *Hints*, ranging from single sentences to long paragraphs of prose, were first published in William Godwin's *Posthumous Works* (1798): see Wollstonecraft, *Vindication*, p. 295.
52 See, for instance, Mary Poovey, *The Proper Lady and the Woman Writer: Ideology as Style in the Works of Mary Wollstonecraft, Mary Shelley, and Jane Austen* (University of Chicago Press, 1984), pp. 82–3.
53 Nancy Yousef, 'Wollstonecraft, Rousseau and the Revision of Romantic Subjectivity', *Studies in Romanticism*, 38:4 (1999), 537–57 (552).
54 Ibid., 555.
55 Mary Wollstonecraft, *The Wrongs of Woman, or Maria*, in *The Works of Mary Wollstonecraft*, ed. Janet Todd and Marilyn Butler, 6 vols. (London: Pickering, 1989), I, 123. All page references are to this edition and will appear in parentheses in the text.

56 For instance: 'the inflamed, volatile emotions Wollstonecraft castigates as weakness, folly and madness in her polemic infuse, motivate, and elevate the heroines of both novels'. Susan Gubar, 'Feminist Misogyny: Mary Wollstonecraft and the Paradox of "It Takes One to Know One"', *Feminist Studies*, 20:3 (1994), 543–74, reprinted in Jump, ed., *Mary Wollstonecraft and the Critics*, p. 153. Anne K. Mellor responds with the 'parodic' argument in 'Righting the Wrongs of Woman: Mary Wollstonecraft's *Maria*', *Nineteenth-Century Contexts*, 19 (1996), 413–24, reprinted in the above volume, pp. 198–210. Mellor, 'Righting the Wrongs of Woman', p. 203.

57 Taylor, *Feminist Imagination*, p. 139.

58 Simon Swift, 'Mary Wollstonecraft and the Reserve of Reason', *Studies in Romanticism*, 45:1 (2006), 3–24 (5).

59 See Swift, *Expressive Rationality*, passim. Claudia Johnson has also argued that Wollstonecraft was influenced by Johnson's *Rasselas*, and that text's account of how our restless desire for happiness 'activates' us, 'Mary Wollstonecraft's Novels', in *The Cambridge Companion to Mary Wollstonecraft* (Cambridge University Press, 2002), pp. 189–208 (p. 192).

60 A search for 'social pleasure' and 'social enjoyment' in the InteLex Past Masters philosophical texts database reveals their occurrence in the work of Shaftesbury, David Hume, Adam Smith and Samuel Johnson.

61 *The Works of Mary Wollstonecraft*, ed. Todd and Butler, IV, p. 131.

62 Theodor Adorno, No. 55, 'May I be so bold?', *Minima Moralia: Reflections on a Damaged Life*, trans. E.F.N. Jephcott, 2nd edn (London: Verso, 2005), pp. 90–1 (p. 91).

63 Peter Hallward, *Out of This World: Deleuze and the Philosophy of Creation* (London: Verso, 2006), p. 61.

64 Laurence Cooper, 'Between Eros and the Will to Power: Rousseau and "The Desire to Extend Our Being"', *American Political Science Review*, 98:1 (2004), 105–19, repr. in John T. Scott, ed., *Jean-Jacques Rousseau: Critical Assessments of Leading Political Philosophers*, 4 vols. (London: Routledge, 2006), II, pp. 443–75 (p. 466).

65 Cooper, 'Between Eros and the Will to Power', p. 447.

66 Eve Grace, 'The Restlessness of "Being": Rousseau's Protean Sentiment of Existence', *History of European Ideas*, 27 (2001), 133–51, repr. in Scott, ed., *Critical Assessments*, II, pp. 397–415 (p. 413).

67 Ibid., p. 413.

68 Ibid., p. 405.

69 Ibid., p. 408.

70 Ibid., p. 408.

3 POETICS OF PLEASURE IN *LYRICAL BALLADS*

1 Charles Lamb, letter to Manning, 15 February 1801, in Robert Woof, *William Wordsworth: The Critical Heritage*, I: *1793–1820* (Abingdon: Routledge, 2001), p. 100.

2 Thomas De Quincey, letter of 14 March 1804, in ibid., p. 123.

3 John Wilson, letter to Wordsworth, 24 May 1802, in ibid., pp. 112, 113.

4 Wordsworth, letter to John Wilson, undated, June 1802, in William Words-worth, *The Early Letters of William and Dorothy Wordsworth (1787–1805)*, ed. Ernest De Selincourt (Oxford: Clarendon, 1935), p. 294.

5 Ibid., p. 295.

6 Ibid., p. 298.

7 Wordsworth, 1850 (=1802) 'Preface' to *Lyrical Ballads*, ll. 399–400 (l. 413). All further references to the prose documents associated with the *Lyrical Ballads* are from Owen and Smyser, eds., *Prose Works*, I, pp. 116–65; for the convenience of readers with different editions, line references not page numbers for each text will be given in parentheses in the text.

8 The examples of these arguments are numerous in Romantic criticism of the past two decades, but lucid and nuanced discussions may be found in Thomas Pfau, *Wordsworth's Profession: Form, Class, and the Logic of Early Romantic Cultural Production* (Stanford University Press, 1997), which compared the models of readerly pleasure as passive consumption to the middle-class 'logic of self-surveillance', experienced as an active pleasure; and Mee, *Romanticism*.

9 See Manning, 'Burns and Wordsworth', and Tim Milnes, *Knowledge and Indifference in English Romantic Prose* (Cambridge University Press, 2003), pp. 89–90.

10 William Wordsworth, 'Lines Written in Early Spring' (1798), in *Lyrical Ballads and Other Poems 1797–1800*, ed. James Butler and Karen Green (Ithaca: Cornell University Press, 1992), p. 76. A significant alteration was made to the final stanza for the 1820 *Miscellaneous Poems*; it reads 'If this belief from Heaven is sent, / If such be nature's holy plan', *Lyrical Ballads*, p. 76.

11 Yousef, 'The Revision of Romantic Subjectivity', 548.

12 'Periwinkles', in Maud Grieve, *A Modern Herbal: The Medicinal, Culinary, Cosmetic and Economic Properties, Cultivation and Folk-Lore of Herbs, Grasses, Fungi, Shrubs & Trees with their Modern Scientific Uses*, 2 vols. (New York: Hafner, 1931; repr. 1967), II, pp. 629–30.

13 Rousseau, *Confessions and Correspondence*, in *Collected Writings of Jean-Jacques Rousseau*, ed. Kelly and Masters, V, p. 190.

14 William Hazlitt, 'On the Character of Rousseau', from *The Round Table: A Collection of Essays on Literature, Men and Manners*, 2 vols. (Edinburgh: Archibald, 1817), II, p. 55.

15 Ben Ross Schneider, *Wordsworth's Cambridge Education* (Cambridge University Press, 1957); Wu, *Wordsworth's Reading 1770–1799*, p. 110.

16 Heller-Roazen, *Inner Touch*, pp. 101–15.

17 William Paley, *Moral and Political Philosophy* (London: R. Faulder, 1785), Chapter VI, 'Human Happiness', pp. 33–4.

18 See, for instance, the Cornell *Lyrical Ballads*, p. 349; Richard Matlak, 'Wordsworth's Reading of *Zoönomia* in "Early Spring"', *Wordsworth Circle*, 21:2 (1990), 76–81; Ashton Nicholls, 'The Loves of Plants and Animals:

Romantic Science and the Pleasures of Nature', in James McKusick, ed., *Romantic Ecology*, November 2001, *Romantic Circles*, www.rc.umd.edu/praxis/ecology/nichols/nichols.html.

19 Paley, *Moral and Political Philosophy*, p. 34.

20 William Paley, *Reasons for Contentment: Addressed to the Labouring Part of the British Public* (Carlisle: F. Jollie, 1792), p. 16.

21 Owen and Smyser, eds., *Prose Works*, I, p. 103. Hazlitt commented that Wordsworth 'approves of Walton's *Angler*, Paley and some other writers of an inoffensive modesty of pretension', in William Hazlitt, *The Spirit of the Age, or, Contemporary Portraits*, ed. E.D. Mackerness (London: Collins, 1969), p. 148.

22 For the dominance of pleasure-pain ethics in Cambridge in the 1780s and 1790s, see Schneider, *Wordsworth's Cambridge Education*, p. 121.

23 Paley, *Reasons for Contentment*, p. 18.

24 Ibid., p. 20.

25 Ibid., p. 8.

26 Ibid., p. 11.

27 'The Barberry-Tree', in William Wordsworth, *Poems, in Two Volumes, and Other Poems, 1800–1807*, ed. Jared Curtis (Ithaca: Cornell University Press, 1983), pp. 576–9. Jonathan Wordsworth, in *William Wordsworth: The Borders of Vision* (Oxford: Clarendon Press, 1982), reads it as a response to Coleridge's *Dejection: An Ode*; though I think these blissful questions are central to Wordsworth's whole oeuvre.

28 The word counts of other positive affect terms: 1798 Advertisement: 'gratification' (1). 1800 'Preface': 'pleased' (7); 'pleasurable' (1); 'enjoy'/'enjoyments' (5); 'joys' (1); 'delight' (1). 1802 'Preface': 'please' (10); 'enjoy' and variants (7); 'delight' (4); 'gratification' (3); 'joys' (1).

29 Entry for 1808, Henry Crabb Robinson, *Diary, Reminiscences, and Correspondence*, I, ed. Thomas Sadler (London: Macmillan, 1869), p. 265.

30 Owen and Smyser, eds., *Prose Works*, I, pp. 173–83.

31 Allen, *Wordsworth*, p. 70.

32 Adela Pinch claims that the 'principle of similitude in dissimilitude' is heterosexist, in *Strange Fits of Passion: Epistemologies of Emotion, Hume to Austen* (Stanford University Press, 1999), p. 88. Wordsworth does not write about homosexuality (unlike the imaginative and open-minded Bentham); yet surely his account of erotic passion as simultaneous feelings of sameness and difference would be applicable to any pair of lovers.

33 Kenneth Johnston, *The Hidden Wordsworth* (London: Pimlico, 2000), p. 549.

34 Coleridge, letter to Southey, 29 July 1802, in Woof, *Wordsworth*, p. 118.

35 C.P. Snow, *The Two Cultures* (Cambridge University Press, 2012). On the development of the idea of objectivity, see Lorraine Daston and Peter Galison, *Objectivity* (New York: Zone, 2007).

36 See Joseph Priestley, *The History and Present State of Electricity, with Original Experiments* (London: Dodsley, 1767). A theoretical account of analogy

appears in Michel Foucault, *The Order of Things: The Archaeology of Human Sciences* (London: Routledge, 2001), p. 21.

37 The question of the scientist's *actual* solitude in the period is much discussed; for instance, see Ludmilla Jordanova, 'Melancholy Reflections: Constructing an Identity for the Unveilers of Nature', in Stephen Bann, ed., *Frankenstein: Creation and Monstrosity* (London: Reaktion, 1994), pp. 60–76 (pp. 63–4).

38 On the specialization of knowledge in the late eighteenth century, see Foucault, *Order of Things*, and more recently Valenza, *The Rise of the Intellectual Disciplines*.

39 Humphry Davy, *A Discourse Introductory to a Course of Lectures on Chemistry, Delivered in the Theatre of the Royal Institution*, on 21 January 1802, in *The Collected Works of Sir Humphry Davy*, II, ed. John Davy (London: Smith, Elder and Co., 1839), pp. [307]–26 (p. 325).

40 This seems a point missed by Milnes when he argues that Wordsworth moves away from a '"cognitive theory" of pleasure' because, 'qualitatively, pleasure is a leveller: it is always undifferentiated, and varies only in degrees of quantity', pp. 89–90.

41 Philip Connell, *Romanticism, Economics and the Question of 'Culture'* (Oxford University Press, 2001), p. 30.

42 Frances Ferguson, 'Wordsworth and the Meaning of Taste', in Stephen Gill, ed., *The Cambridge Companion to Wordsworth* (Cambridge University Press, 2003), pp. 90–107 (pp. 96–7).

43 Ibid., p. 98.

44 Ibid., p. 102.

45 Note the same metaphor in Kant's description of man's pleasure in nature as an indication of his ontological security: 'Die Schöne Dinge zeigen an, daß der Mensch in die Welt passe und selbst seine Anschauung der Dinge mit den Gesetzen seiner Anschauung stimme', Reflexion aus dem Jahr 1771 (Refl. 1820a), *Kants gesammelte Schriften*, 29 vols. (Berlin: de Gruyter, 1924), XVI, p. 127. Hannah Arendt's translation brings out the idea of 'affection': 'The fact that man is affected by the sheer beauty of nature proves that he is made for and fits into this world', *Lectures*, p. 30.

46 Blake scrawled a paratextual rebellion on the copy of *The Excursion* he borrowed from Henry Crabb Robinson around 1825: 'You shall not bring me down to believe such fitting & fitted I know better and Please Your Lordship', G.T. Bentley, Jr, *William Blake's Writings*, II: *Writings in Conventional Typography and in Manuscript* (Oxford: Clarendon Press, 1978), p. 1507.

47 Brendan O'Donnell, *The Passion of Meter: A Study of Wordsworth's Metrical Art* (Kent State University Press, 1995), p. 43.

48 Ibid., pp. 45–6.

49 Owen and Smyser, eds., *Prose Works*, I, p. 103.

50 Corngold, *Complex Pleasure*, p. 50.

51 Ibid., p. 55.

52 Ibid., pp. 56–7.

53 Ibid., p. 57.
54 Wordsworth appears to have owned a copy of Thomas Creech, trans., *Titus Lucretius Carus: His Six Books of Epicurean Philosophy, Done into English Verse* (London: T. Bradyll, 1699), from the 1780s, see Wu, *Wordsworth's Reading 1800–1815*, p. 256. He may also have studied the original at Hawkshead, and read James Beattie's translation in *Original Poems and Translations* (1760); see Wu, *Wordsworth's Reading 1770–1799*, p. 90. On allusions and similarities, see Willard Spiegelman, 'Some Lucretian Elements in Wordsworth', *Comparative Literature*, 37 (1985), 27–47.
55 Creech, trans., *Titus Lucretius Carus*, p. 41 (Lucretius, *De Rerum Natura*, II. 216–24).
56 Harold Bloom, *The Anxiety of Influence: A Theory of Poetry*, 2nd edn (Oxford University Press, 1997), p. 14.
57 Gilles Deleuze, *Difference and Repetition*, trans. Paul Patton, 2nd edn (London: Continuum, 2001), p. 232.
58 Nancy, 'The Inoperative Community', in *The Inoperative Community*, trans. Connor et al., pp. 3–4.

4   ECONOMIES OF AFFECT IN *THE PRELUDE* AND *HOME AT GRASMERE*

1 References are to William Wordsworth, *The Prelude, 1799, 1805, 1850*, ed. Jonathan Wordsworth, M.H. Abrams and Stephen Gill (New York: W.W. Norton, 1979), and will be given as book and line numbers in the text.
2 Milnes notes that *The Prelude* 'oscillates' between 'ontological exploration' and 'demonstration and argumentation', *Knowledge and Indifference*, p. 93.
3 On the relationship between Hartley's doctrine and Wordsworth, see Arthur Beatty, 'Wordsworth, Hartley and English Philosophy', in *William Wordsworth: His Doctrine and Art in their Historical Relation* (Madison: University of Wisconsin Press, 1922), pp. 89–116. On Coleridge's debt to Hartley see Jerome Christensen, *Coleridge's Blessed Machine of Language* (Ithaca: Cornell University Press, 1981). On Wordsworth's relation to Brunonianism see Paul Youngquist, 'Lyrical Bodies: Wordsworth's Physiological Aesthetics', *European Romantic Review*, 10:2 (1999), 152–62. On Wordsworth and Erasmus Darwin, see Matlak, 'Wordsworth's Reading of *Zoönomia* in "Early Spring"'.
4 David Hartley, *Observations on Man*, 2 vols. (London: Richardson, 1749), I, Proposition 33, p. 143. Hartleian associationism describes pleasures and pains as 'internal Feelings' arising from impressions produced by external objects, as distinct from Ideas; these feelings differ not in kind but in degree. Moderate impressions gently agitate the tiny particles of the medullary substance, causing pleasure; whereas when they are pulled violently apart, and cannot return to their normal situation, pain occurs. Pains can in time become pleasures; vivid pleasures can become faint, because upon the regular impact of painful vibration, the receiving organ gradually changes so that weaker vibrations will be sent to the brain.

5 Ibid., p. 143.

6 Ibid., p. 144.

7 See, for instance, Sharon Ruston, *Shelley and Vitality* (Basingstoke: Palgrave Macmillan, 2005), and Denise Gigante, *Life: Organic Form and Romanticism* (New Haven and London: Yale University Press, 2009). Health, on the other hand, is a somewhat neglected topic in scholarship.

8 John Brown, *Elementa Medicinae* (Edinburgh: Denovan, 1784); Thomas Beddoes, ed., *The Elements of Medicine of John Brown, M.D., Translated from the Latin, with Comments and Illustrations by the Author*, 2 vols. (London: J. Johnson, 1795). All references are to Beddoes' translation. 'Brunonianism' had a huge influence over two generations of Romantics both in Britain and Germany, with quite different inflections, materialist and transcendental. See W.F. Bynum and Roy Porter, eds., *Brunonianism in Britain and Europe* (= *Medical History*, Supplement No. 8, London: Wellcome Institute, 1988), and Neil Vickers, *Coleridge and the Doctors 1795–1806* (Oxford: Clarendon Press, 2004), pp. 43–62.

9 Beddoes, ed., *Elements*, I, p. 102.

10 Ibid., I, pp. 102–3.

11 Beddoes, an ambivalent disseminator of Brunonianism, borrowed Claudius Secundus' aphorism to epitomize Brunonianism: 'Balnea, vina, venus, corrompunt copora nostra / sed vitam faciunt balnea, vina, venus' ('Wine, warmth and love our vigour drain / Yet wine, warmth and love our life sustain'), ibid., I, pp. cxxxi, 112.

12 Ibid., I, pp. 1, 55. 'Perfect health, which consists in the middle point solely, or forty degrees, rarely occurs; in consequence of the variation of the stimuli to which man is continually exposed', 'Table of Excitement and Excitability', ibid., I.

13 Ibid., I, pp. 44–5, 58.

14 Wordsworth may also have been influenced by Erasmus Darwin's physiology, outlined in his prose work *Zoönomia* (1794–5), which shared many of the features of Brown's *Elementa*, though with a more explicit role for pleasure. But Darwin also noted his own debt to Brown: 'The coincidence of some parts of this work with correspondent deductions in the Brunonian Elementa Medicina, a work (with some exceptions) of great genius, must be considered as confirmations of the truth of the theory, as they were probably arrived at by different trains of reasoning', Martin Priestman, ed., *The Collected Writings of Erasmus Darwin*, 9 vols. (Bristol: Thoemmes, 2003), V, p. 75. Paul Youngquist notes that Wordsworth's notion of pleasure sounds like Cullen's 'nervous energy' or Whytt's 'sentient principle', p. 158.

15 Here I disagree with Youngquist, who sees Wordsworth's use of pleasure as a placeholder for Brown's 'excitability', but feels that Wordsworth refuses the 'tragic' implications of Brunonianism and that all is ideologically guarded by the centrality of the 'rational mind', 'Lyrical Bodies', p. 158.

16 William Hazlitt, 'On Burns, and the Old Ballads', in *Selected Writings of William Hazlitt*, ed. Duncan Wu, 9 vols. (London: Pickering, 1998), II,

p. 286. A more recent example is Denise Gigante, *Taste: A Literary History* (New Haven and London: Yale University Press, 2005), p. 76.

17 Empson, 'Sense in *The Prelude*', in *Complex Words*, pp. 289–305 (p. 298).

18 The references to hunger and appetite here are controversial: Gigante has argued in her discussion of the 'feeding mind' image that Wordsworth seems to want to allow for appetite but not excretion, the man of 'taste' but not the gusto or guts of the mob, *Taste*, pp. 72–3 (p. 82). Yet, Wordsworth seems to want to resist transcendentalizing this passage; as the Norton editors point out, he retains the word 'organic' in the phrase 'pure organic pleasure' in every version, and removes the term 'eternal beauty' from the 1850 version, *The Prelude*, p. 61.

19 For instance: 'According to a Christian philosophical tradition, pleasure constitutively depends on a mental act of loving that may be directed toward different cognitively presented things. To some contemporary analytic philosophers influenced by them, pleasure itself is a single propositional attitude, like belief, that, similarly, may be directed toward diverse propositional contents ... If there are representationally contentless but phenomenally conscious pleasant moods, such claims and theories cannot be correct', Katz, 'Pleasure'.

20 Ryle, 'Pleasure'.

21 Michel Henry, *The Genealogy of Psychoanalysis*, trans. Douglas Brick (Stanford University Press, 1993), reverses traditional views of Cartesianism, suggesting that we have missed the correct emphasis when Descartes writes in the *Meditations*: 'At the very least, it *seems to me* that I see' (At certe videor videre; a different translation is given in René Descartes, *Meditations on First Philosophy with Selections from the Objections and Replies*, ed. John Cottingham (Cambridge University Press, 1996), p. 19). Instead, Henry calls it a 'primal sensing', which is 'identical to the being defined by that sensing. I sense that I think, therefore I am', *Genealogy*, p. 21.

22 Jarvis, *Philosophic Song*, pp. 165–9.

23 Noel Jackson, *Science and Sensation in Romantic Poetry* (Cambridge University Press, 2008), p. 71.

24 Ibid., pp. 74–5.

25 The eroticism here is slightly, but not entirely, moralized in the 1850 version, with the replacement of l. 326 with 'Whose transient pleasure mounted to the head', *Prelude*, p. 141.

26 See Simpson's discussion of the agrarian ideal in *Historical Imagination*, pp. 56–78.

27 Hunter Davies, *William Wordsworth: A Biography*, rev. edn (Stroud: Sutton Publishing Ltd, 1997), p. 320.

28 Wordsworth, *Poems, in Two Volumes*, p. 232.

29 Jarvis has argued that 'The poem thus opens a wish which animates the whole authorship: for an unconscious reciprocity of excess', *Philosophic Song*, p. 106.

30 Rousseau, *Reveries*, in *Collected Writings of Rousseau*, ed. Kelly and Masters, VIII, p. 47.

31 ' "Joy" is associated in both his [Wordsworth's] poetry and critical writings not with weakness or impermanence but with the consciousness of power, of master and control not only over himself, but in relation to everything which lies beyond him, be it language, other people, or the natural universe', Manning, 'Burns and Wordsworth', p. 206.

32 The 1850 *Prelude* makes a comparison with the biblical 'peace / Which passeth understanding', and becomes a little more religious: man may seek 'in vain' for peace from another source.

33 In the 1850 version, Wordsworth changes this unfailing delight to 'peace / Which passeth understanding'; he also changes 'the highest bliss / That can be known' to 'the highest bliss / That flesh can know' (XII. 126–7, 113–14); in changing delight to peace, he reduces the implicit hedonism; but at the same time, insists on the sensuality of bliss.

34 Thomas Kavanagh, *Enlightened Pleasures: Eighteenth-Century France and the New Epicureanism* (New Haven and London: Yale University Press, 2010).

35 John Milton, *Paradise Lost*, ed. Scott Elledge (New York: W.W. Norton, 1975), VIII. 365–6.

36 Ibid., VIII. 513–16.

37 Johnson, *Dictionary*, s.v. 'Congratulation'.

38 William Wordsworth, *Home at Grasmere*, ed. Beth Darlington (Ithaca: Cornell University Press, 1977). There are several manuscript versions of this poem for *The Recluse*. The text used here is MS B, the earliest full text, much of which was drafted in 1800 and, after an interlude, completed in late summer 1806. A later version, MS D, was worked on from 1812 to 1814 and 1831–2. See the extended discussion in *Home at Grasmere*, pp. 3–32. All line references are to MS B and will be given in parentheses in the text. See *Home at Grasmere*, pp. 455–62, on why the poem remained unpublished until 1888 and its rather patchy reputation.

39 William Minto, 'Wordsworth's Great Failure' (1889), reprinted in A.W. Thomson, ed., *Wordsworth's Mind and Art* (New York: Barnes and Noble, 1969), pp. 10–27 (p. 13).

40 Stephen C. Gill, 'Wordsworth's "Never Failing Principle of Joy"', *ELH*, 34 (1967), 208–24 (223–4).

41 The tension around Wordsworth's relationship to Coleridge in this poem is pressed by Raimonda Modiano, 'Blood Sacrifice, Gift Economy and the Edenic World: Wordsworth's *Home at Grasmere*', *Studies in Romanticism*, 32 (1993), 418–521. Simpson refers to the poem's 'intensity of hyperbole' in Simpson, *Historical Imagination*, p. 133, and has 'suspicions of a highly unstable psyche', p. 134. One of the best readings of the poem emphasizes its 'insuperable intrinsic contradictions that doubtless had as much to do with Wordsworth's inability to finish *The Recluse* as the sum total of all the external difficulties of his late years', Kenneth Johnston, '*Home at Grasmere*: Reclusive Song', *Studies in Romanticism*, 14:1 (1975), 1–28 (22).

42 Sally Bushell, 'The Making of Meaning in Wordsworth's *Home at Grasmere*: Speech Acts, Micro-Analysis and "Freudian Slips"', *Studies in Romanticism*, 49:3 (2009), 391–420 (400).
43 *The Tempest*, 3.11.130–1, Peter Alexander, ed., *William Shakespeare: The Complete Works* (London: Collins, 1951), p. 17.
44 Edmund Spenser, *The Faerie Qveene*, ed. A.C. Hamilton et al. (Edinburgh: Longman, 2001), iii, vi, 46.4–6.
45 On tautology, see Johnston, '*Home at Grasmere*: Reclusive Song', 8–12.
46 Rousseau, *Reveries*, in *Collected Writings of Rousseau*, ed. Kelly and Masters, viii, p. 46.
47 Modiano claims the boy is 'blissfully unaware' of his deathly hints, 'Blood Sacrifice', 485.
48 Georges Bataille, 'The Notion of Expenditure', in *Visions of Excess: Selected Writings 1927–39*, ed. and trans. Allan Stoekl (Minneapolis: University of Minnesota Press, 1985), pp. 116–29. Bataille was strongly interested in the affective economy of the French Revolution and its thinkers, especially de Sade. For discussion, see Jacques Derrida, 'From Restricted to General Economy: A Hegelianism without Reserve', in Alan Bass, trans., *Writing and Difference* (London and New York: Routledge, 1978, 2001), pp. 317–50.
49 Bataille, 'The Notion of Expenditure', p. 116.
50 Ibid., p. 118.
51 Ibid., pp. 118, 127.
52 Ibid., p. 116.
53 Johnston, '*Home at Grasmere*: Reclusive Song', 12.
54 Ibid., 5; Bataille, 'The Notion of Expenditure', p. 125.
55 Modiano, 'Blood Sacrifice', 486.
56 Johnston, '*Home at Grasmere*: Reclusive Song', 14.
57 Milton, *Paradise Lost*, viii. 365–6.
58 Matthew Arnold, 'St Paul and Protestantism', in R.H. Super, ed., *Dissent and Dogma* (Ann Arbor: University of Michigan Press, 1968), pp. 5–33 (p. 10). Arnold's essays on Spinoza include 'Spinoza and the Bible' and 'Tractatus Theologico-Politicus', in *Lectures and Essays in Criticism*, ed. Super, pp. 158–82, 56–64.
59 Spinoza, 'Of the Affects', P58, *Ethics*, p. 102.
60 Deleuze, *Spinoza: Practical Philosophy*, pp. 50–1.
61 See the discussion in Derrida, 'From Restricted to General Economy', pp. 321–3.
62 At moments in his career, Bataille did indeed want to recuperate these flights of desire to determined 'ends', particularly in his left-wing political engagement.
63 On the economy of pleasure, see Sigmund Freud, *Beyond the Pleasure Principle*, pp. 9–10, and 'Project for a Scientific Psychology', passim, both in Sigmund Freud, *Beyond the Pleasure Principle, Group Psychology and Other Works*, trans. and ed. James Strachey et al. (The Standard Edition of the Complete Psychological Works of Sigmund Freud; London: Hogarth Press,

1955); as well as 'The Economic Problem of Masochism', in *The Ego and the Id, and Other Works*, trans. and ed. James Strachey et al. (The Standard Edition of the Complete Psychological Works of Sigmund Freud; London: Hogarth Press, 1961), pp. 159–72.

64 Simpson, *Historical Imagination*, p. 134.

65 Ibid., pp. 134–5.

66 This may also be a rebuttal of Descartes' promise to 'make ourselves [like] the lords and masters of nature', *Discourse on Method*, VI, in *The Philosophical Writings of Descartes*, trans. John Cottingham et al., 3 vols. (Cambridge University Press, 1995), I, pp. 142–3.

67 Derrida emphasizes that sovereignty subtends mastery, in 'From Restricted to General Economy', passim.

68 Wordsworth, *Poems, in Two Volumes*, p. 133.

69 For Modiano, both positions – absolute possession and absolute sharing – represent Wordsworth's desire for the 'power of self-sufficiency' in breaking from Coleridge; my reading accords with hers in recognizing Wordsworth's desire to transform the meaning of ownership, but it does not perceive the language of pleasure and consummation to be 'threatened' by sacrifice and death, 'Blood Sacrifice', 520–1.

70 Wordsworth, *Home at Grasmere*, p. 18.

71 On the tropes of labour and idleness see Simpson, *Historical Imagination*, passim.

72 Modiano, 'Blood Sacrifice', 520.

73 Ibid., 520.

74 Ibid., 521.

75 Force, *Self-Interest*, pp. 50–2.

76 William Wordsworth, *Last Poems, 1821–1850*, ed. Jared Curtis (Ithaca: Cornell University Press, 1999), pp. 193–5. My attention was drawn to this poem by Susan Wolfson's May 2011 talk at Trinity College, Cambridge, on 'MJJ' (Maria Jane Jewsbury).

77 This is 'katastematic' pleasure, or *ataraxia*, most commonly associated with Epicurus. See Gosling and Taylor, *The Greeks on Pleasure*, pp. 365–96.

78 There are some similarities here with what Anne-Lise François calls Romanticism's ethos of 'minimal contentment', though unlike her I find its roots in the Enlightenment and earlier, and find in it political utopianism rather than resignation or defeat, *Open Secrets*, p. xix.

79 Theodor Adorno, 'Sur l'eau', *Minima Moralia*, pp. 156–7. Simon Jarvis has suggested to me that this passage also alludes to Stendhal and the opening of Hegel's *Logic*.

80 Adorno, 'Sur l'eau', pp. 155–6.

81 Ross Wilson, 'Voluptuousness and Asceticism in Adorno', *German Life and Letters*, 62:3 (2009), 270–83 (278).

82 Sebastiano Timpanaro, *On Materialism*, trans. Lawrence Garner (London: NLB, 1975), pp. 17–18.

83 Ibid., p. 20.

84 Ibid., p. 21.

85 Keston Sutherland, 'Happiness in Writing', *world picture*, 3 (2009), 7–13 (9).

5 THE POLITICS OF HAPPINESS IN *THE EXCURSION*

1 Opening lines of 'Character of the Happy Warrior', in Wordsworth, *Poems, in Two Volumes*, pp. 84–6 (ll. 1–26). Further line references will be given in parentheses in the text.

2 The related poems are 'Elegiac Verses', 'Elegiac Stanzas', 'To the Daisy' and 'Distressful Gift'. See R.C. Townsend, 'John Wordsworth and his Brother's Poetic Development', *PMLA*, 81:1 (1966), 70–88.

3 Wordsworth mentions both John and Lord Nelson in relation to the poem in Isabella Fenwick's notes; see Wordsworth, *Poems, in Two Volumes*, pp. 86, 405.

4 Richard Matlak, *Deep Distresses: William Wordsworth, John Wordsworth, Sir George Beaumont, 1800–1808* (Cranbury, NJ: Associated University Presses / University of Delaware Press, 2003), pp. 123–6.

5 Townsend, 'John Wordsworth and his Brother's Poetic Development', p. 74.

6 Edith Batho, *The Later Wordsworth* (Cambridge, 1933), p. 35n, cited in Townsend, 'John Wordsworth and his Brother's Poetic Development', p. 74.

7 William Hazlitt, 'Guy Faux', in *Selected Writings*, IX, pp. 45–9 (p. 53).

8 Ibid., pp. 50, 48.

9 Ibid., pp. 58–9.

10 J.L. Austin, '*Agathon* and *Eudaimonia* in the *Ethics* of Aristotle', in J.O. Urmson and G.J. Warnock, eds., *Philosophical Papers*, 2nd edn (Oxford University Press, 1970), pp. 1–31 (p. 20).

11 Martha C. Nussbaum, 'Mill between Aristotle and Bentham', *Daedalus*, 133:2 (2004), 60–8 (61).

12 Martha C. Nussbaum, *The Fragility of Goodness: Luck and Ethics in Greek Tragedy and Philosophy*, 2nd edn (Cambridge University Press, 2001), p. 2; see also her 'Who Is the Happy Warrior? Philosophy Poses Questions to Psychology', in Eric A. Posner and Cass R. Sunstein, eds., *Law and Happiness* (University of Chicago Press, 2010), pp. 81–113.

13 Adorno, *Minima Moralia*, p. 157.

14 Aristotle, *Nicomachean Ethics*, I.VII.15–16, trans. H. Rackham (Loeb Classical Library; London: Heinemann, 1976), p. 33.

15 Claire Colebrook, 'Happiness, Theoria and Everyday Life', *symploke*, 11:1–2 (2003), 132–51 (135).

16 Jonathan Lear, *Happiness, Death, and the Remainder of Life* (Cambridge, MA: Harvard University Press, 2000), p. 56.

17 Ibid., p. 36.

18 John Dryden, *Dryden: Selected Poems*, ed. Paul Hammond and David Hopkins (Harlow: Pearson, 2007), pp. 350–1.

19 William Wordsworth, *The Excursion*, ed. Sally Bushell, James A. Butler and Michael C. Jaye (Ithaca: Cornell University Press, 2008). All references (book and line) are to this edition and will be given in parentheses in the text.

20 John Barrell, *Poetry, Language and Politics* (Manchester University Press, 1988), pp. 111–12.

21 Woof, *Critical Heritage*, pp. 369, 382, 499. But perhaps *The Excursion*'s time has come: the past fifteen years have witnessed not only the 2008 Cornell edition but Alison Hickey's *Impure Conceits: Rhetoric and Ideology in Wordsworth's* Excursion (Stanford University Press, 1997) and Sally Bushell's *Re-Reading 'The Excursion': Narrative, Response and the Wordsworthian Dramatic Voice* (Aldershot: Ashgate, 2002). On its positive Victorian reception, see Stephen Gill, *Wordsworth and the Victorians* (Oxford University Press, 2001), pp. 17–19 and passim.

22 Connell, *Romanticism*, pp. 123–4.

23 Ibid., p. 132.

24 Louis-Antoine de Saint-Just, 'Sur le mode d'exécution du décret contre les ennemis de la Révolution' (3 March 1794), in *Discours et rapports*, ed. Albert Souboul (Paris: Messidor/Éditions Sociales, 1988), pp. 149–51 (p. 150).

25 Slavoj Žižek, *For They Know Not What They Do: Enjoyment as a Political Factor*, 2nd edn (London: Verso, 2002), pp. 273–4.

26 For other literary influences on the poem, see Wordsworth, *Excursion*, p. 7.

27 Stuart Peterfreund, 'In Free Homage and Generous Subjection: Miltonic Influence on *The Excursion*', *Wordsworth Circle*, 9 (1978), 173–7.

28 Milton, *Paradise Lost*, xii. 636, 634.

29 Ibid., ix. 254–5.

30 Ibid., iv. 327–30, 417.

31 Ibid., x. 1019.

32 Ibid., x. 1052, 1054–6.

33 Ibid., x. 1082–5.

34 Ibid., xii. 646–9.

35 Undeniably, Wordsworth's relation to Protestantism is complex, as can be seen from the Wanderer's description of the Reformation in vii. 1044–9, and the sympathetic treatment of monasticism in the *Tuft of Primroses*.

36 McMahon, *Happiness: A History*, pp. 172, 173.

37 Maren-Sofie Rostvig, *The Happy Man: Studies in the Metamorphosis of a Classical Ideal, 1600–1700* (Oslo: Akademisk Forlag; Oxford: Basil Blackwell, 1954), pp. 71–116.

38 Samuel Taylor Coleridge, *Philosophical Lectures*, ed. Kathleen Coburn (London: Pilot Press, 1949), p. 141.

39 Samuel Taylor Coleridge, *Opus Maximum*, ed. Thomas McFarland (Princeton University Press, 2002), p. 27.

40 Coleridge, *Opus Maximum*, p. xliv.

41 Letter to William Wordsworth, *c.* 10 Setember 1799, Letter 290, in Earl Leslie Griggs, *The Collected Letters of Samuel Taylor Coleridge*, 6 vols. (Oxford: Clarendon Press, 1956), I, p. 527.

42 Coleridge's own planned philosophical system, in some ways a parallel to the planned *Recluse*, has been described as driven by a 'continuing subtext' of anti-Epicureanism, Coleridge, *Opus Maximum*, p. xliv.

43 On Wordsworth's Stoicism see Michael G. Cooke, *The Romantic Will* (New Haven: Yale University Press, 1976), and Jane Worthington, *Wordsworth's Reading of Roman Prose* (New Haven: Yale University Press, 1946).

44 Samuel Taylor Coleridge, *The Major Works*, ed. H.J. Jackson (Oxford University Press, 1985), pp. 114–18, ll. 93, 69.

45 This passage, and particularly that last controversial sentence, has a complex composition history: see Wordsworth, *Excursion*, p. 76.

46 Simpson, *Historical Imagination*, p. 201.

47 See Bertrand Russell, *History of Western Philosophy: And its Connection with Political and Social Circumstances from the Earliest Times to the Present Day* (London: Allen and Unwin, 1946), pp. 275–93. For an account of Stoicism stressing the perverse possibilities 'where everything is permitted', see Gilles Deleuze, *The Logic of Sense*, trans. Mark Lester (London: Continuum, 2004), pp. 148–9.

48 'All things which participate in anything which is common to them all move towards that which is of the same kind with themselves ... But in the things which are still superior, even though they are separated from one another, unity in a manner exists, as in the stars. Thus the ascent to the higher degree is able to produce a sympathy even in things which are separated.' George Long, trans. and ed., *The Meditations of Marcus Aurelius*, IX. 9 (London: Blackie & Son, 1910), pp. 121–2.

49 Aristotle, *Nicomachean Ethics*, I.v, trans. J.A.K. Thomson (Harmondsworth: Penguin, 1976), p. 68.

50 Friedrich Nietzsche, *Untimely Meditations*, trans. R.J. Hollingdale (Cambridge University Press, 1997), p. 60.

51 Ibid., p. 62.

52 Ibid., p. 62.

53 Lines 374–410 were originally written for the *Tuft of Primroses* in 1808; in an earlier draft of *The Excursion* they appeared as the Poet's words in Book V. See Wordsworth, *Excursion*, pp. 68–73.

54 Rousseau, *Reveries*, in *Collected Writings of Rousseau*, ed. Kelly and Masters, VIII, pp. 42, 46.

55 See editorial notes to Wordsworth, *Excursion*, p. 145. 'Blow, winds, and crack your cheeks; rage, blow', *King Lear*, 3.II.I, Alexander, ed., *Complete Works*, p. 1092.

56 If the attack on unspecified 'Philosophers' draws from conversations with Coleridge, as is plausible, one might note that Coleridge referred to Aristippus as the first philosopher of 'self-love', but also used the phrase with reference to Kant (*selbst-liebe*) and Paley; see the editorial note to *Opus Maximum*, p. 29.

57 Owen and Smyser, eds., *Prose Works*, I, p. 103.

58 Immanuel Kant, *Critique of Practical Reason*, Theorem II, Remark II, in *Practical Philosophy*, trans. and ed. Mary J. Gregor (Cambridge University Press, 1996), p. 159.

59 Ibid., p. 214.

60 Immanuel Kant, *Groundwork of the Metaphysics of Morals*, in *Practical Philosophy*, trans. and ed. Gregor, p. 71. See the similar statement in 'On the Common Saying: That May be Correct in Theory', in ibid., p. 288.

61 Kant, 'On the Common Saying', p. 297.

62 Kant, *Critique of Practical Reason*, p. 170.

63 Ibid., p. 161; Kant, 'On the Common Saying', p. 301.

64 The Cornell editors identify eight stages of work on the poem from 1809 to 1814, with books VI, VII, VIII and IX worked on probably between January 1813 and May 1814, and book V being harder to place, Wordsworth, *Excursion*, p. 428.

65 The first *Essay on Epitaphs* was printed as a footnote to *The Excursion* as well as appearing in *The Friend*, February 1810, whilst Essays II and III were not published until 1876. See Ferguson, *Counter-Spirit*; Michael O'Neill, '"The Words He Uttered . . .": A Reading of Wordsworth', *Romanticism on the Net*, 3 (1996), www.erudit.org/revue/ron/1996/v/n3/005725ar.html.

66 Aristotle, *Poetics*, §6, ed. and trans. Stephen Halliwell (Loeb Classical Library; Cambridge, MA: Harvard University Press, 1995), p. 51.

67 Owen and Smyser, eds., *Prose Works*, II, p. 64.

68 On happiness and 'trial' more broadly, see Vivaswan Soni, *Mourning Happiness: Narrative and the Politics of Modernity* (Ithaca: Cornell University Press, 2010), which claims that interference between older, narrative-based (Aristotelian) models of happiness and novel-based 'trial narratives' in the eighteenth century ultimately emptied classical happiness of its political and moral structure, 'denarrativizing' it and making it merely 'sentimental', pp. 10–12.

69 Wordsworth, *Excursion*, p. 44.

70 Paley, *Reasons for Contentment*, p. 8.

71 Cited in Schneider, *Wordsworth's Cambridge Education*, which also gives useful context for these 'soothing pamphlet arguments upon the blessings of the *status quo*', p. 205.

72 Owen and Smyser, eds., *Prose Works*, I, pp. 38–88.

73 Simpson, *Historical Imagination*, p. 48.

74 Ibid., p. 64.

75 Kant, *Practical Philosophy*, p. 159.

76 1845, VI. 791–6. See editorial note, Wordsworth, *Excursion*, p. 216.

77 These two stories were originally intended for *Home at Grasmere*.

78 William Hazlitt, 'Character of Mr. Wordsworth's New Poem, *The Excursion*', *The Examiner* (28 August 1814), 555–8 (555).

79 Kevis Goodman, *Georgic Modernity and British Romanticism: Poetry and the Mediation of History* (Cambridge University Press, 2004), p. 117.

80 Ibid., pp. 123, 124.

81 Ibid., p. 142.

82 *An Essay on Man*, Epistle I (ll. 217–18), in *The Poems of Alexander Pope*, ed. John Butt (London: Methuen, 1963), p. 512.

83 *King Richard the Second*, 2.1.45–50, Alexander, ed., *Complete Works*, p. 454.

84 McMahon, *Happiness*, pp. 234–5.

85 Linda Colley, *Britons: Forging the Nation 1707–1837*, 2nd edn (London: Pimlico, 2003). For a critique see J.C.D. Clark, 'Protestantism, Nationalism and National Identity, 1660–1832', *Historical Journal*, 43:1 (2000), 249–76.

86 Colley, *Britons*, p. 32.

87 Milton, *Paradise Lost*, VII. 31.

88 *The Excursion* editors compare the active principle to Newton's explanation of motion in terms of 'active principles', and Shaftesbury's quotation of the *Aeneid*, 'The active Mind, infus'd thro' all the Space, Unites and mingles with the mighty Mass', in *Characteristics*; see Wordsworth, *Excursion*, p. 419.

89 Wordsworth was reading Bell in December 1811; see Mark Reed, *Wordsworth: The Chronology of the Middle Years, 1800–1815* (Cambridge, MA: Harvard University Press, 1975), pp. 675–84. On Wordsworth's, Coleridge's and Southey's support for Bell's scheme from 1808, see Alan Richardson, *Literature, Education and Romanticism: Reading as Social Practice, 1780–1832* (Cambridge University Press, 1994).

90 Wordsworth, *Excursion*, p. 314.

91 Richardson comments: 'Wordsworth seems blinded by fears of "disorder" to the contradiction involved in criticizing the factory system for rendering children (and adults) parts of a "machine" and then recommending an educational system which he himself characterizes, in his note to line 200, as a "simple engine"', *Literature*, p. 102. Alison Hickey argues that Wordsworth's and Bell's 'happy union' of bodies is 'a blending that denies hierarchical and individual difference and uses metaphors of shared substance to mask an appropriation of otherness, or an imposition of sameness', 'Dark Characters, Native Grounds: Wordsworth's Imagination of Imperialism', in Alan Richardson and Sonia Hofkosh, eds., *Romanticism, Race, and Imperial Culture 1780–1834* (Bloomington: Indiana University Press, 1996), pp. 283–307 (p. 296). However, a simplistic division between individualism-otherness and systematicity-sameness is not corroborated in Bentham's own writing. He wrote against the 'body politic' metaphor, arguing that the happiness of community was nothing more than the happiness of its individuals; see Élie Halévy, *The Growth of Philosophical Radicalism*, trans. Mary Morris (New York: Macmillan), p. 500. Frances Ferguson has suggested utilitarianism *does* involve 'difference': monitorial education can be seen as 'self-analyzing evaluative systems that aimed to make individuals distinctive and to reward them with what Bentham called "proportionable shares of general respect"', *Pornography, the Theory*, p. 18.

92 Jeremy Bentham, *The Panopticon: Or, the Inspection-House* (Dublin: Thomas Byrne, 1791), 'Letter XXI: Schools', p. 108.

93 James Mill, *The Article* 'COLONY', *Reprinted from The Supplement to the Encyclopedia Britannica* (London: J. Innes, 1820), p. 12.

94 Bees symbolize the movement and continuation of life in Virgil's *Georgics*, IV: in Dryden's translation, they 'take the Forms his Prescience did ordain, / And into him at length resolve again', John Dryden, *The Works of Virgil: Containing his Pastorals, Georgics, and Aeneis: Translated into English Verse;*

by Mr. Dryden, 3rd edn, 3 vols. (London: J. Tonson, 1709), I, p. 193. On bee imagery, see Hattie Ellis, *Sweetness & Light: The Mysterious History of the Honey-Bee* (London: Hodder and Stoughton, 2004).

95 Halévy, *Philosophic Radicalism*, p. 503.

96 Hickey, *Impure Conceits*, p. 145.

97 *The Excursion* editors point to Christian readers' discomfiture with this ending, for example James Montgomery, 'Wordsworth's Excursion', *Eclectic Review* (January 1815), 13–39 (and suggest that an open-ended model may have been Minucius Felix's *Octavius*). See Reeve Parker, '"Finer Distance": The Narrative Art of Wordsworth's "The Wanderer"', *English Literary History*, 39 (1972), 87–111 (110), for praise of the 'perplexity' the poem generates.

98 Nussbaum, *Fragility*, p. xviii. The same move could be traced through the virtue ethics of Elizabeth Anscombe, Philippa Foot and Alasdair MacIntyre.

99 Paul Hamilton connects *The Excursion* with Kantian and post-Kantian (especially Marx's) attempts to find new discursive forms for the purpose of 'an adequate description of our species being', in 'The Excursion and Wordsworth's Special Remainder', in Alexander Regier and Stefan Uhlig, eds., *Wordsworth's Poetic Theory* (Basingstoke: Palgrave Macmillan, 2010), pp. 139–57 (p. 155).

100 Kant, *Practical Philosophy*, p. 189.

CONCLUSION

1 William Hazlitt, 'My First Acquaintance with Poets', in *Selected Writings*, IX.

2 Todorov, *Imperfect Garden*, p. 41.

3 Walter Benjamin, 'On the Image of Proust', in Rodney Livingstone et al., eds., *Selected Writings*, II, Part I: *1927–1930* (Cambridge, MA, 1999), pp. 237–47 (p. 239).

Bibliography

Adelman, Richard, *Idleness, Contemplation and the Aesthetic, 1750–1830* (Cambridge University Press, 2011)

Adorno, Theodor, *Minima Moralia: Reflections on a Damaged Life*, trans. E.F.N. Jephcott, 2nd edn (London: Verso, 2005)

Adorno, Theodor and Max Horkheimer, *Dialectic of Enlightenment*, trans. John Cumming (London: Verso, 1979)

Agamben, Giorgio, 'On Friendship', trans. Joseph Falsone, in *Contretemps*, 5 December 2004, http://sydney.edu.au/contretemps/5december2004/agamben.pdf

Ahmed, Sara, 'The Happiness Turn', *New Formations*, 63 (2007–8), 7–14

Alexander, Peter, ed., *William Shakespeare: The Complete Works* (London: Collins, 1951)

Allen, Robert J., ed., *Addison and Steele: Selections from the Tatler and the Spectator* (Orlando: Holt, Rinehart and Winston, 1970)

Allen, Stuart, *Wordsworth and the Passions of Critical Poetics* (Basingstoke: Palgrave Macmillan, 2010)

Allison, Henry E., *Kant's Theory of Taste: A Reading of the 'Critique of Aesthetic Judgment'* (Cambridge University Press, 2001)

Ansell Pearson Keith, *Nietzsche contra Rousseau: A Study of Nietzsche's Moral and Political Thought* (Cambridge University Press, 1991)

Arendt, Hannah, *Between Past and Future: Eight Exercises in Political Thought* (London: Penguin, 1977)

The Human Condition (University of Chicago Press, 1958; repr. 1970)

Lectures on Kant's Political Philosophy, ed. Ronald Beiner (Brighton: Harvester Press, 1982)

The Life of the Mind: One/Thinking (New York and London: Harcourt Brace Jovanovich, 1971)

The Origins of Totalitarianism (London: André Deutsch, 1986)

Arendt, Hannah and Karl Jaspers, *Correspondence, 1926–1969*, trans. Robert and Rita Kimber (New York and London: Harcourt Brace, 1992)

Aristotle, *Nicomachean Ethics*, trans. H. Rackham (Loeb Classical Library; London: Heinemann, 1976)

Nicomachean Ethics, trans. J.A.K. Thomson (Harmondsworth: Penguin, 1976)

On the Soul, trans. W.S. Hett (Loeb Classical Library; Cambridge, MA: Harvard University Press, 1985)

Poetics, ed. and trans. Stephen Halliwell (Loeb Classical Library; Cambridge, MA: Harvard University Press, 1995)

Arnold, Matthew, *Lectures and Essays in Criticism*, ed. R.H. Super (Ann Arbor: University of Michigan Press, 1962)

'Preface' to *Poems of Wordsworth* (London: Macmillan, 1879), pp. v–xxvi (reprinted as 'Wordsworth' in *Essays in Criticism: Second Series* (London: Macmillan, 1888), pp. 122–62)

'St Paul and Protestantism', in R.H. Super, ed., *Dissent and Dogma* (Ann Arbor: University of Michigan Press, 1968), pp. 5–33

Austin, J.L., '*Agathon* and *Eudaimonia* in the *Ethics* of Aristotle', in J.O. Urmson and G.J. Warnock, eds., *Philosophical Papers*, 2nd edn (Oxford University Press, 1970), pp. 1–31

Babbitt, Irving, *Rousseau and Romanticism* (Boston, MA: Houghton, 1919)

Badowska, Ewa, 'The Anorexic Body of Liberal Feminism: Mary Wollstonecraft's *A Vindication of the Rights of Woman*', *Tulsa Studies in Women's Literature*, 17:2 (1998), 283–303

Baker, Eric, 'Lucretius in the European Enlightenment', in Stuart Gillespie and Philip Hardie, eds., *The Cambridge Companion to Lucretius* (Cambridge University Press, 2007), pp. 274–305

Barker-Benfield, G.J., *The Culture of Sensibility: Sex and Society in Eighteenth-Century Britain* (University of Chicago Press, 1992)

Barrell, John, *Poetry, Language and Politics* (Manchester University Press, 1988)

Barthes, Roland, *The Neutral: Lecture Course at the College de France (1977–1978)*, trans. Rosalind F. Krauss and Denis Hollier (New York: Columbia University Press, 2005)

The Pleasure of the Text, trans. Richard Miller (New York: Hill & Wang, 1975)

Bataille, Georges, *Eroticism, trans. Mary Dalwood* (London: Penguin, 2001)

Visions of Excess: Selected Writings 1927–39, ed. and trans. Allan Stoekl (Minneapolis: University of Minnesota Press, 1985)

Bateson, F.W., ed., *The Twickenham Edition of the Poems of Alexander Pope*, 10 vols. (London: Methuen, 1951)

Batho, Edith, *The Later Wordsworth* (Cambridge, 1933)

Beatty, Arthur, *William Wordsworth: His Doctrine and Art in their Historical Relation* (Madison: University of Wisconsin Press, 1922)

Beddoes, Thomas, trans. and ed., *The Elements of Medicine of John Brown, M.D., Translated from the Latin, with Comments and Illustrations by the Author*, 2 vols. (London: J. Johnson, 1795)

Beiner, Ronald, 'Rereading Hannah Arendt's Kant Lectures', in Ronald Beiner and Jennifer Nedelsky, eds., *Judgment, Imagination and Politics* (Lanham: Rowman and Littlefield, 2001), pp. 91–101

Benjamin, Walter, 'On the Image of Proust', in Rodney Livingstone et al., trans., *Selected Writings*, II, Part 1: *1927–1930* (Cambridge, MA: Harvard University Press, 1999), pp. 237–47

Bentham, Jeremy, *The Panopticon: Or, the Inspection-House* (Dublin: Thomas Byrne, 1791)
   Selected Writings on Utilitarianism, with an introduction by Ross Harrison (Ware: Wordsworth Editions, 2000)
Bentley, G.T., Jr, *William Blake's Writings*, II: *Writings in Conventional Typography and in Manuscript* (Oxford: Clarendon Press, 1978)
Berg, Maxine, *Luxury and Pleasure in Eighteenth-Century Britain* (Oxford University Press, 2005)
Bernstein, Jay, *The Fate of Art: Aesthetic Alienation from Kant to Derrida and Adorno* (Cambridge: Polity, 1992)
Bernstein, John Andrew, *Shaftesbury, Rousseau, and Kant* (New Jersey: Associated University Presses, 1980)
Berry, C.J., *The Idea of Luxury: A Conceptual and Historical Investigation* (Cambridge University Press, 1994)
Bialostosky, Don, *Making Tales: The Poetics of Wordsworth's Narrative Experiments* (University of Chicago Press, 1984)
Blanchot, Maurice, *The Unavowable Community*, trans. Pierre Joris (New York: Station Hill Press, 1988)
Bloom, Harold, *The Anxiety of Influence: A Theory of Poetry*, 2nd edn (Oxford University Press, 1997)
Bourke, Richard, *Romantic Discourse and Political Modernity: Wordsworth, the Intellectual and the Cultural Critique* (Hemel Hempstead: Harvester Wheatsheaf, 1993)
Boyson, Rowan, 'Walking Back to Happiness', *New Formations*, 63 (2007–8), 138–44
Brennan, Teresa, *The Transmission of Affect* (Ithaca: Cornell University Press, 2004)
Broglio, Ron, ed., *Romanticism and the New Deleuze* (= *Romantic Circles Praxis Series*, January 2008), www.rc.umd.edu/praxis/deleuze/index.html
Brown, John, *Elementa Medicinae* (Edinburgh: Denovan, 1784)
Brown, Marshall, 'Romanticism and Enlightenment', in Stuart Curran, ed., *The Cambridge Companion to British Romanticism* (Cambridge University Press, 1993), pp. 25–47
Bushell, Sally, 'The Making of Meaning in Wordsworth's *Home at Grasmere*: Speech Acts, Micro-Analysis and "Freudian Slips"', *Studies in Romanticism* 49:3 (2009), 391–420
   Re-Reading 'The Excursion': Narrative, Response and the Wordsworthian Dramatic Voice (Aldershot: Ashgate, 2002)
Bynum, W.F. and Roy Porter, eds., *Brunonianism in Britain and Europe* (= *Medical History*, Supplement No. 8, London: Wellcome Institute, 1988)
Carey, Daniel, *Locke, Shaftesbury and Hutcheson – Contesting Diversity in the Enlightenment and Beyond* (Cambridge University Press, 2006)
Carlyle, Thomas, *Carlyle's Latter-Day Pamphlets*, ed. Michael K. Goldberg and Jules P. Seigel (Ottawa: Canadian Federation for the Humanities, 1983)

Cassirer, Ernst, *The Philosophy of the Enlightenment*, trans. F.C.A. Koelln and J.P. Pettegrove (Princeton University Press, 1951)

The Platonic Renaissance in England, trans. James Pettegrove (Edinburgh: Thomas Nelson, 1953)

The Question of Jean-Jacques Rousseau, trans. and ed. Peter Gay (New York: Columbia University Press, 1954)

Caygill, Howard, *The Art of Judgement* (Oxford: Basil Blackwell, 1989)

Kant Dictionary (Oxford: Blackwell, 1995)

'Life and Aesthetic Pleasure', in Andrea Rehberg and Rachel Jones, eds., *The Matter of Critique: Readings in Kant's Philosophy* (Manchester: Clinamen Press, 2000), pp. 79–92

'The Shared World – Philosophy, Violence, Freedom', in Darren Sheppard, Simon Sparks and Colin Thomas, eds., *On Jean-Luc Nancy: The Sense of Philosophy* (London and New York: Routledge, 1997), pp. 19–31

Chandler, James K., *Wordsworth's Second Nature: A Study of the Poetry and Politics* (University of Chicago Press, 1984)

Chandler, James and Maureen N. McLane, eds., *The Cambridge Companion to Romantic Poetry* (Cambridge University Press, 2008)

Christensen, Jerome, *Coleridge's Blessed Machine of Language* (Ithaca: Cornell University Press, 1981)

Clark, David L., 'We "Other Prussians": Bodies and Pleasures in De Quincey and Late Kant', *European Romantic Review*, 14 (2003), 261–87

Clark, J.C.D., 'Protestantism, Nationalism and National Identity, 1660–1832', *Historical Journal*, 43:1 (2000), 249–76

Colebrook, Claire, 'Happiness, Theoria and Everyday Life', *symploke*, 11:1–2 (2003), 132–51

Coleridge, Samuel Taylor, *The Major Works*, ed. H.J. Jackson (Oxford University Press, 1985)

Opus Maximum, ed. Thomas McFarland (Princeton University Press, 2002)

Philosophical Lectures, ed. Kathleen Coburn (London: Pilot Press, 1949)

Table Talk, ed. Carl Woodring, 2 vols. (Princeton University Press, 1990)

Colley, Linda, *Britons: Forging the Nation 1707–1837*, 2nd edn (London: Pimlico, 2003)

Collini, Stefan, *Arnold* (Oxford University Press, 1988)

Connell, Philip, *Romanticism, Economics and the Question of 'Culture'* (Oxford University Press, 2001)

Cooke, Michael G., *The Romantic Will* (New Haven: Yale University Press, 1976)

Cooper, Laurence, 'Between Eros and the Will to Power: Rousseau and "The Desire to Extend Our Being"', *American Political Science Review*, 98:1 (2004), 105–19

Rousseau, Nature, and the Problem of the Good Life (University Park, PA: Pennsylvania State University Press, 1999)

Cooper, Thomas, *Thesaurus linguae Romanae & Britannicae* (London: Wykes, 1565)

Corngold, Stanley, *Complex Pleasure: Forms of Feeling in German Literature* (Stanford University Press, 1998)

Cowan, Brian, 'Reasonable Ecstasies: Shaftesbury and the Language of Libertinism', *Journal of British Studies*, 37:2 (1998), 111–38

Crabb Robinson, Henry, *Diary, Reminiscences, and Correspondence*, I, ed. Thomas Sadler (London: Macmillan, 1869)

Craciun, Adriana, 'Violence against Difference: Mary Wollstonecraft and Mary Robinson', in Greg Clingham, ed., *Making History: Textuality and the Forms of Eighteenth-Century Culture* (= *Bucknell Review*, 42:1 (1997)), 111–41

Creech, Thomas, trans., *Titus Lucretius Carus: His Six Books of Epicurean Philosophy, Done into English Verse* (London: T. Bradyll, 1699)

Crowley, John E., *The Invention of Comfort: Sensibilities and Design in Early Modern Britain and Early America* (Baltimore: Johns Hopkins University Press, 2000).

Damasio, Antonio, *Looking for Spinoza: Joy, Sorrow and the Feeling Brain* (Orlando: Harcourt, Inc., 2003).

Damrosch, Leopold, *Jean-Jacques Rousseau: Restless Genius* (Boston, MA: Houghton Mifflin, 2005)

Dart, Gregory, *Rousseau, Robespierre and English Romanticism* (Cambridge University Press, 1999)

Darwall, Stephen, *The British Moralists and the Internal Ought, 1640–1740* (Cambridge University Press, 1995).

Daston, Lorraine and Peter Galison, *Objectivity* (New York: Zone, 2007)

Daston, Lorraine and Katharine Park, *Wonders and the Order of Nature, 1150–1750* (New York: Zone Books, 1998)

Davies, Hunter, *William Wordsworth: A Biography*, rev. edn (Stroud: Sutton Publishing Ltd, 1997)

Davy, Humphry, *The Collected Works of Sir Humphry Davy*, II, ed. John Davy (London: Smith, Elder and Co., 1839)

De Bolla, Peter, *Art Matters* (Cambridge, MA: Harvard University Press, 2001)

De Man, Paul, 'Phenomenality and Materiality in Kant', in Andrzej Warminski, ed., *Aesthetic Ideology* (Minneapolis: University of Minnesota Press, 1995), pp. 70–90

'The Rhetoric of Temporality', in *Blindness and Insight: Essays in the Rhetoric of Contemporary Criticism*, 2nd edn (Minneapolis: University of Minnesota Press, 1983), pp. 187–228

Deleuze, Gilles, *Desert Islands and Other Texts (1953–1974)*, trans. Mike Taormina (Los Angeles: Semiotext(e), 2004)

'Désir et plaisir', *Magazine Littéraire*, 325 (October 1994), 59–65

Difference and Repetition, trans. Paul Patton, 2nd edn (London: Continuum, 2001)

'Dualism, Monism and Multiplicities (Desire-Pleasure-*Jouissance*): Seminar of 26 March 1973', trans. Daniel Smith, *Contretemps*, 2 (2001), 92–108

Kant's Critical Philosophy: The Doctrine of the Faculties, trans. Hugh Tomlinson and Barbara Habberjam (London: Athlone Press, 1984)

The Logic of Sense, trans. Mark Lester (London: Continuum, 2004)

Spinoza: Practical Philosophy, trans. Robert Hurley (San Francisco: City Lights Books, 1988)

Dent, N.J.H., *Rousseau: An Introduction to his Psychological, Social and Political Theory* (Oxford: Basil Blackwell, 1988)

A Rousseau Dictionary (Oxford: Blackwell, 1992)

Derrida, Jacques, *Of Grammatology*, trans. Gayatri Chakravorty Spivak, 2nd edn (Baltimore and London: Johns Hopkins University Press, 1998)

The Post Card: From Socrates to Freud and Beyond, trans. Alan Bass (University of Chicago Press, 1987)

'From Restricted to General Economy: A Hegelianism without Reserve', in Alan Bass, trans., *Writing and Difference*, 2nd edn (London and New York: Routledge, 2001), pp. 317–50

Descartes, René, *Meditations on First Philosophy with Selections from the Objections and Replies*, ed. John Cottingham (Cambridge University Press, 1996)

The Philosophical Writings of Descartes, trans. John Cottingham et al., 3 vols. (Cambridge University Press, 1995)

Diderot, Denis and Jean Le Rond D'Alembert, *The Encyclopedia of Diderot & d'Alembert*, collaborative translation project (Ann Arbor: Scholarly Publishing Office of the University of Michigan Library, 2007), http://hdl.handle.net/2027/spo.did2222.0000.826

Encyclopédie, ou Dictionnaire raisonné des sciences, des arts et des métiers, par une société de gens de lettres, 35 vols. (Paris [Geneva]: Briasson et al., 1751–80)

Dix, Robin, *The Literary Career of Mark Akenside: Including an Edition of his Non-Medical Prose* (Cranbury, NJ: Rosemont, 2006)

Dixon, Thomas, *The Invention of Altruism: Making Moral Meanings in Victorian Britain* (Oxford University Press, 2008)

From Passions to Emotions: The Creation of a Secular Psychological Category (Cambridge University Press, 2003)

Driscoll, E.A., 'The Influence of Gassendi on Locke's Hedonism', *International Philosophical Quarterly*, 12 (1972), 87–110

Dryden, John, *Dryden: Selected Poems*, ed. Paul Hammond and David Hopkins (Harlow: Pearson, 2007)

The Works of Virgil: Containing his Pastorals, Georgics, and Aeneis: Translated into English Verse; by Mr. Dryden, 3rd edn, 3 vols. (London: J. Tonson, 1709)

Duffy, Edward, *Rousseau in England: The Context for Shelley's Critique of the Enlightenment* (Berkeley: University of California Press, 1979)

Eagleton, Terry, *The Function of Criticism: From the Spectator to Post-Modernism* (London: Verso, 1984)

The Ideology of the Aesthetic (Oxford: Basil Blackwell, 1990)

Ehrenreich, Barbara, *Dancing in the Streets: A History of Collective Joy* (London: Granta Books, 2007)

Ellis, Hattie, *Sweetness & Light: The Mysterious History of the Honey-Bee* (London: Hodder and Stoughton, 2004)

Ellis, Markman, *The Politics of Sensibility: Race, Gender and Commerce in the Sentimental Novel* (Cambridge University Press, 1996)

Empson, William, *The Structure of Complex Words*, 3rd edn (London: Penguin, 1995)

Entick, John, *The New Latin and English Dictionary* (London, 1771)

Fenves, Peter, *Late Kant: Towards Another Law of the Earth* (London: Routledge, 2003)

Ferguson, Frances, *Pornography, the Theory: What Utilitarianism Did to Action* (Chicago University Press, 2004)

Solitude and the Sublime: Romanticism and the Ethics of Individuation (New York: Routledge, 1992)

'Wordsworth and the Meaning of Taste', in Stephen Gill, ed., *The Cambridge Companion to Wordsworth* (Cambridge University Press, 2003), pp. 90–107

Wordsworth: Language as Counter-Spirit (New Haven and London: Yale University Press, 1977)

Fitz Gerald, Jennifer, 'Wordsworth's Natural Philosophy: Phlogiston and Physiology in Wordsworth's Poetry, 1798–1800' (unpublished Ph.D. thesis, University of Cambridge, 1984)

Force, Pierre, *Self-Interest before Adam Smith: A Genealogy of Economic Science* (Cambridge University Press, 2003)

Foucault, Michel, *Discipline and Punish: The Birth of the Prison*, trans. Alan Sheridan (London: Allen Lane, 1977)

The History of Sexuality: An Introduction, I, trans. Robert Hurley (New York: Random House, 1978)

The Order of Things: The Archaeology of Human Sciences (London: Routledge, 2001)

François, Anne-Lise, *Open Secrets: The Literature of Uncounted Experience* (Stanford University Press, 2008)

Freud, Sigmund, *Beyond the Pleasure Principle, Group Psychology and Other Works*, trans. and ed. James Strachey et al. (The Standard Edition of the Complete Psychological Works of Sigmund Freud; London: Hogarth Press, 1955)

The Ego and the Id, and Other Works, trans. and ed. James Strachey et al. (The Standard Edition of the Complete Psychological Works of Sigmund Freud; London: Hogarth Press, 1961)

Fridén, Bertil, *Rousseau's Economic Philosophy: Beyond the Market of Innocents* (Dordrecht and London: Kluwer Academic, 1998)

Fullmer, June Z., *Young Humphry Davy: The Making of an Experimental Chemist* (Philadelphia: American Philosophical Society, 2000)

Gadamer, Hans-Georg, *Truth and Method*, trans. and revised by Joel Weinsheimer and Donald G. Marshall, 2nd edn (London: Sheed & Ward, 1989)

Gassendi, Pierre, *De vita et moribus Epicuri libri octo* (Lugduni: Barbier, 1647)

Gigante, Denise, *Life: Organic Form and Romanticism* (New Haven and London: Yale University Press, 2009)

Taste: A Literary History (New Haven and London: Yale University Press, 2005)

Gill, Stephen, *Wordsworth and the Victorians* (Oxford University Press, 2001)

'Wordsworth's "Never Failing Principle of Joy"', *ELH*, 34 (1967), 208–24

Gillespie, S. and P.R. Hardie, *The Cambridge Companion to Lucretius* (Cambridge University Press, 2007)

Goodman, Kevis, *Georgic Modernity and British Romanticism: Poetry and the Mediation of History* (Cambridge University Press, 2004)

Gosling, J.C.B. and C.C.W. Taylor, *The Greeks on Pleasure* (Oxford: Clarendon Press, 1982)

Grace, Eve, 'The Restlessness of "Being": Rousseau's Protean Sentiment of Existence', *History of European Ideas*, 27 (2001), 133–51

Grieve, Maud, *A Modern Herbal: The Medicinal, Culinary, Cosmetic and Economic Properties, Cultivation and Folk-Lore of Herbs, Grasses, Fungi, Shrubs & Trees with their Modern Scientific Uses*, 2 vols. (New York: Hafner, 1931; repr. 1967)

Griggs, Earl Leslie, *The Collected Letters of Samuel Taylor Coleridge*, 6 vols. (Oxford: Clarendon Press, 1956)

Gubar, Susan, 'Feminist Misogyny: Mary Wollstonecraft and the Paradox of "It Takes One to Know One"', *Feminist Studies*, 20:3 (1994), 543–74

Guyer, Paul, 'Beauty, Freedom and Morality', in *Values of Beauty: Historical Essays in Aesthetics* (Cambridge University Press, 2005), pp. 287–305

Kant and the Claims of Taste, 2nd edn (Cambridge, MA: Harvard University Press, 1997)

Hadot, Pierre and A.I. Davidson, *Philosophy as a Way of Life: Spiritual Exercises from Socrates to Foucault* (Oxford: Blackwell, 1995)

Halévy, Élie, *The Growth of Philosophical Radicalism*, trans. Mary Morris (New York: Macmillan, 1928)

Hallward, Peter, *Out of This World: Deleuze and the Philosophy of Creation* (London: Verso, 2006)

Hamilton, Paul, *Coleridge and German Philosophy* (London: Continuum, 2007)

'The Excursion and Wordsworth's Special Remainder', in Alexander Regier and Stefan Uhlig, eds., *Wordsworth's Poetic Theory* (Basingstoke: Palgrave Macmillan, 2010), pp. 139–57

Metaromanticism: Literature, Theory, Politics (University of Chicago Press, 2003)

Wordsworth (Brighton: Harvester, 1986)

Hardt, Michael and Antoni Negri, *Multitude: War and Democracy in the Age of Empire* (London: Penguin, 2006)

Hartley, David, *Observations on Man*, 2 vols. (London: Richardson, 1749)

Hartman, Geoffrey, *Wordsworth's Poetry 1787–1814* (New Haven: Yale University Press, 1964)

Hazlitt, William, 'Character of Mr. Wordsworth's New Poem: *The Excursion*', *The Examiner* (28 August 1814), 555–8

Essay on the Principles of Human Action: Being an Argument in Favour of the Natural Disinterestedness of the Human Mind (London: J. Johnson, 1805)

The Round Table: A Collection of Essays on Literature, Men and Manners, 2 vols. (Edinburgh: Archibald, 1817)

Selected Writings of William Hazlitt, ed. Duncan Wu, 9 vols. (London: Pickering, 1998)

The Spirit of the Age, or, Contemporary Portraits, ed. E.D. Mackerness (London: Collins, 1969)

Heller-Roazen, Daniel, *The Inner Touch: The Archaeology of a Sensation* (New York: Zone Books, 2007)

Henry, Michel, *The Genealogy of Psychoanalysis*, trans. Douglas Brick (Stanford University Press, 1993)

Hertz, Neil, 'Lurid Figures', in Lindsay Waters and Wlad Godwich, eds., *Reading de Man Reading* (Minneapolis: University of Minnesota Press, 1989), pp. 82–104

Hickey, Alison, 'Dark Characters, Native Grounds: Wordsworth's Imagination of Imperialism', in Alan Richardson and Sonia Hofkosh, eds., *Romanticism, Race, and Imperial Culture, 1780–1834* (Bloomington: Indiana University Press, 1996), pp. 283–307

Impure Conceits: Rhetoric and Ideology in Wordsworth's Excursion (Stanford University Press, 1997)

Hirschman, Albert, *The Passions and the Interests: Political Arguments for Capitalism before its Triumph* (Princeton University Press, 1977)

Holmes, Richard, *The Age of Wonder: How the Romantic Generation Discovered the Beauty and Terror of Science* (London: Harper Press, 2008)

Hont, Istvan, 'The Early Enlightenment Debate on Commerce and Luxury', in Mark Goldie and Robert Wokler, eds., *The Cambridge History of Eighteenth-Century Political Thought* (Cambridge University Press, 2006), pp. 379–415

Hopkins, David, 'The English Voices of Lucretius from Lucy Hutchinson to John Mason Good', in Stuart Gillespie and Philip Hardie, eds., *The Cambridge Companion to Lucretius* (Cambridge University Press, 2007), pp. 254–73

Ingrams, David, *Reason, History and Politics: The Communitarian Grounds of Legitimation in the Modern Age* (New York: SUNY, 1995)

Inwood, Brad and L.P. Gerson, *The Epicurus Reader: Selected Writings and Testimonia* (Indianapolis: Hackett, 1994)

Israel, Jonathan, *Radical Enlightenment: Philosophy and the Making of Modernity 1650–1750* (Oxford University Press, 2001)

Jackson, Noel, *Science and Sensation in Romantic Poetry* (Cambridge University Press, 2008)

James, Susan, *Passions and Action: The Emotions in Seventeenth-Century Philosophy* (Oxford: Clarendon Press, 1987)

Jameson, Fredric, 'Pleasure: A Political Issue', in *Formations of Pleasure* (London: Routledge and Kegan Paul, 1983), pp. 1–13

Jarvis, Simon, 'Wordsworth and Idolatry', *Studies in Romanticism*, 38 (1999), 3–27

'Wordsworth's Gifts of Feeling', *Romanticism*, 4:1 (1998), 90–103

Wordsworth's Philosophic Song (Cambridge University Press, 2007)

Johnson, Claudia L., 'Mary Wollstonecraft's Novels', in *The Cambridge Companion to Mary Wollstonecraft* (Cambridge University Press, 2002), pp. 189–208

Johnson, Mary Lynn and John E. Grant, *Blake's Poetry and Designs* (New York: W.W. Norton, 1979)

Johnson, Samuel, *A Dictionary of the English Language*, 5th edn, 2 vols. (London: Strahan, 1785)

Johnson, W.R., *Lucretius and the Modern World* (London: Duckworth, 2000)

Johnston, Kenneth, *The Hidden Wordsworth* (London: Pimlico, 2000)

'*Home at Grasmere*: Reclusive Song', *Studies in Romanticism*, 14:1 (1975), 1–28

Jones, Chris, *Radical Sensibility: Literature and Ideas in the 1790s* (London: Routledge, 1993)

Jones, Howard, *The Epicurean Tradition* (London: Routledge, 1989)

Jones, Kath Renark, 'Exposing Community: Towards a Dynamic of Commercium', in Andrea Rehberg and Rachel Jones, eds., *The Matter of Critique: Readings in Kant's Philosophy* (Manchester: Clinamen, 2000), pp. 129–46

Jordanova, Ludmilla, 'Melancholy Reflections: Constructing an Identity for the Unveilers of Nature', in Stephen Bann, eds., *Frankenstein: Creation and Monstrosity* (London: Reaktion, 1994), pp. 60–76

Joughin, John J. and Simon Malpas, eds., *The New Aestheticism* (Manchester University Press, 2003)

Jump, Harriet Devine, ed., *Mary Wollstonecraft and the Critics, 1788–2001*, 2 vols. (London: Routledge, 2003)

Kant, Immanuel, *Anthropology from a Pragmatic Point of View*, trans. and ed. Mary J. Gregor. (The Hague: Martinus Nijhoff, 1974)

Anthropology from a Pragmatic Point of View, trans. and ed. Robert B. Louden (Cambridge University Press, 2006)

Critique of Judgment, trans. Werner S. Pluhar (Indianapolis: Hackett Publishing Company, 1987)

Kants gesammelte Schriften, 29 vols. (Berlin: de Gruyter, 1924)

Philosophical Correspondence, trans. and ed. Arnulf Zweig (Cambridge University Press, 1999)

Practical Philosophy, trans. and ed. Mary J. Gregor (Cambridge University Press, 1996)

Theoretical Philosophy 1755–75, trans. and ed. David Walford (Cambridge University Press, 2006)

Kaplan, Cora, *Sea Changes: Essays in Culture and Feminism* (London: Verso, 1986)

Katz, Leonard, 'Pleasure', in *Stanford Encyclopedia of Philosophy*, http://plato.stanford.edu/entries/pleasure

Kavanagh, Thomas, *Enlightened Pleasures: Eighteenth-Century France and the New Epicureanism* (New Haven and London: Yale University Press, 2010)

Keble, John, *Keble's Lectures on Poetry, 1832–1841*, trans. Edward Kershaw Francis, in Gavin Budge, ed., *Aesthetics and Religion in Nineteenth-Century Britain*, 1 (Bristol: Thoemmes Press, 2003)

Kelly, George Armstrong, 'General Overview', in Patrick Riley, ed., *The Cambridge Companion to Rousseau* (Cambridge University Press, 2001), pp. 8–56

Kristeva, Julia, *Hannah Arendt*, trans. Ross Guberman (New York: Columbia University Press, 2001)

Lange, Frederick Albert, *The History of Materialism*, 3 vols. (New York: Arno Press, 1974)

Lange, Lynda, ed., *Feminist Interpretations of Jean-Jacques Rousseau* (University Park, PA: Pennsylvania State University Press, 2002)

Layard, Richard, *Happiness: Lessons from a New Science* (London: Allen Lane, 2005)

Lear, Jonathan, *Happiness, Death, and the Remainder of Life* (Cambridge, MA: Harvard University Press, 2000)

Leavis, F.R., ed., *Mill on Bentham and Coleridge* (London: Chatto & Windus, 1950)

Leddy, Neven and Avi Lifschitz, eds., *Epicurus in the Enlightenment* (Oxford: Voltaire Foundation, 2009)

Lévesque de Pouilly, L.-J. and J. Vernet, *The Theory of Agreeable Sensations . . . To which is Subjoined, Relative to the Same Subject, a Dissertation on Harmony of Stile. [With a preface by J. J. Vernet.] Translated from the French [of Louis Jean Levesque de Pouilly]* (London: W. Owen, 1749)

Levine, George, *Dying to Know: Scientific Epistemology and Narrative in Victorian England* (University of Chicago Press, 2002)

Levinson, Marjorie, 'A Motion and a Spirit: Romancing Spinoza', *Studies in Romanticism*, 46 (2007), 367–408

Locke, John, *An Essay concerning Human Understanding* (Oxford World's Classics; Oxford University Press, 2008)

Long, George, trans. and ed., *The Meditations of Marcus Aurelius* (London: Blackie & Son, 1910)

Longuenesse, Béatrice, *Kant and the Capacity to Judge: Sensibility and Discursivity in the Transcendental Analytic of the 'Critique of Pure Reason'*, trans. Charles T. Wolfe (Princeton University Press, 1998)

Kant on the Human Standpoint (Cambridge University Press, 2005)

Lucretius, Titus Carus, *De Rerum Natura*, trans. W.H.D. Rouse and ed. M.F. Smith (Loeb Classical Library; Cambridge, MA: Harvard University Press, 1975)

Lyotard, Jean-François, *Lessons on the Analytic of the Sublime*, trans. Elizabeth Rottenberg (Stanford University Press, 1994)

'Sensus Communis', trans. Marion Hobson and Geoff Bennington, *Paragraph*, 11:1 (1988), 1–25

McDonagh, Josephine, *De Quincey's Disciplines* (Oxford: Clarendon Press, 1994)

McFarland, Thomas, *Romanticism and the Heritage of Rousseau* (Oxford: Clarendon Press, 1995)

McIntosh, Carey, *The Evolution of English Prose, 1700–1800: Style, Politeness, and Print Culture* (Cambridge University Press, 1998)

MacIntyre, Alasdair, *After Virtue: A Study in Moral Theory* (London: Duckworth, 1981)

McKendrick, Neil, John Brewer and J.H. Plumb, *The Birth of a Consumer Society: The Commercialization of Eighteenth-Century England* (London: Europa, 1992)

McLane, Maureen, *Romanticism and the Human Sciences: Poetry, Population and the Discourse of the Species* (Cambridge University Press, 2000)

McMahon, Darrin, *Happiness: A History* (New York: Atlantic Monthly Press, 2005)

Mandeville, Bernard, *The Fable of the Bees and Other Writings*, ed. E.F. Hundert (Indianapolis: Hackett, 1997)

Manning, Susan, 'Burns and Wordsworth: Art and "The Pleasure which There Is in Life Itself"', in Roy Porter and Marie Mulvey Roberts, eds., *Pleasure in the Eighteenth Century* (Basingstoke: Macmillan, 1996), pp. 183–206

Marx, Karl and Frederick Engels, 'Critique of Modern German Philosophy according to its Representatives Feuerbach, B. Bauer and Stirner', in *Collected Works*, 50 vols. (London: Lawrence and Wishart, 1975–90), v: 1845–7

Mason, Emma and Isobel Armstrong, eds., *Languages of Emotion* (= *Textual Practice*, 22:1 (2008))

Masson, David, ed., *Collected Writings of Thomas De Quincey*, 14 vols. (London: A. & C. Black, 1897)

Matlak, Richard, *Deep Distresses: William Wordsworth, John Wordsworth, Sir George Beaumont, 1800–1808* (Cranbury, NJ: Associated University Presses / University of Delaware Press, 2003)

  'Wordsworth's Reading of *Zoönomia* in "Early Spring"', *Wordsworth Circle*, 21:2 (1990), 76–81

Maurer, Christian, 'Self-Love in Early Eighteenth-Century British Moral Philosophy: Shaftesbury, Mandeville, Hutcheson, Butler and Campbell', Institut de philosophie, Universite de Neuchatel, Neuchatel (2009)

Mauzi, Robert, *L'idée du bonheur dans la littérature et la pensée françaises au XVIIIe siècle* (Paris: Éditions Albin Michel, 1979; repr. 1994)

Mee, Jon, *Romanticism, Enthusiasm, and Regulation: Poetics and the Policing of Culture in the Romantic Period* (Oxford University Press, 2003)

Meld Shell, Susan, *The Embodiment of Reason: Kant on Spirit, Generation, and Community* (Chicago University Press, 1997)

  'Emile: Nature and the Education of Sophie', in Patrick Riley, ed., *The Cambridge Companion to Rousseau* (Cambridge University Press, 2001), pp. 272–301

  'Kant's "True Economy of Human Nature": Rousseau, Count Verri and the Problem of Happiness', in Brian Jacobs and Patrick Kain, eds., *Essays in Kant's Anthropology* (Cambridge University Press, 2003), pp. 194–229

Mellor, Anne K., 'Righting the Wrongs of Woman: Mary Wollstonecraft's *Maria*', *Nineteenth-Century Contexts*, 19 (1996), 413–24

Romanticism and Gender (New York: Routledge, 1993)

Michael, Fred S. and Emily Michael, 'Gassendi's Modified Epicureanism and British Moral Philosophy', *History of European Ideas*, 21:6 (1995), 743–61

Mill, James, *The Article 'COLONY', reprinted from The Supplement to the Encyclopedia Britannica* (London: J. Innes, 1820)

Mill, John Stuart, *Autobiography and Literary Essays*, ed. John M. Robson and Jack Stillinger (University of Toronto Press, 1981)

Milnes, Tim, *Knowledge and Indifference in English Romantic Prose* (Cambridge University Press, 2003)

Milton, John, *Paradise Lost*, ed. Scott Elledge (New York: W.W. Norton, 1975)

Minto, William, 'Wordsworth's Great Failure' (1889), reprinted in A.W. Thomson, eds., *Wordsworth's Mind and Art* (New York: Barnes and Noble, 1969), pp. 10–27

Mintz, Sidney W., *Sweetness and Power: The Place of Sugar in Modern History* (New York and Harmondsworth: Viking Penguin, 1985)

Modiano, Raimonda, 'Blood Sacrifice, Gift Economy and the Edenic World: Wordsworth's *Home at Grasmere*', *Studies in Romanticism*, 32 (1993), 418–521

Moller Okin, Susan, *Women in Western Political Thought* (Princeton University Press, 1979)

Montgomery, James, 'Wordsworth's Excursion', *Eclectic Review* (January 1815), 13–39

Moriarty, Michael, *Roland Barthes* (Cambridge: Polity, 1991)

Mullan, John, *Sentiment and Sociability: The Language of Feeling in the Eighteenth Century* (Oxford: Clarendon Press, 1988)

Nadel, G.H., 'Pouilly's Plagiarism', *Journal of the Warburg and Courtauld Institutes*, 30 (1967), 438–44

Nancy, Jean-Luc, *A Finite Thinking*, trans. and ed. Simon Sparks (Stanford University Press, 2003)

　　The Inoperative Community, trans. Peter Connor et al. (Minneapolis: University of Minnesota Press, 1991)

　　Le plaisir au dessin: carte blanche à Jean-Luc Nancy (Paris: Hazan; Lyon: Museée des Beaux-Arts de Lyon, 2007)

Neuhouser, Frederick, *Rousseau's Theodicy of Self-Love: Evil, Rationality, and the Drive for Recognition* (Oxford University Press, 2008)

Newlyn, Lucy, *Coleridge, Wordsworth and the Language of Allusion* (New York: Oxford University Press, 1986)

Niblett, Matthew, 'Man, Morals and Matter: Epicurus and Materialist Thought in England from John Toland to Joseph Priestley', in Neven Leddy and Avi Lifschitz, eds., *Epicurus in the Enlightenment* (Oxford: Voltaire Foundation, 2009), pp. 137–59

Nicholls, Ashton, 'The Loves of Plants and Animals: Romantic Science and the Pleasures of Nature', in James McKusick, ed., *Romantic Ecology*, November 2001, *Romantic Circles*, www.rc.umd.edu/praxis/ecology/nichols/nichols.html

Nietzsche, Friedrich, *On the Genealogy of Morals: A Polemic*, trans. Douglas Smith (Oxford University Press, 1996)
    Untimely Meditations, trans. R.J. Hollingdale (Cambridge University Press, 1997)
Nussbaum, Martha C., *The Fragility of Goodness: Luck and Ethics in Greek Tragedy and Philosophy*, 2nd edn (Cambridge University Press, 2001)
    'Mill between Aristotle and Bentham', *Daedalus*, 133:2 (2004), 60–8
    'Who Is the Happy Warrior? Philosophy Poses Questions to Psychology', in Eric A. Posner and Cass R. Sunstein, eds., *Law and Happiness* (University of Chicago Press, 2010), pp. 81–113
O'Donnell, Brennan, *The Passion of Meter: A Study of Wordsworth's Metrical Art* (Kent State University Press, 1995)
O'Hagan, Timothy, 'Taking Rousseau Seriously', *History of Political Thought*, 25:1 (2004), 73–85
O'Neill, Michael, '"The Words He Uttered ...": A Reading of Wordsworth', *Romanticism on the Net*, 3 (1996), www.erudit.org/revue/ron/1996/v/n3/005725ar.html
Owen, W.J.B., *Wordsworth as Critic* (University of Toronto Press, 1969)
Owen, W.J.B. and Jane Worthington Smyser, eds., *The Prose Works of William Wordsworth*, 3 vols. (Oxford: Clarendon Press, 1974)
Paley, William, *Moral and Political Philosophy* (London: R. Faulder, 1785)
    Reasons for Contentment: Addressed to the Labouring Part of the British Public (Carlisle: F. Jollie, 1792)
Park, Roy, ed., *Lamb as Critic* (London: Routledge, 1980)
Parker, Reeve, '"Finer Distance": The Narrative Art of Wordsworth's "The Wanderer"', *English Literary History*, 39 (1972), 87–111
Peterfreund, Stuart, 'In Free Homage and Generous Subjection: Miltonic Influence on *The Excursion*', *Wordsworth Circle*, 9 (1978), 173–7
Pfau, Thomas, *Romantic Moods: Paranoia, Trauma and Melancholy, 1790–1840* (Baltimore: Johns Hopkins University Press, 2005)
    Wordsworth's Profession: Form, Class, and the Logic of Early Romantic Cultural Production (Stanford University Press, 1997)
Pinch, Adela, *Strange Fits of Passion: Epistemologies of Emotion, Hume to Austen* (Stanford University Press, 1996)
Poovey, Mary, *The Proper Lady and the Woman Writer: Ideology as Style in the Works of Mary Wollstonecraft, Mary Shelley, and Jane Austen* (University of Chicago Press, 1984)
Pope, Alexander, *The Poems of Alexander Pope*, ed. John Butt (London: Methuen, 1963)
Porter, Roy and Marie Mulvey Roberts, eds., *Pleasure in the Eighteenth Century* (Basingstoke: Macmillan, 1996)
Potkay, Adam, *The Story of Joy: From the Bible to Late Romanticism* (Cambridge University Press, 2007)
Priestley, Joseph, *The History and Present State of Electricity, with Original Experiments* (London: Dodsley, 1767)

Priestman, Martin, 'Lucretius in Romantic and Victorian Britain', in Stuart Gillespie and Philip Hardie, eds., *The Cambridge Companion to Lucretius* (Cambridge University Press, 2007), pp. 289–305

ed., *The Collected Writings of Erasmus Darwin*, 9 vols. (Bristol: Thoemmes, 2003)

Rand, Benjamin, ed., *The Life, Unpublished Letters and Philosophical Regimen of Anthony, Earl of Shaftesbury* (London: Swan Sonnenschein, 1900)

Ray, William, 'Reading Women: Cultural Authority, Gender and the Novel: The Case of Rousseau', *Eighteenth-Century Studies*, 27 (1994), 421–47

Reddy, William M., *The Navigation of Feelings: A Framework for the History of Emotions* (Cambridge University Press, 2001)

Reed, Mark, *Wordsworth: The Chronology of the Middle Years, 1800–1815* (Cambridge, MA: Harvard University Press, 1975)

Regier, Alexander and Stefan Uhlig, eds., *Wordsworth's Poetic Theory* (Basingstoke: Palgrave Macmillan, 2010)

Richardson, Alan, *Literature, Education and Romanticism: Reading as Social Practice, 1780–1832* (Cambridge University Press, 1994)

Riley, Patrick, 'Hannah Arendt on Kant, Truth and Politics', *Political Studies*, 35:3 (1987), 379–92

Rivers, Isabel, *Reason, Grace, and Sentiment: A Study of the Language of Religion and Ethics in England, 1660–1780*, 2 vols. (Cambridge University Press, 2000)

Robertson, John, *The Case for the Enlightenment: Scotland and Naples, 1680–1760* (Cambridge University Press, 2005)

Rose, Gillian, *Hegel contra Sociology* (London: Athlone, 1981)

Rosenfeld, Sophia, *Common Sense: A Political History* (Cambridge, MA: Harvard University Press, 2011)

Rostvig, Maren-Sofie, *The Happy Man: Studies in the Metamorphoses of a Classical Ideal* (Oslo: Akademisk Forlag; Oxford: Basil Blackwell, 1954)

Rousseau, Jean-Jacques, *The Collected Writings of Rousseau*, ed. Christopher Kelly and Roger D. Masters, 12 vols. (Hanover: University Press of New England, 1990–2007)

Emile, or, On Education, trans. Allan Bloom (New York: Basic Books, 1979)

Russell, Bertrand, *History of Western Philosophy: And its Connection with Political and Social Circumstances from the Earliest Times to the Present Day* (London: Allen and Unwin, 1946)

Ruston, Sharon, *Shelley and Vitality* (Basingstoke: Palgrave Macmillan, 2005)

Rylance, Rick, *Roland Barthes* (New York: Harvester, 1994)

Ryle, Gilbert, *Collected Papers*, 2 vols. (London: Hutchinson, 1971)

Saint-Just, Louis-Antoine de, *Discours et rapports*, ed. Albert Soboul (Paris: Messidor/Éditions Sociales, 1988)

Schmid, Thomas H. and Michelle Faubert, *Romanticism and Pleasure* (New York: Palgrave Macmillan, 2010)

Schneider, Ben Ross, *Wordsworth's Cambridge Education* (Cambridge University Press, 1957)

Scott, John T., *Jean-Jacques Rousseau: Critical Assessments of Leading Political Philosophers*, 4 vols. (London: Routledge, 2006)

Shaftesbury (Cooper, Antony Ashley, Third Earl of Shaftesbury), *Characteristics of Men, Manners, Opinions, Times*, ed. Lawrence E. Klein (Cambridge University Press, 1999)

Exercises, trans. Laurent Jaffro (Paris: Aubier, 1993)

The Shaftesbury Project, at www.amerikanistik.phil.unierlangen.de/shaftesbury/index.html

Simpson, David, 'Romanticism, Criticism and Theory', in Stuart Curran, ed., *The Cambridge Companion to British Romanticism* (Cambridge University Press, 1993), pp. 1–24

Wordsworth's Historical Imagination: The Poetry of Displacement (New York: Methuen, 1987)

Smith, Adam, *Lectures on Rhetoric and Belles Lettres*, ed. J.C. Bryce (Indianapolis: Liberty Fund, 1993)

Snow, C.P., *The Two Cultures* (Cambridge University Press, 2012)

Soni, Vivasvan, 'Communal Narcosis and Sublime Withdrawal: The Problem of Community in Kant's Critique of Judgment', *Cultural Critique*, 64 (2006), 1–39

Mourning Happiness: Narrative and the Politics of Modernity (Ithaca: Cornell University Press, 2010)

Spenser, Edmund, *The Faerie Qveene*, ed. A.C. Hamilton et al. (Edinburgh: Longman, 2001)

Spiegelman, Willard, 'Some Lucretian Elements in Wordsworth', *Comparative Literature*, 37 (1985), 27–47

Spinoza, Benedict de, *Ethics*, trans. Edwin Curley (London: Penguin, 1996)

Stallknecht, Newton P., *Strange Seas of Thought: Studies in William Wordsworth's Philosophy of Man and Nature* (New York: Edwin Mellen, 2000)

Starobinski, Jean, *Jean-Jacques Rousseau: Transparency and Obstruction*, trans. Arthur Goldhammer (University of Chicago Press, 1988)

Strauss, Leo, *Political Philosophy: Six Essays*, ed. H. Gilden (Indianapolis: Bobbs-Merrill, 1975)

Sutherland, Keston, 'Happiness in Writing', *world picture*, 3 (2009), 7–13

Swift, Simon, 'Hannah Arendt's Tactlessness: Reading Eichmann in Jerusalem', *New Formations*, 71 (2011), 79–94

'Mary Wollstonecraft and the Reserve of Reason', *Studies in Romanticism*, 45:1 (2006), 3–24

Romanticism, Literature and Philosophy: Expressive Rationality in Rousseau, Kant, Wollstonecraft and Contemporary Theory (London: Continuum, 2006)

Taylor, Barbara, *Mary Wollstonecraft and the Feminist Imagination* (Cambridge University Press, 2003)

Terada, Rei, *Feeling in Theory: Emotion after the 'Death of the Subject'* (Cambridge, MA: Harvard University Press, 2001)

'The Life Process and Forgettable Living: Arendt and Agamben', *New Formations*, 71 (2011), 95–109

Timpanaro, Sebastiano, *On Materialism*, trans. Lawrence Garner (London: NLB, 1975)

Todorov, Tzvetan, *Imperfect Garden: The Legacy of Humanism* (Princeton University Press, 2002)

Townsend, Dabney, 'From Shaftesbury to Kant: The Development of the Concept of Aesthetic Experience', *Journal of the History of Ideas*, 48:2 (1987), 287–305

Townsend, R.C., 'John Wordsworth and his Brother's Poetic Development', *PMLA*, 81:1 (1966), 70–88

Trilling, Lionel, 'The Fate of Pleasure', in *Beyond Culture: Essays on Literature and Learning* (Oxford University Press, 1980), pp. 57–88

Valenza, Robin, *Literature, Language, and the Rise of the Intellectual Disciplines in Britain, 1680–1820* (Cambridge University Press, 2009)

Vickers, Neil, *Coleridge and the Doctors 1795–1806* (Oxford: Clarendon Press, 2004)

Vico, Giambattista, *The New Science of Giambattista Vico*, an abridged trans. of the 3rd edn (1744), ed. Thomas Goddard Bergin and Max Harold Fisch (Ithaca: Cornell University Press, 1970)

On the Study Methods of Our Time, trans. Elio Gianturco (Indianapolis: Bobbs-Merrill Company, 1965)

Voitle, Robert, *The Third Earl of Shaftesbury: 1671–1713* (Baton Rouge: Louisiana State University Press, 1984)

Wade, Allan, *The Letters of W.B. Yeats* (London: Hart-Davis, 1954)

Warren, James, *The Cambridge Companion to Epicureanism* (Cambridge University Press, 2009)

Weiskel, Thomas, *The Romantic Sublime: Studies in the Structure and Psychology of Transcendence* (Baltimore: Johns Hopkins University Press, 1976)

Williams, Gareth, ed., *Hannah Arendt: Critical Assessments of Leading Political Philosophers*, 4 vols. (London: Routledge, 2006)

Williams, Raymond, *Keywords: A Vocabulary of Culture and Society* (London: Croom Helm, 1976)

Wilson, Catherine, 'Epicureanism in Early Modern Philosophy', in J. Warren, ed., *The Cambridge Companion to Epicureanism* (Cambridge University Press, 2009), pp. 266–86

Epicureanism at the Origins of Modernity (Oxford University Press, 2010)

Wilson, Ross, *Subjective Universality in Kant's Aesthetics* (Oxford: Peter Lang, 2008)

'Voluptuousness and Asceticism in Adorno', *German Life and Letters*, 62:3 (2009), 270–83

Wollstonecraft, Mary, *A Vindication of the Rights of Men, with, A Vindication of the Rights of Woman*, ed. Sylvana Tomaselli (Cambridge University Press, 1995)

The Works of Mary Wollstonecraft, ed. Janet Todd and Marilyn Butler, 6 vols. (London: Pickering, 1989)

Wood, Allen W., *Kant's Ethical Thought* (Cambridge University Press, 1999)

Woof, Robert, *William Wordsworth: The Critical Heritage*, I: *1793–1820* (Abingdon: Routledge, 2001)

Wordsworth, Jonathan, *William Wordsworth: The Borders of Vision* (Oxford: Clarendon Press, 1982)

Wordsworth, William, *The Early Letters of William and Dorothy Wordsworth (1787–1805)*, ed. Ernest De Selincourt (Oxford: Clarendon, 1935)

The Excursion, ed. Sally Bushell, James A. Butler and Michael C. Jaye (Ithaca: Cornell University Press, 2008)

Home at Grasmere, ed. Beth Darlington (Ithaca: Cornell University Press, 1977)

Last Poems, 1821–1850, ed. Jared Curtis (Ithaca: Cornell University Press, 1999)

Lyrical Ballads and Other Poems 1797–1800, ed. James Butler and Karen Green (Ithaca: Cornell University Press, 1992)

Poems, in Two Volumes, and Other Poems, 1800–1807, ed. Jared Curtis (Ithaca: Cornell University Press, 1983)

The Prelude, 1799, 1805, 1850, ed. Jonathan Wordsworth, M.H. Abrams and Stephen Gill (New York: W.W. Norton, 1979)

The Prose Works of William Wordsworth, ed. W.J.B. Owen and Jane Worthington Smyser, 3 vols. (Oxford: Clarendon Press, 1974)

Worthington, Jane, *Wordsworth's Reading of Roman Prose* (New Haven: Yale University Press, 1946)

Wu, Duncan, *Wordsworth's Reading 1770–1799* (Cambridge University Press, 1993)

Wordsworth's Reading 1800–1815 (Cambridge University Press, 1996)

Youngquist, Paul, 'Lyrical Bodies: Wordsworth's Physiological Aesthetics', *European Romantic Review*, 10:2 (1999), 152–62

Yousef, Nancy, *Isolated Cases: The Anxieties of Autonomy in Enlightenment Philosophy and Romantic Literature* (Ithaca: Cornell University Press, 2004)

'Wollstonecraft, Rousseau and the Revision of Romantic Subjectivity', *Studies in Romanticism*, 38:4 (1999), 537–57

Zammito, John H., *The Genesis of Kant's Critique of Judgment* (University of Chicago Press, 1992)

Kant, Herder and the Birth of Anthropology (Chicago University Press, 2002)

Zerilli, Linda M.G., '"We Feel Our Freedom": Imagination and Judgment in the Thought of Hannah Arendt', *Political Theory*, 33 (2005), 158–88

Žižek, Slavoj, *For They Know Not What They Do: Enjoyment as a Political Factor*, 2nd edn (London: Verso, 2002)

Zuckert, Rachel, *Kant on Beauty and Biology: An Interpretation of the Critique of Judgment* (Cambridge University Press, 2007)

Index

238

CAMBRIDGE STUDIES IN ROMANTICISM

General Editor
JAMES CHANDLER, *University of Chicago*